13.50

Library of
Davidson College

VOID

**Soccer Coaching the Modern Way**

# SOCCER COACHING THE MODERN WAY

Eric Batty

FABER AND FABER
London

*First published in 1969*
*This edition published 1975*
*by Faber and Faber Limited*
*3 Queen Square London WC1*
*Printed in Great Britain by*
*Whitstable Litho Straker Brothers Ltd*
*All rights reserved*

*ISBN 0 571 10648 X (Faber Paperbacks)*
*ISBN 0 571 08289 O (Hard bound editions)*

© *1969, 1975 Eric Batty*

# Contents

Introduction *page* 9

1. The evolution of the game to date. Football has leaned more and more towards defence and though defences now seem to be dominant there are still inherent weaknesses which must be sought    11

2. The effect of modern tactics on the old playing positions, the new positions which have been created, and the redistribution of duties and responsibilities throughout the team    33

3. The tactics of defenders in relation to space, and the relationship between open spaces in midfield with shooting spaces in the penalty area    46

4. Creating space in attack and exploiting this space by coming from behind    63

5. Push the ball and run spotlights the wall-pass, but tighter marking makes 'push and run' obsolete. With an extra twist it leads directly to the 'Whirl' predicted by Willy Meisl    81

6. The overlap developed in England, or place-changing on the wings. The method of coaching wing combinations and some of the problems we meet when coaching modern football    92

7. Variations of wing combinations and further development after the initial break-through    113

8. Central combinations    139

9. An analysis of the four major phases of the contemporary game and place-changing within this context. The demands made by modern football on the abilities of the players and the aims of coaching    167

## Contents

| | |
|---|---|
| 10. Drills and exercises aimed at developing the techniques required in place-changing and combination play *page* | 179 |
| 11. The importance of talking in the game | 204 |
| 12. Combinations for attack only | 212 |
| 13. Place-changing in relation to the super-defence and the free-back | 237 |
| 14. The ideal team shape | 258 |
| 15. The theory of modern coaching, which must be related to the demands of the game and the importance of the correct psychological approach | 264 |

Drawings between pages 186 and 187

Turning on the ball

1. Stretch the left foot out to meet the ball.
2. Receive the ball with the inside of the left foot.
3. Withdraw the left foot immediately on contact.
4. Left foot takes first step towards enemy goal.
5. Ball runs on while body weight is shifted.
6. Right foot comes round to push the ball on.
7. The turn completed with minimum delay.

**NOTES**

Throughout this book the numbering of players is based on the prevailing system in Great Britain.

In all the diagrams an unbroken line ⎯⎯→ is used to indicate the path of the ball. A broken line - - - - → is used to indicate the path of a player *running off the ball*. An unbroken wriggling line ∼∼∼→ is used to indicate the path of a player running with the ball in his possession.

# Introduction

This book really begins in the 1953–54 season when Hungary beat England 6–3 at Wembley. After seeing the outstanding team of 1953–56, many people became convinced that the Hungarians had developed a form of telepathy. At that time, the tremendous understanding exhibited by Puskas, Hidegkuti, Kocsis and Boszik was attributed to a wide variety of factors but the most popular conclusions drawn, were that the individual players were great and that their understanding developed naturally as a result of playing together over long periods. To a handful of the world's leading coaches it was immediately clear that the Hungarians had developed a new approach to the game. Observation of players *running off the ball* revealed a series of frequently repeated patterns, but these movements were not noticed by the vast majority of spectators who made the basic error of watching the ball to the exclusion of everything else.

I failed to see what the Hungarians were doing in 1953 and those who did, being engaged in a highly competitive and lucrative field, had no reason to publicize their discoveries. My introduction to pattern-plays came several years later when watching teams coached by men who had recognized the advance made by the Hungarians. Prominent amongst these men were Albert Batteux (Reims and France), Bela Guttmann (Benfica), Helenio Herrera (CF Barcelona and FC Internazionale) and Sepp Herberger the West German National coach.

It was through observation of the teams coached by these men that I became aware of pattern-plays and they became even more pronounced in the attacking football developed by Anton Malatinsky (Spartak Trnava) and Ron Greenwood (West Ham United).

To have noted the patterns through observation was one thing but to develop a method of coaching along these lines presented a far greater problem. Finally, after considerable experiment over many months, the method presented in this book was evolved.

Before writing this book I presented the ideas and the method to Dr. Geza Kalocsai, the Hungarian coach of Gornik Zabrze. In correspondence, Dr. Kalocsai had already intimated that *coming from behind* was the key to success against tightly packed defences

## *Introduction*

but his views were important to me for two other reasons. First, he is, with Ron Greenwood, the only top-class coach I know who is prepared to enter into full and frank discussions on all aspects of the game. Although the attitude of the many other coaches I have met is understandable, they prefer not to discuss their methods. Secondly, and this was an equally important reason, Dr. Kalocsai was one of a team of three coaches who worked under Gustav Szebes with the Hungarian National team around 1953.

Outlining my ideas in detail and explaining the method of coaching presented in this book, I was told by Dr. Kalocsai that combination-plays were indeed the basis of the apparently telepathic understanding developed within the great Hungarian team.

It was, said Dr. Kalocsai, the senior coach, Marton Bukovi, who developed the idea of combinations in 1951. At first they were limited to two players and the simple wall-pass but later they were developed more fully and became more intricate.

Dr. Kalocsai added that he has been working along the lines of *coming from behind* and *place-changing* since 1962. It is hard work, he said, but also very interesting and in my experience there is no other way of teaching players to look and to think.

It should be clearly understood that although the combinations will first appear in match play 'parrot-fashion' this is only the first stage in the coaching plan. The players should be encouraged to express their individuality and particular skills within this framework of team-play.

The essentials that will come from coaching in this manner will be the good habits that form an integral part of each combination. These habits that are all desirable in good players include moving off into space after playing the ball; making a pass first-time when being challenged from behind and taking up supporting positions on colleagues caught in such a situation. Above all perhaps, to get players to 'lift their heads' and look around when in possession. So many skilful players with their heads down, eyes glued to the ball, fail to appreciate when to let the ball go to advantage for a colleague who has made a good run into space.

*January 1974*　　　　　　　　　　　　　　　　　　　　Eric Batty

# 1 — The evolution of the game to date. Football has leaned more and more towards defence and though defences now seem to be dominant there are still inherent weaknesses which must be sought

The goal-less draw is not a phenomenon of the 1960s as many people claim, though this is clearly the most likely result of a game in which both teams play to avoid defeat. Neither is it true to say that pulling eight men into defence when your goal is under pressure is negative. What is important is the attitude within the team towards victory and defeat. If it is common sense to withdraw eight men in defence of our goal when the enemy are in possession of the ball then it is no less sensible to commit at least eight men to attack when, in our turn we regain possession. In 1872 tactics were virtually unknown though team formations were already beginning to develop. In that year England and Scotland took part in the first official International match. Staged in Glasgow, the game attracted an estimated 4,000 spectators and in spite of the apparently overwhelming numerical superiority of the respective sets of forwards the result was a goalless draw. Scotland were tactically the most advanced at that time, fielding: a goalkeeper; two full-backs; two half-backs and six forwards. England's team was distributed less evenly between defence and attack with: a goalkeeper; one half-back; one three-quarterback and eight forwards.

It seems incredible that fourteen forwards could not manage to score even one goal but the game in those days was very different from that which we know today. With the emphasis on dribbling, both sets of forwards tended to bunch together around the ball and inevitably this brought the eight English forwards back to help in defence when the Scots had possession and pressed deep into the England half. The passing game which evolved later was to change the shape of the team from 2–2–6 or 1–1–8 to a disposition of players which gave a

## *The evolution of the game*

more even balance between defence and attack, but there is an important psychological point to be digested here. One would think that playing to a 1-1-8 formation would necessarily lead to a great many goals being conceded. This did not occur because when the enemy was in possession the eight forwards fell back to reinforce the defence.

In a modern context we now assume that if both teams in a game play to an 8-1-1 formation then no goals will be scored, but this will only be so if the defenders are unwilling to race upfield to reinforce the attack once their team gains possession. Willingness to attack is essential if the dominance of defences is to be ended. But the will to attack is not enough and no matter how much a manager or coach may urge his players to attack, the individual player will not respond unless the expenditure of physical effort on his part can be seen to have a beneficial result.

Ordered to move up and support the attack, a full-back will sprint forward with pleasure. He will do so because attacking is always more enjoyable than defending, but when the attack fails and possession of the ball is lost, the defender must sprint back in order to fulfil his primary role. The joy of racing forward will be more than counter-balanced by the agony of forcing his tiring body back into defence and unless his sorties are bringing tangible results he will soon lose his new spirit for attack.

To bring tangible results we must somehow 'link' defence and attack. We must give defensive players a clear role in attack which will be both enjoyable and effective, and we must train harder (physically) than ever before, to eliminate the fatigue which will inevitably overtake any player who attempts to play a full role in both defence and attack.

We shall return to this theme later but first we should consider the development of the game from England's 1-1-8 formation of 1872 to the 4-3-3 and 1-4-2-3 systems which predominate in the modern game. These changes did not occur haphazardly but for sound, logical reasons. Whenever attacking play exposed an inherent weakness in the defensive system, the game sought a remedy. Inevitably, this meant pulling more and more players back from attack to defence, as each weakness was exposed. When we reached catenaccio, the super-defensive system adopted by many of the inferior Italian clubs, this movement towards defence could go no further. The 1-4-3-2 is very close to the limit to which we can go without rejecting

## The evolution of the game

even the slightest hope of winning. Any movement now must be positive and if we cannot hope for a swing towards attack we must at least attempt to counter-attack.

## THE EARLY CHANGES FORCED BY THE PASS

During the early years following the final break between Rugby and Association Football, dribbling predominated within a team formation which closely resembled the Rugby pack. Heading and shooting at goal from long range were still unknown.

The player in possession of the ball attempted to break through by dribbling, with his team-mates in close support to pick up the ball if he should lose control of it. Inevitably the opposition massed in front of the player with the ball.

Scotland has been given the credit for introducing the pass, and this innovation led to a new game being developed, based on dribbling and passing. This forced everyone to think about re-distributing their players. No longer was it enough to mass directly in the path of the player in possession for at any moment the new *weapon* might be used. A pass could leave any number of players out of position, i.e. in a position from which they could not prevent an attack developing into a shot at goal.

With the introduction of passing, the team formation moved quite quickly to that which is now known as the system based on the attacking centre-half. Again it was Scotland which led the way and in the match against England in 1872, already referred to, the Scots fielded two backs, two half-backs and six forwards. Five of Scotland's six forwards are still with us today while the sixth was an additional centre-forward. Finally the extra centre-forward was withdrawn to become first a half-centre (forward) and later a centre-half.

Essentially the centre-half remained an attacking player and for more than half a century the attacking centre-half game remained. For the first time we had an even balance between defence and attack with five forwards and five supporting players behind the attack who also had defensive duties.

In Britain we still number our players according to their disposition in the attacking centre-half system and we still refer to the eleven playing positions as they were fifty years ago. The change in the offside law brought the conversion of the centre-half who became

## *The evolution of the game*

in fact, but not in name, a centre-back. Elsewhere the game was even less eager to accept the implications of WM. In Hungary the centre-back was not introduced until several years after the Second World War, while Uruguay, Austria and Switzerland remained true to the old game until after the 1954 World Cup.

From the Scottish 2-2-6 formation to WM is a big step and in reality two big steps. The first was taken after the adaptation of the Scottish pass into the long pass, while the second did not come until after the offside law was changed.

As the passing game developed it became clear that a great advantage could be gained if play were switched from one side of the field to a player positioned on the other flank. It should be understood that at this time the game was still dominated by dribbling and short passing and the three half-backs were always positioned well upfield in support of the forwards. Thus a quick long pass to a player positioned on one of the flanks (the modern winger) was often able to effect a break-through, for five forwards and three half-backs could be left out of position by one long pass.

When this move became popular it was found necessary to guard against it by asking the wing-halves to accept responsibility for coping with the enemy wingers and leave the backs to defend the area in front of goal. This formation remained for more than two decades, the true 2-3-5 system.

If Scotland had played the major role in the evolving game, now it was England's turn to force the next step. Five forwards and three supporting half-backs clearly placed the two full-backs in many difficult situations and now with an ingenious master stroke, the backs gained the upper hand. In the orthodox short-passing game both sets of eight attacking players remained relatively compact. Every attack therefore was contested by the five opposing forwards and three half-backs. The longer pass brought a very different problem for the two backs, for particularly against very quick forwards, the long pass could isolate them from their colleagues in attack. Without support, the two lone defenders could be outflanked by a long cross-field pass, and the backs countered this threat by introducing their offside trap.

At that time the law ruled, in effect, that a player was offside if there were less than three opponents between the attacking player and the goal-line, when the pass was made. By anticipating the long pass and moving upfield, the full-backs were able to turn the long

## The evolution of the game

pass attack to their own advantage. For a while the backs and their offside trap held the upper hand, though there is little doubt that given time the forwards would have found an effective answer. Football was already a thriving industry however and it was clear to all that the public would not continue to pay to watch games dominated by offside tactics. Prematurely, the legislators amended the offside law and henceforth it was necessary for a forward to have only two (instead of three) opponents between him and the goal-line at the moment the ball was played.

## THE THREE-BACK GAME—WM

With the change in the offside law the number of goals soared once more and inevitably the defenders found themselves out-thought and out-played. Had football remained a game, there would have been no problem but by now the working class had taken to football as spectators. The clubs with the largest following and the biggest bank balances were those who were most successful, and league points became more and more important. As each goal conceded reduced the chances of ultimate victory, the safety-first policy was evolved.

Arsenal Manager, Herbert Chapman, is the man generally credited with reorganizing the defence and introducing the third back. Certainly it was Arsenal who attracted most publicity and achieved most success in this period by effectively limiting the number of goals conceded. Moving the full-backs out to the flanks where they assumed responsibility for covering the opposing wing-forwards, Chapman withdrew the centre-half from his old attacking role to fill the gap between the full-backs and complete the apparently impregnable defensive wall. For more than twenty-five years, football was then dominated by the most negative player of all time: the stopper centre-half. Tall, strongly built and essentially a very good header of the ball, the centre-half became the key player in defence.

Critics who remember the old attacking centre-half game have never ceased to complain that the art and beauty of the game were killed by the introduction of the stopper, but in retrospect it must be admitted that forwards had so dominated the game after the change in the offside law that something had to be done to bolster the defence. The introduction of the third back was inevitable.

Accepting the reorganization of the defence into a well-balanced

*The evolution of the game*

unit, it was not inevitable however, that art and beauty should disappear and be replaced by speed and power. It was not the stopper who put an end to craft and skill, but a lack of ingenuity within the game as a whole.

## THE DOUBLE-STOPPER GAME (4-2-4)

The introduction of the centre-back certainly brought fresh problems but there was no reason why the game should have allowed the new villain to dominate. Analysing the situation we can see now that the centre-back specialized in dealing with long high passes intended for the centre-forward and the game as a whole played right into his hands. Twenty-five years later the Hungarians 'assassinated' the centre-back but until the Hungarians exposed the weakness in the three-back system, the stopper was allowed to dominate.

To do battle with the big, strong stopper, the tank-type centre-forward replaced the speedy ball player who had previously led the attack. Now the centre-forward had to be strong and fearless; willing to chase long passes hit over the head of the centre-back, and withstand vigorous shoulder charges. In addition he had to be able to outjump his new opponent and 'head' into goal a stream of high centres from the wings.

No wonder the art and beauty seemed to disappear from the game. Previously the old-style centre-half and the old centre-forward had both been artists with the ball and the most creative players in the side. Suddenly they were transformed, becoming bigger and stronger and far less skilful. Skill was the last requirement demanded of the new stopper. He had only to clear the ball from the danger area (in front of goal) with head or foot. If his clearance went to a colleague then so much the better, but if it did not, then no matter.

Neither did it matter if the new centre-forward was skiful or not. He was required to get the ball into the net and if he was neither graceful nor agile, he was forgiven if he got a goal or two in each game.

From around 1926 until 1953, the new centre-back was allowed to dominate, though in reality there was an inherent weakness in the three-back game. This weakness stemmed from the fact that the apparently unbeatable centre-back had in reality to fulfil a dual role. While the full-backs positioned themselves on the flanks to mark their respective wingers they were also required to drop back and

## The evolution of the game

cover the centre-half. Thus a long cross-field pass from inside-left—hit over the head of the centre-back into the space behind him—should be dealt with by the left-back who dropped back to cover. When the opposition attempted to make progress on their right flank, then it was the responsibility of the right-back to fall back and cover. With the full-backs marking the wingers and the wing-halves now keeping an eye on the opposing inside-forwards, the centre-back was left to concentrate on blotting the centre-forward out of the game. Finally the Hungarians discovered that the centre-back had in fact a secondary role to fulfil in addition to marking the enemy centre-forward. In the light of what the Hungarians did we can now say that the centre-back had two primary tasks:

1. He had to mark the centre-forward.
2. He had to cover the central defensive zone.

As long as the centre-forward remained a tank-type, operating as a central spearhead then the centre-back could fulfil both roles without difficulty. In Britain the centre-forwards remained true to type, varying in size and shape perhaps, but always playing as a spearhead thrust deep into the enemy defence. But on the Continent and more particularly in Central Europe a new style centre-forward was seen as early as the late 1930s. Reluctant to replace the skilful ball-playing leader with a 'tank' the Central Europeans withdrew the centre-forward into a midfield role.

The Hungarians have been given the credit for developing this innovation but in fact Nandor Hidegkuti who fulfilled this role between 1953 and 1958 was certainly not the first withdrawn centre-forward. Neither was he a truly withdrawn leader.

What the Hungarians did was to develop a new-style centre-forward who was a cross-breed between the British spearhead and the Central European leader who led the attack from behind. Hidegkuti, who wore the number 9 shirt for Hungary with great distinction, would have been better described as a *withdrawing* centre-forward. By withdrawing—dropping back to meet a pass *played at his feet*—Hidegkuti clearly demonstrated that the centre-back could no longer fulfil both his primary duties effectively. If the stopper advanced to challenge the number 9 as he withdrew to meet the ball, then the central defensive zone was left uncovered.

If the Hungarian XI which developed during the years 1949 to 1953 had a British-style centre-forward then it was probably not Hidegkuti at all but inside-right Sandor Kocsis. Wearing the number 8 shirt,

## The evolution of the game

Kocsis was seldom very far away from Hidegkuti and as the number 9 withdrew to meet a pass from midfield, Kocsis edged forward ready to spring. It is now clear that the master-mind behind this outstanding Hungarian team was Marton Bukovi, coach of the Budapest club Voros Loboga (now MTK) and chief assistant to Gustav Szebes the Hungarian National team manager.

Through a series of training drills, which were known as combinations, the Hungarian players Puskas, Kocsis, Bozsik and Hidegkuti built up a great understanding. Other combinations involving the wingers and their inside partners were developed too, but the key feature in the Hungarian game was undoubtedly the central combinations.

First developed around 1951 the combinations were largely based on positional switching allied to the wall-pass (double-pass on the Continent). Later, between 1954 and 1956, these combinations were further developed to involve not two players as in a wall-pass but three. Diagrams 1 (a) and 1 (b) show the two basic combinations developed shortly before the team broke up in 1956, and in 1 (c) an alternative which was to be used as a variation when a less gullible opponent decided to tight mark Kocsis.

Hidegkuti was the key player in all the central thrusts to goal for in his *withdrawing* role he was used as a decoy to lure forward the centre-back and thus expose the direct approach to goal. From an orthodox advanced position, Hidegkuti would drop back to meet a pass, play it away first time to a midfield colleague, usually Puskas or Bozsik, and they would pop the ball into the space behind the advancing centre-back to send the inside-forward running through for a shot at goal. Though all four—Kocsis, Hidegkuti, Puskas and Bozsik—were great individual players it must be emphasized that these simple yet devastating moves did not happen naturally. They were perfected only after hours and hours of practice spread over many months.

At the time of Hungary's 6–3 victory over England at Wembley in 1953, the central combinations were still based on the wall-pass. Though the combinations developed later were to be even more effective, the 1953 Hungarians created space in the centre by asking their wingers Budai and Czibor to operate close to the touchlines and drop back slightly. This in turn forced the English full-backs to position themselves wider than usual and prevented them giving the customary cover to the centre-back.

## The evolution of the game

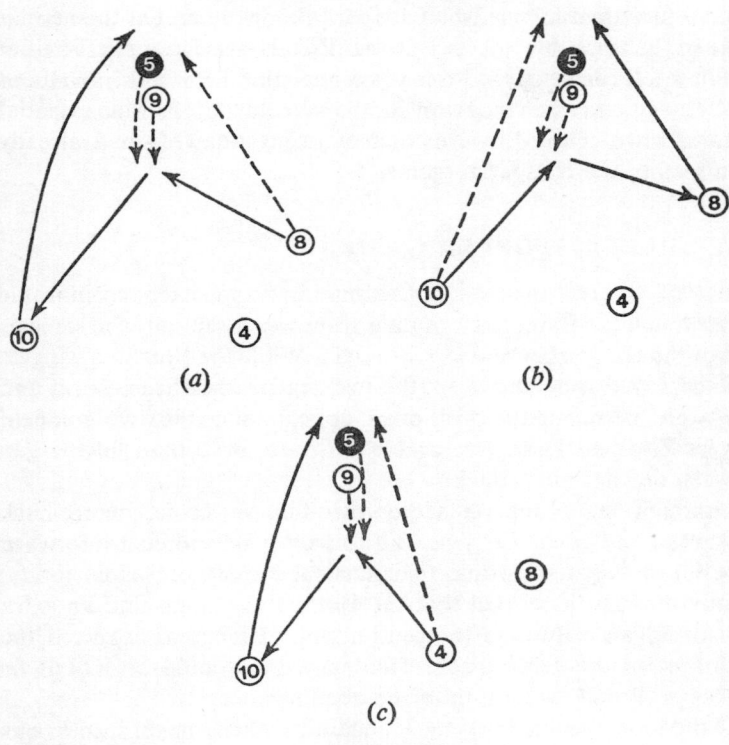

*Diagram 1*

In May 1954 the Hungarians met England again in a return match in Budapest, and this time the margin of victory was even more pronounced. By seven goals to one Hungary thrashed England, and though the game as a whole was not quick to grasp the full implications behind the Hungarian achievements they had effectively put an end to the WM system. Soon it was to become clear that the centre-back could not mark the centre-forward who withdrew and at the same time cover the central approach to goal. The answer was to be found by converting one of the wing-halves to play a purely defensive role alongside the old centre-back. Henceforth there would be two centre-backs—right centre-back and left centre-back. One would challenge for the ball while the other would cover space, but significantly the Hungarian team of 1953–54 included one player who was generally judged to be inferior to his colleagues. At the time no one

## *The evolution of the game*

could understand how left-half Joszef Zakarias managed to keep his place in the team. Now it is clear that Zakarias was not a left-half at all but a left centre-back. Four years later the Brazilians introduced the 4–2–4 system when they won the 1958 World Cup, but the essential features—two centre-forwards and two centre-halves—had already been seen in the Hungarian game.

### THE TREBLE-STOPPER GAME

In 1958 the Brazilian's 4–2–4 formation was clearly recognizable for although the framework of their team was essentially the same as that of the Hungarians it was more rigid. While the Brazilian wingers were deployed wide and deep, the two central spearheads Vava and Pele were permanently positioned upfield, and the two midfield players Zito and Didi were asked to do no more than fill the gap between defence and attack.

Although the Hungarians did introduce a second centre-back (Zakarias) and could fairly be said to have a second centre-forward (Kocsis) the key-note within their tactical formation was flexibility. At any moment it seemed that the Hungarians could find an extra man to advance through the centre, while Hidegkuti attracted the attentions of the centre-back. This extra man could be Kocsis or Puskas or Bozsik according to the circumstances.

At the time it seemed that the Hungarians' phenomenal success was entirely due to the fact that they could field four *great* players. 'By chance' the Hungarians had produced Kocsis, Hidegkuti, Puskas and Bozsik at the same period, and the thought that they had also developed a new approach to the game was dismissed.

Certainly the four Hungarians were great, but their individual skills had in fact been linked together by revolutionary yet basically simple training drills. Opponents who attempted to tight-mark Kocsis by withdrawing the left-half to play a fully defensive role were only partially successful for both Puskas and Bozsik had also been drilled in place-changing with Hidegkuti and they, too, were frequently seen sneaking in round behind the centre-back, to become a temporary centre-forward. Thus it can truly be said that the Hungarians had no less than four centre-forwards, Hidegkuti and the three players who had been drilled with him in place-changing.

Although it was the Hungarians who introduced the essential features of 4–2–4 they had good reason to let the rest of the world

## The evolution of the game

believe they were still playing WM. From around 1951 to 1956 they baffled everyone with their new approach and the fact that their opponents were unaware of what they were doing gave the performances of Puskas, Kocsis, Hidegkuti and Bozsik even greater effect.

The Brazilian version of 4–2–4 was another matter entirely for now it was clear that inside-right Didi was operating exclusively on the left; that Pele was always up in close support of the centre-forward and that Orlando was permanently positioned between centre-half and left-back. The Hungarians were able to conceal their game by place-changing, because for lengthy periods the Hungarian players were seen to be operating in zones which were consistent with the numbers on their backs. Brazil's rigid team formation brought the second centre-back and the second centre-forward out into the open for all to see, and almost overnight the numbers game was invented. With Vava and Pele operating as twin centre-forwards it was no longer possible for any realistic opponent to play the one centre-back. Had anyone done so then the Brazilians would have had two against one in the centre whenever they succeeded in giving a pass to either Vava or Pele. Clearly everyone now had to play with two centre-backs. Withdrawing one of the wing-halves to play a purely defensive role alongside the old stopper inevitably left a gap in midfield, and to fill the gap one of the inside-forwards had to be withdrawn. It followed also that the old centre-forward could no longer be expected to battle alone against two centre-backs, and once the first step was taken towards 4–2–4 the other changes had to be made.

Within twelve months of Brazil's World Cup success almost the entire world had switched to 4–2–4. Some had made the change simply because the system had been proved good enough to win the World Cup but inherent within the new system was recognition of a fundamental football truth that had been hidden for years; the old centre-back had two duties to perform and when the centre-forward moved from the middle then one man could not fulfil both duties. The stopper had to choose whether to mark the centre-forward *or* cover the central zone. He could not do both against a *withdrawing* centre-forward. With the introduction of the second centre-back it appeared that greater stability had been given to the defence. Each of the centre-backs marked one of the enemy centre-forwards and depending on the circumstances they covered each other (and the central defensive zone). Thus if the right centre-forward (9) and the left

## The evolution of the game

centre-back (6) were involved in a duel for the ball—on the ground or in the air—then the right centre-back (5) would drop back to cover as illustrated in Diagram 2 (a). When it was the turn of the left centre-

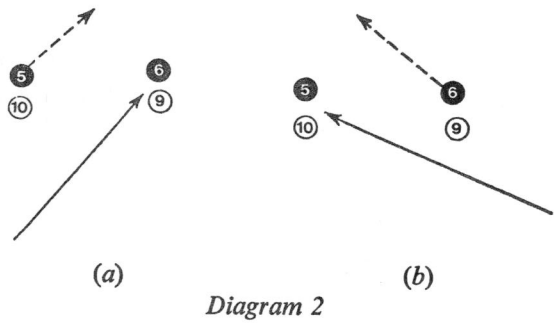

*(a)*        *(b)*
*Diagram 2*

forward (10) and right centre-back (5) to challenge for the ball then the left centre-back would drop back to cover as in Diagram 2 (b).

In reality, however, the greater defensive stability obtained by playing with twin stoppers was just as illusory as the *stability* given to the defence by the conversion of the old attacking centre-half which gave us the WM system. Had opponents limited themselves to one centre-forward all would have been well, but faced by two centre-forwards who moved across the pitch *or* withdrew, the two centre-backs were unable to mark men and cover the central zone. Now it became clear that two centre-backs were not enough against two centre-forwards unless they were both 'tank' types and they both remained permanently positioned in the centre.

The crux of this problem will become clear if we consider a Kocsis, Hidegkuti, Puskas, Bozsik-type 'combination' based on an orthodox 4–2–4 playing team. With both teams in a game playing 4–2–4 the disposition of forces just outside the penalty area would be roughly that shown in Diagram 3 (a). Withdrawn a little in right-midfield Kocsis pushes the ball forward to Hidegkuti *and runs around behind the man he has passed to* (place-changing). To cover this threat because the left centre-back (6) cannot challenge Hidegkuti *and* cover space, the right centre-back (5) drops back to cover. Now, however, he leaves the left centre-forward Puskas wide open, and a touch with head or foot from Hidegkuti gives Puskas the ball some 20–25 yards from goal. Outstanding players don't need to be asked to shoot from

## The evolution of the game

such positions and they shoot today with both power and accuracy. Clearly the defence must have depth (which means cover) but it is also clear that we cannot afford to leave top-class forwards unmarked. In the attack outlined above the centre-backs were powerless to intervene for they were outnumbered three against two when Kocsis came from behind.

To withstand such attacks we must do three things in the central defensive zone:
1. We must challenge Hidegkuti or he will turn on the ball and shoot.
2. We must mark Puskas tight or he will be free to take a pass from Hidegkuti and shoot.
3. We must have someone to cover the centre against the thrust made by Kocsis.

Two men cannot possibly do all three things and it now follows that two centre-backs are not enough against a top-class team which has two centre-forwards. We must have three centre-backs—twin stoppers each tight-marking one of the centre-forwards and the third centre-back covering space. If we do not have three centre-backs but only two, then an attack well drilled in *place-changing combinations* will repeatedly create a shooting position for someone. Each of the two centre-backs has two alternatives—he can mark a man or cover space, but he cannot do both. If 6 marks his man and 5 drops back to cover space then the attack will develop as shown in Diagram 3 (a).

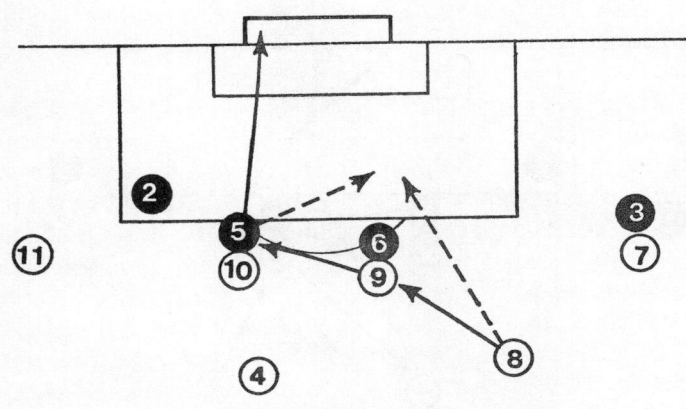

*Diagram 3 (a)*

## The evolution of the game

If 6 declines to challenge 9 and lays off to cover space while 5 remains tight on 10 then 9 will turn on the ball and shoot as illustrated in Diagram 3 (b).

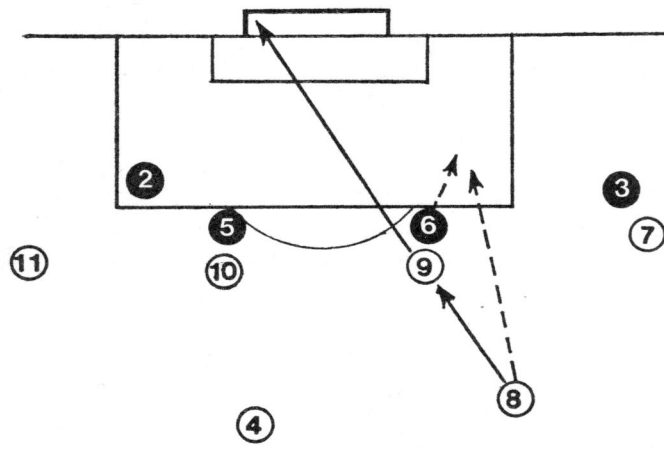

*Diagram 3 (b)*

If both 5 and 6 stay tight on their respective opponents then 9 will play the ball back to 4 who chips the ball first time over the defenders to create a shooting position for 8 as outlined in Diagram 3 (c).

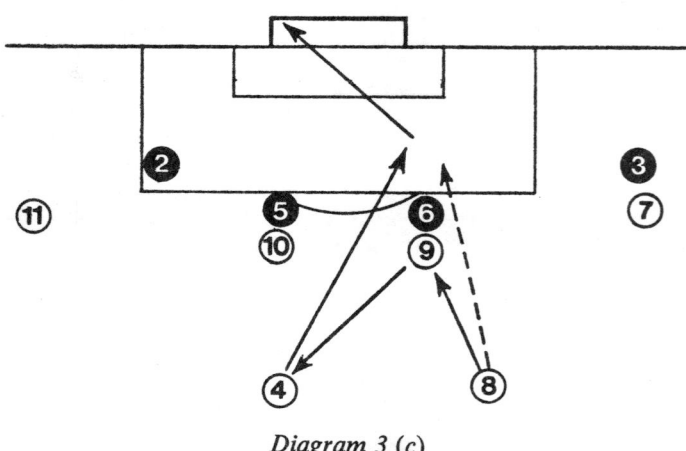

*Diagram 3 (c)*

## The evolution of the game

Finally, if both 5 and 6 elect to cover; 6 moving over to pick up 8 as he moves in and 5 coming across to support his colleague then 9 will 'turn' on the ball and can either shoot himself as in Diagram 3 (b) or push the ball forward for 10 to shoot from even closer range as shown in Diagram 3 (d).

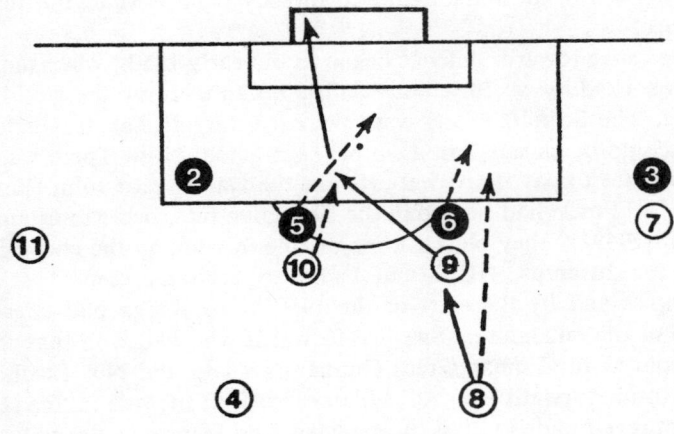

*Diagram 3 (d)*

It will now be clear that a team based on 4–2–4 with two good centre-forwards well drilled in *place-changing combinations* will tear apart any defence. If the defenders challenge they are wrong; if they lay off to cover they are wrong; and if one centre-back challenges while his colleague covers, they are still wrong!

For the attacking side the key to success lies in the place-changing combinations for if 8 (or another player) does not come from behind the defenders will not be outnumbered and will close-mark their opponents. For the defending side there is no chance unless they have three centre-backs which is the basis of the defensive tactics developed in Italy.

## CATENACCIO

The Italians' defensive tactics developed naturally as a direct result of the bigger clubs signing outstanding forwards from all over the world. Poorer opponents who could not afford to compete in the

## The evolution of the game

transfer market found themselves swamped by the stars bought by AC Milan, Juventus and FC Internazionale, and step by step the lowly clubs tightened up their defences. Tracing the evolutionary process to which the game has been subjected we can now see that 4–2–4 and 4–3–3 are intermediate systems between WM and catenaccio. While the rest of the world stepped slowly from WM to 4–2–4 and later to 4–3–3, the Italians moved directly from WM to the super-defence.

The move towards defence began in the early 1950s, when the big clubs backed by wealthy industrialists began to comb the world for talent. The Scandinavians were the early targets, for as amateurs they could be engaged on a simple contractual basis. There was no transfer fee to pay. Early imports like the Danish pair John Hansen and Karl Praest had starred in the 1948 Olympics soccer tournament and in 1949/50 they played a major role in winning the championship for Juventus. AC Milan had also been represented at the Olympics and by the start of the 1950/51 campaign had engaged three of the outstanding Swedish forwards who had won that competition. With Gunnar Gren, Gunnar Nordahl and Nils Liedholm their inside-forward trio, AC Milan carried off the title in fine style. Juventus responded to this by engaging Karl Hansen, a third Danish international to win back the championship in 1951/52. Then it was the turn of FC Internazionale (Milan) and with Lennart Skoglund (Sweden) and Stefan Nyers (Hungary) in their side, they won the first of two consecutive championships in 1952/53.

By this time defences had already become tighter and though worse was to come, it is clear from the champions goals for totals that the emphasis was changing:

| | | |
|---|---|---|
| 1949/50 | Juventus | 100 |
| 1950/51 | AC Milan | 107 |
| 1951/52 | Juventus | 98 |
| 1952/53 | Internazionale | 64 |
| 1953/54 | Internazionale | 67 |

At this period the imported stars so dominated the game in Italy that lesser teams were swamped by big scores. This was neither surprising nor unusual, for the outstanding teams in every country were no less successful. But in Italy there were few clubs who were prepared to accept heavy reverses and when small clubs began to dismiss their managers after conceding 6, 7 or 8 goals to a crack team, the

## The evolution of the game

unfortunate bosses began to devise methods of limiting the number of goals conceded by their inferior players.

Double-marking the star forwards formed the basis of most early attempts to prevent teams like Juventus and AC Milan scoring goals. Gunnar Nordahl, Italy's leading scorer in five seasons out of six, was a particular target for double-marking and it became quite common for the smaller clubs to play with two centre-backs. One wore the number 5 shirt and played the normal stopper's game while the other centre-back might wear the number 9 shirt, line up at centre-forward but spend the entire ninety minutes marking Nordahl 'tight'.

Now it can be seen that for practical rather than theoretical reasons the Italians decided that the way to limit the number of goals being scored was to play with two centre-backs. One was nominated to mark the centre-forward while the other centre-back simply covered the central approach to goal.

Double-marking became increasingly popular and the move towards defence accelerated rapidly when it was realized that with sound planning and disciplined players, the star-studded teams could be stopped. Not only stopped, but beaten!

From primitive beginnings the Italians soon developed an overall defensive plan geared to the conception that one centre-back was not enough. Against an outstanding player the lone centre-back could be drawn out of position and while wingers did the same to the full-backs, the inside-forwards took full advantage of the spaces which were created. Fielding two players against one was uneconomical, however, and by adapting the Swiss *'bolt'* system the Italians formed the ideal solution. If a team thought it necessary to double-mark only one opponent a comprehensive system was not needed, but when as many as four opponents merited this distinction another solution had to be found. Thus it was that catenaccio was developed from the bolt. Devised by Karl Rappan in the thirties, the bolt, or verrou as it was known in Switzerland, was designed to give an extra man in defence when needed, without depleting the attack.

Adapted directly from the old attacking centre-half game, the wing-halves continued to cover the opposing wingers; the centre-half remained in midfield and the backs played the vital covering role in the central defensive zone.

In midfield, one of the inside-forwards dropped back to join the centre-half and in the attacking phase the wing-halves were also encouraged to attack.

## The evolution of the game

When the attack broke down and possession of the ball was lost the players with defensive duties sprinted back to take up the positions illustrated in Diagram 4. Clearly the system called for stamina, in-

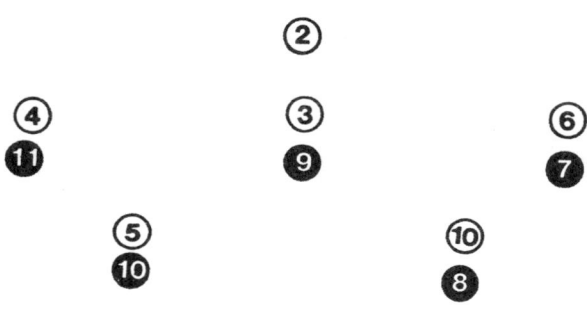

*Diagram 4*

telligence and adaptability, but there were distinct advantages to the system. The most important being the extra stability in defence which accrued from the free-back who marked the space behind the line of three 'backs'.

It is not clear who was responsible for adapting the defensive phase of the 'bolt' and producing catenaccio, but by the late 1950s the Italians were convinced that this was the only way to play. By delegating one player to give cover behind the defence, the other defenders were allowed complete freedom to concentrate on their particular opponent. No longer was it necessary for the stopper or the full-backs to cover their zones as well as marking a man.

Compared with the general policy of double-marking the advantages of catenaccio were enormous. Playing against AC Milan for example, a lowly team once attempted to double-mark all three inside-forwards Gren, Nordahl and Liedholm. With three players committed to tight marking in addition to the orthodox six-men defence this left only two players free to attack.

With the coming of catenaccio, defenders still played 'tight' on their man but the free-back gave cover to each defender in turn. Thus whichever forward happened to be in possession of the ball at any given moment, the defenders were able to double-mark him by the man 'tight' and the free-back who positioned himself according

## The evolution of the game

to the movement of the ball and covered the space immediately behind the defender who was challenging the man in possession. Catenaccio can now be seen in several different forms but in general terms we can say that the system seeks to provide three essential features:
1. Tight-marking defenders for each enemy 'front' player.
2. A free-back to give depth (and cover) to the defence as a whole.
3. Two or three midfield players who are expected to forage for the ball and by loosely 'marking' the enemy midfield players, prevent defenders being drawn away from their man by an opponent who carries the ball into a shooting position.

It will be evident that against a team expected to play to a 4–2–4 formation the catenaccio would be 1–4–2–3 *or* 1–4–3–2.

Against a team expected to play to 4–3–3 the catenaccio would be 1–3–3–3, 1–3–4–2 *or* 1–3–2–4.

The exact disposition of players in midfield and in attack depends on many factors including the relative strength of the opposition and the nature of the game. In an away European Cup tie or a home league match in which a draw would be considered a moral victory, 1–4–3–2 could be anticipated. But in a home European Cup tie or a league game which *must* be won, a more offensive line up may be expected, perhaps 1–3–2–4. Everything depends on the strength of the opposition and the overall aim in terms of a result.

If catenaccio were in fact nothing more than a purely defensive and negative system it would not have acquired the popularity it has today with managers and coaches. It has already been stated that even against outstanding teams the system has been proved successful and by adopting catenaccio, inferior teams have not only prevented vastly superior sides from scoring and thus earned a draw but have on many occasions scored themselves and won. It is the hard truth of this statement which has persuaded the Italians and many more coaches that catenaccio is the only way to play.

To see this clearly, let us return to the early days of catenaccio when only the poorer Italian clubs played the defensive game. A lowly club faced by the Gren-Nordahl-Liedholm team of AC Milan decides to play two forwards up and concentrate on defence in the hope of earning a draw. They give their team the shape described in Diagram 5 while Milan play to the old 3–2–5, WM system. Clearly it will be a game dominated by Milan, but midfield superiority frequently bears no relationship to the result of a game. What really

*The evolution of the game*

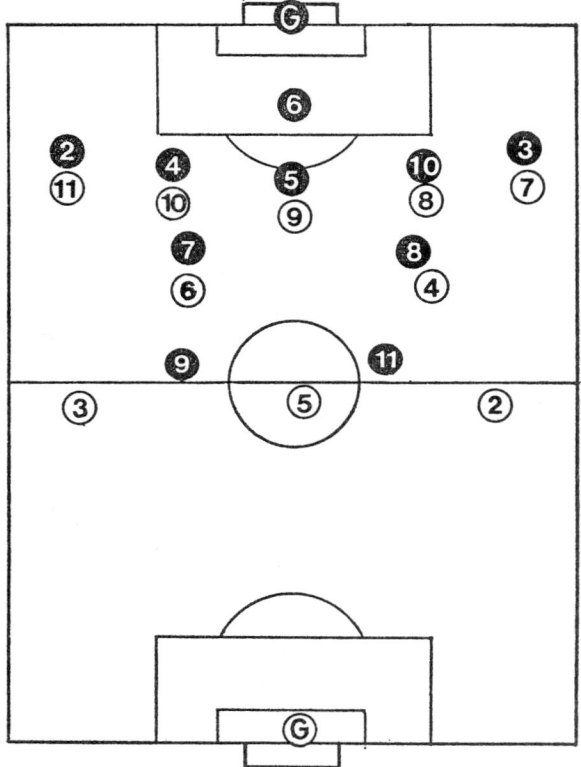

*Diagram 5*

matters is what happens in and around the respective penalty areas which might be more realistically re-named shooting areas.

A well-organized defence will retreat in good order and make its stand just outside their penalty area, where every opponent is marked; the man in possession is challenged, and the free-back is covering every possible break-through. With a reliable and agile goalkeeper it is practically impossible to score.

Wave after wave of attack rolls towards the goal, and time after time the moves break down. Being human, the enemy defenders 2, 3 and 5 are tempted to move up in a bid to break the deadlock. Gaining possession near the half way line, the right-back moves up-

## The evolution of the game

field with the ball but as he gets closer to goal, the marking on his team-mates becomes tighter. There is no unmarked colleague to whom he can pass and if he tries to pass, it could be intercepted. If he tries to dribble he may well be dispossessed and if he tries a high centre it will almost certainly be the goalkeeper's ball.

Once possession is lost, the defending team attempts to get the ball forward to one of their front players 9 and 11. To a very great extent the play will be concentrated in one half of the field but occasionally the defensive team will manage to break away. If their two front players do manage to reach their opponent's penalty area quickly then they will certainly have a much better chance of scoring. There is no free-back covering them, and the penalty area is not crowded with players as it is at the other end.

As the teams adopting catenaccio became more skilled at their game, they became more successful at engineering quick breakaway attacks. So successful were they that the top teams soon became aware that superior skill was no guarantee of success. In one good breakaway, the defensive team could score a goal, while the attacking team found this beyond them in spite of perhaps thirty minutes constant pressure.

Finally, the top teams realized that they must have insurance against conceding a breakaway goal. They too must have a *libero* or free-back, and catenaccio in one form or another became established. To play any other way was to invite disaster for experience showed that to concede the first goal was fatal. Even the most talented and skilful teams could not guard against the breakaway goal in any other way.

Once they had scored, the negative teams were happy to waste time; keep the ball, and give away tactical free kicks in midfield. Calling everyone back into defence, the defensive teams with a goal lead proved very difficult to beat. If it was difficult to score against a team playing 1–4–3–2, then it became almost impossible against a 2–4–4–0 framework which often resembled 10–0–0. Now it became clear that if a team could not score themselves it was vital that they should not concede a goal which would allow their opponents to go completely defensive. Everyone must now have a free-back: catenaccio was the only way to play!

Reviewing the developments in the game to date, we can now see that inherent weaknesses in defence have enforced changes once they have been discovered. WM was discarded because the lone centre-back

## *The evolution of the game*

had two roles to play: he had to mark the centre-forward *and* cover space.

The dual centre-back game which is the heart of the 4-2-4 and 4-3-3 defensive systems, has been rejected because the two centre-backs have three major duties: they have each to mark a man *and* between them to cover space.

Now it appears that the three centre-back system has finally settled all defensive problems. Two of the centre-backs each marks a centre-forward, while the third centre-back marks the space behind his colleagues in turn as they challenge for the ball.

The central approach to goal now seems to have been closed but in reality the free (covering) back also has two primary roles to fulfil:
1. He has to cover the space immediately behind the defender who challenges for the ball.
2. He has to watch for, and cover, any opponent who *comes from behind*.

## 2 — The effect of modern tactics on the old playing positions, the new positions which have been created, and the redistribution of duties and responsibilities throughout the team

The creation of the *libero* (free-back) and the disappearance of the left-wingers who have been very largely withdrawn into midfield, has created a great deal of misunderstanding particularly amongst those brought up in the era of the attacking centre-half. If we are to make a realistic appraisal of the modern team then we must clearly understand that the numbers worn by the players can no longer be taken as a guide to *how* they will play. A player's role in any particular game can no longer be predicted by a glance at his number and to determine a player's position we must watch him closely during the game.

In general terms we can state quite simply that wing-halves have almost ceased to exist. Like the centre-halves who became centre-backs in the thirties the wing-halves have virtually disappeared. Some people may no doubt wish to argue this point, but considering the 4-2-4 system developed by Brazil in 1958 it will be difficult to explain convincingly the difference between number 4 (Zito) and number 8 (Didi). Zito the right-half and Didi the inside-right (who withdrew across the pitch to play on the left) were Brazil's midfield link-men. Was Zito still a right-half and could Didi's role be adequately described by the term inside-forward? The new game becomes simpler if we accept that in 1958 the Brazilians fielded two *midfield* players—Zito on the right and Didi on the left. They should now be referred to as *right-midfield* and *left-midfield*. To trace the effects of modern tactics on the various playing positions we can begin with the WM system where there was only one misnomer—the centre-half. Following the change in the offside law the centre-half was in reality the centre-back.

## *The new playing positions*

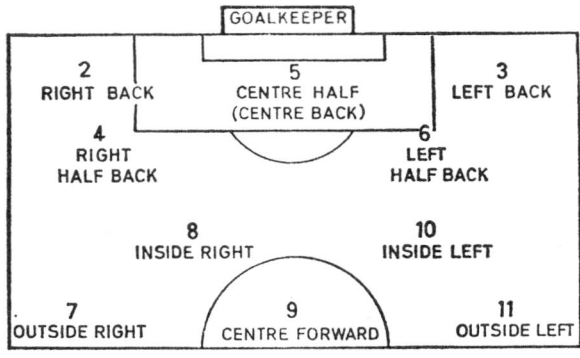

*Diagram 6*

In the WM system the eleven playing positions and the numbers worn by the players were as shown in Diagram 6 and with minor variations the team retained this shape until 1958. In the thirties a withdrawn centre-forward was introduced in central Europe and in the early fifties Hungary withdrew left-half Zakarias to play a purely defensive role. Later still the Real Madrid centre-forward Alfredo di Stefano was to play a wandering game which still defies description but as late as 1957 it was possible to observe right-wingers, inside-rights and right half-backs. But with the development of Brazil's 4–2–4 system the functions of many players began to change and *new* playing positions emerged. 4–2–4 made important changes in all three phases of the game. In defence we saw the introduction of the *right centre-back* and *left centre-back*—achieved by withdrawing the left-half to play alongside the old centre-half. In attack the inside-left was relieved of his midfield responsibilities in order that he could play alongside the old centre-forward, and thus we now had a *right centre-forward* and a *left centre-forward*.

Having withdrawn the left-half and advanced the inside-left the Brazilians now had a huge gap in midfield between left-back and outside-left and they filled this void by withdrawing their inside-right and moving him across to the left flank. We could conceivably continue to refer to the midfield players by their old names or alternatively we could call them right and left *link-man*. However, I prefer to call the two men linking defence and attack midfield players—in 4–2–4—*right-midfield* and *left-midfield*. Later we shall find we also have a centre-midfield and two more players whose duties

## The new playing positions

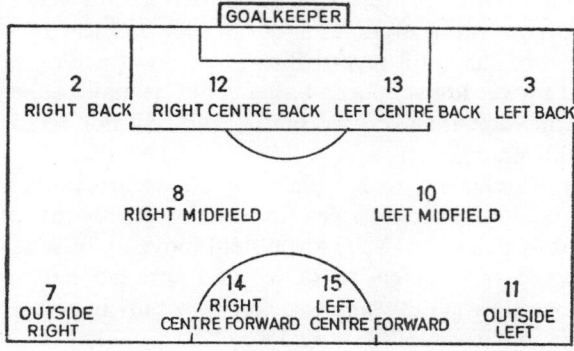

*Diagram 7*

keep them between defence and attack but they will not be true midfield players.

Diagram 7 shows the distribution of players in the 4-2-4 system as applied to the Brazilian team of 1958. Though other teams may withdraw their right-half into defence and play with the old inside-right and left-half as the link-men, my description of the playing positions in 4-2-4 covers all the possible variations. It will be seen that I have given four of the positions new numbers—12, 13, 14 and 15—for while the midfield players may be fairly described as hard working inside-forwards of the old WM system we have not previously seen two centre-backs nor two centre-forwards. These four playing positions are completely new compared with WM.

Since the Brazilians demonstrated that the old relationship between a player's number and his role in the team was not sacrosanct others have made further experiments. Indeed, in some cases these experiments were forced on coaches and managers because some players were quite unable to adapt their style of play, and amongst professional teams playing 4-2-4 I have seen centre-backs wearing numbers 10, 8 and 7.

Having had considerable experience of adapting players brought up on WM to other systems of play it is my conclusion that some players are quite incapable of playing their normal (and natural) game unless they wear the number with which they are familiar.

Adapting a WM team to 4-2-4 it seems logical to withdraw one of the wing-halves to play alongside the old stopper and though this

## The new playing positions

may present no problem to the player chosen we now have to fill the gap left by his withdrawal. This is the real problem for a former inside-forward may still regard himself as an attacking player. He will sprint forward to support an attack, but he may not be prepared to accept his defensive responsibilities and will not return to midfield quickly enough.

Former wing-halves with a flair for attack are probably better suited to the near midfield roles for psychologically they do regard themselves as defenders. They always did move up in WM, but they also accepted their defensive duties and sprinted back when the attack broke down. But—and this can be vitally important—which players are to wear numbers 4 and 6?

Needing another centre-half we may prefer to promote a reserve stopper rather than convert a wing-half and giving the number 6 shirt to the newcomer we now have to find another number for the former left-half. We may give him 8 or 10 or 9 or 11 for in theory it matters little which number he wears.

In fact, however, the former left-half may now be unwilling to accept his defensive responsibilities for wearing the inside-left shirt changes his outlook. For weeks after these changes are made there may be a deficiency in left midfield where opponents are allowed to bring the ball into the danger area and force the left-back to leave his winger to make a challenge.

Very often such problems can be overcome quite simply for example by giving the promoted centre-half the number 10 shirt. Now both wing-halves are wearing their familiar numbers and if the former left-half cannot play *left-midfield* with a 10 on his back he certainly can when his old shirt is returned to him. As a general rule when problems of this kind present themselves, give the player who has difficulty 'playing out of position' the number from WM which most closely resembles his new role.

To return to the main theme we find that in defence 4–3–3 is based on the same basic principles as 4–2–4 and there are no new roles. In midfield there are now three players as against two in 4–2–4 and we can now add a *centre-midfield* to our growing list of playing positions and give him the number 16.

In general terms the three midfield players in 4–3–3 have similar duties. Like the midfield links in 4–2–4 they will all act as supporting players behind the attack and competing with their opponents midfield players will challenge for the ball in front of their defensive

## The new playing positions

wall. From time to time they may be asked to pay particular attention to a particular opponent but though they may be more restricted in this case they remain in essence midfield players.

Catenaccio has produced two further playing positions which cannot be fairly compared with the duties of players already mentioned. The first is the key man in any catenaccio—the *libero*—and the second I have called a *defensive-screen*.

Originally the *libero* was the old-style centre-back who was left to cover the central defensive zone when double-marking was the fashion and a withdrawn forward assumed the task of tight marking the enemy centre-forward. As catenaccio developed the old centre-back slipped further back and he now lies in a covering position behind the line of tight-marking defenders. Clearly, he is a newcomer in the development of tactics from WM via 4–2–4 to 4–3–3. I have given him number 17.

The defensive-screen has been seen in 4–3–3 playing in a more or less fixed position in front of the two centre-backs but he originated from the 1–4–2–3 form of catenaccio. Teams playing 1–4–2–3 often found that their opponents fielded only one centre-forward and one of the two orthodox centre-backs then had no one to mark. With the *libero* covering space and the second centre-back marking the enemy centre-forward, the first centre-back had no clear role. Reluctant to reduce their permanent defence from 5 to 4 a new role was created for the superfluous centre-back.

Preparing his team to play 1–4–2–3 the Italian coach decided in advance which of his twin stoppers would mark the centre-forward and made it clear that if there was not a second centre-forward the 'free' centre-back would step forward and play in front of the defence. In his new position the 'free' centre-back has two primary duties:

1. To challenge any opponent who evades the midfield players and brings the ball forward. Unopposed, such a player would either reach a shooting position or force a defender to leave his immediate opponent free when he came to challenge.
2. To make it difficult for the opposition to lay passes at the feet of their centre-forward.

In England where the *defensive-screen* has already been seen, he has been called the 'sweeper in front of the defence'. Originally the *centre-midfield*, he was withdrawn by some teams to play a purely defensive role. His duties are precisely the same as those developed

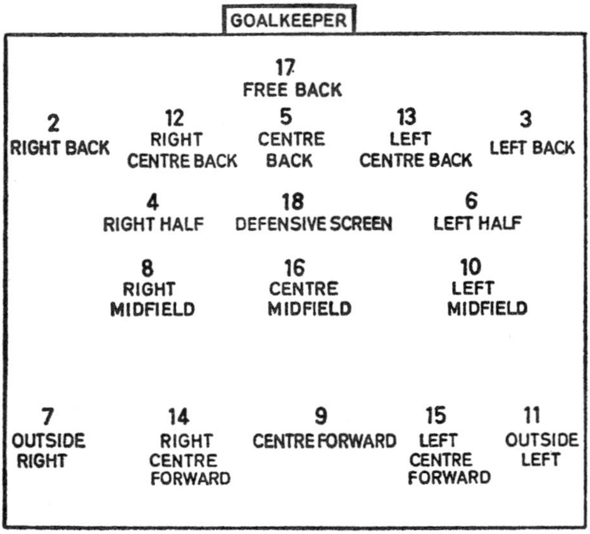

## The new playing positions

```
                    | GOALKEEPER |

                         17
                      FREE BACK
     2          12          5          13          3
  RIGHT BACK   RIGHT      CENTRE      LEFT      LEFT BACK
              CENTRE BACK  BACK    CENTRE BACK

                 4          18          6
             RIGHT HALF DEFENSIVE SCREEN LEFT HALF

                 8          16          10
               RIGHT      CENTRE       LEFT
             MIDFIELD    MIDFIELD    MIDFIELD

     7          14          9          15          11
  OUTSIDE     RIGHT    CENTRE FORWARD  LEFT      OUTSIDE
   RIGHT     CENTRE                  CENTRE       LEFT
            FORWARD                 FORWARD
```

*Diagram 8*

in Italy for the spare centre-back, but screening the defence as he does, I prefer to call him a screen. I have given him number 18.

In Diagram 8 we can now review the eighteen playing positions which can be clearly seen in the modern game and then we can consider a most important point.

Ten years ago a player would ask his manager or coach 'Where am I playing today?' and the manager could reply 'Right-back'. The conversation would have ended there and the player would have put on his number 2 shirt and played as he understood a right-back should play. Today it is quite different for, as an example, many teams do not field left-wingers, and if our opponents are not going to have an outside-left we do not need an orthodox right-back. In the enemy dressing-room the manager will be telling one of his players, 'Wear 11 and line up at outside-left. But as soon as the game starts, sprint back and play left centre-back'. Against an immature team the modern manager knows that in these circumstances the opposing right-back will spend the entire afternoon looking for the left-winger, and contributing very little to the team effort.

In amateur football this is very common and on one occasion I overheard a brief conversation between a right-half and his manager.

## The new playing positions

Approaching his manager on the trainer's bench the right-half asked, 'Where is the inside-left? I can't find him'. The player was told, 'He's there somewhere. Find him and mark him'. In reality this particular inside-left was playing the *libero* (free-back) game at position number 17. No wonder the right-half couldn't find him!

Before we can enter the realm of modern soccer we must accept the fact that players' numbers no longer indicate how they will play. In a match programme, numbers serve only to enable spectators to identify the individual players, and if we are to follow the game intelligently or by coaching, prepare players for a game, we must accept that there are now eighteen playing positions.

Today, when a player asks his manager, 'Where am I playing?' it is no longer enough. In fact he should ask two questions.
1. What number shall I wear?
2. What role shall I play?

As already stated it has been my experience that some players are unable to forget the implications of the old numbering system, and very largely this stems from the fact that the new game has not been explained to them. If coaches and players are to communicate and if spectators and critics are to understand modern soccer we must recognize the new roles and define the duties of the players in various positions.

We must also understand that although I define eighteen quite different playing positions each team is still limited to eleven players and they will be numbered (for the benefit of spectators) from 1 to 11. The manager or coach must decide which eleven positions he will use for each game and this will depend to a very great extent on the 'shape' of the team the opposition is expected to field.

Before going further into this field we should now define the modern playing positions. Where once we had backs, half-backs and forwards I believe that we should now be more realistic and I have accordingly renamed the three major groupings of players. Backs become defenders, half-backs become midfield players and the forwards become front players.

### Goalkeeper

Although goalkeepers have assumed additional responsibilities and developed new techniques in recent years it is not my intention to delve into this aspect of the game. Broadly speaking the goalkeeper's duties remain what they were in WM.

## The new playing positions

### DEFENCE PLAYERS

**Free-back**

Known as the *libero* in Italy, the free-back is so named because he does not have to mark an opponent. Positioned behind the defenders who are marking men, the free-back covers each of his defensive colleagues in turn as his team mates are drawn into a challenge for the ball. In particular he is responsible for covering the central approach to goal when the centre-back(s) are drawn out of position.

**Right-back**

The new tactics have made little impact on the full-backs and the right-back is still responsible for marking the opposing left-winger. In 4-2-4 and 4-3-3 the right-back will also be asked to give cover on the centre when the enemy attacks on the other flank or through the centre. In any form of catenaccio, full responsibility for covering is taken by the free-back and the right-back is left to concentrate on the left-winger.

**Left-back**

Like his partner on the other flank the left-back is expected to mark the opposing right-winger and in 4-2-4 and 4-3-3 also to cover the centre. In any form of catenaccio he is also relieved of covering responsibilities.

*N.B.*—If it was anticipated that the opposition would play 4-2-4 with wingers and once the game begins, one of the 'wingers' withdraws to fulfil another role, it is essential that the spare back should be re-deployed. There are now four possibilities:
  (a) the spare back can be used as a second centre-back if the enemy has two centre-forwards and we have only one centre-back.
  (b) the spare back can be used as a free-back behind the defence.
  (c) the spare back can be used as a defensive-screen in front of the defence.
  (d) the spare back can be used in midfield.

The decision will depend on the abilities of the full-back and the playing 'shape' adopted by the opposition.

**Right centre-back**

Where there are two centre-forwards to be faced the right centre-

## The new playing positions

back should mark the left centre-forward. In 4-2-4 and 4-3-3 he will also be expected to cover the right-back and the left centre-back. In catenaccio he concentrates solely on preventing the left centre-forward from making any contribution to the game.

**Centre-back**

The old-style stopper is still to be seen—for example in a 1-3-3-3 team facing opposition which plays with three players up front—two wingers and a lone centre-forward. Here the duties of the centre-back will be confined exclusively to a personal duel with the centre-forward. In certain circumstances it may still be possible to see an old-fashioned stopper centre-half, for example in a two-legged cup tie where the home team needs to make up for a heavy defeat in the first leg and is prepared to gamble on all-out attack. In such circumstances the centre-back will be expected to give cover to either full-back as may be required.

**Left centre-back**

In the dual centre-back game of 4-2-4 and 4-3-3 the left centre-back will be expected to mark the right centre-forward and give cover to the left-back and the right centre-back. With a free-back playing behind, however, he will be free to give all his attention to his immediate opponent.

**Defensive-screen**

A purely defensive player who is asked to patrol across the front of the defensive wall, intercepting passes intended for the opposition's front players. From whichever direction an attack might develop it will be the screen who moves across to challenge the player who has possession, thus making it more difficult for opponents to pull a tight-marking defender away from his man.

**Right-half**

Normally used only in matches where the emphasis is on defence. His duties will be to cover the opposing left-midfield and also to act as a permament *screen* on the right flank.

**Left-half**

Exactly the same duties as the right-half—a defensive midfield player asked to cover the enemy right-midfield and act as a screen on the left flank.

## *The new playing positions*

**Right-midfield**

A combination of old WM-type right-half and inside-right, but with greater freedom of action. Will be expected to support his front colleagues but also be in a position to 'screen' the defensive players when required.

**Centre-midfield**

Perhaps best described as the old-style attacking centre-half (pre-WM) or later as a withdrawn centre-forward. Positioned between right-midfield and left-midfield his duties will be to support the front players and also help in defence when necessary.

**Left-midfield**

Like his partner at right-midfield, this player is expected to challenge for the ball in midfield, support the attack and help in defence.

*N.B.*—It should be noted that any of the midfield players, 4, 6, 8, 16 or 10 may be asked to pay particular attention to a key opponent who plays in midfield.

## FRONT PLAYERS

**Outside-right**

Although wingers are less common than they were ten years ago, their duties have changed very little. In addition to carrying out raids from the flanks, they are also expected to move across field cutting in when the attack develops on the other flank to score goals themselves.

**Centre-forward**

Still predominantly regarded as a spearhead, the orthodox centre-forward plays very much as his predecessors did.

**Right centre-forward**

Only to be seen in teams which employ two front players in the central zone, he positions himself as the central European inside-right did when the inside-forwards played as spearheads and the centre-forward was withdrawn into midfield.

## *The new playing positions*

**Left centre-forward**

Like the right centre-forward his objectives are similar to those of the old-style centre-forward except that he positions more to the left. By providing close support for each other the two centre-forwards are better able to create space for themselves than the lone centre-forward could ever hope to do.

**Outside-left**

The left-winger's duties have changed little compared with the old-style outside-left. Though he is a rarity today his presence helps to add width in attack and thus prevent the defenders from concentrating.

Having defined the new playing positions we can now briefly describe some of the common team *shapes* to be seen today. But before we go any further let it be clearly understood that WM is dead. In top-class football the old 3-2-5 game cannot be found anywhere in the world.

In general the British teams still seem to favour 4-2-4 with a sprinkling of clubs switching to 4-3-3 following England's success in the 1966 World Cup.

Elsewhere it is clear that 4-2-4 still has many advocates but the vast majority of European club sides are now playing to various forms of catenaccio.

In West Germany 1-3-2-4 is very popular—two backs and a stopper, with a free-back behind; two midfield players and two wingers and two centre-forwards in attack.

The Hungarians, once the most attack-conscious of all, have also adopted catenaccio, though they are generally even more defensive than the Germans. In Budapest the common rule is now 1-4-2-3, with some favouring two wingers and others preferring two centre-forwards.

It is in Italy, however, that the game is most advanced in terms of defence, and it is there that the most negative forms of catenaccio can be seen.

F.C. Internazionale have been the most successful Italian team in recent years but they are not quite typical. Other clubs, less endowed with money and therefore not so well equipped in terms of talented players, are even more negative, but Inter provide an excellent guide to catenaccio.

Diagram 9 illustrates the shape of the Inter team in 1966/67

```
                    1
                  SARTI
               (GOALKEEPER)


                    6
                  PICCHI
               (FREE BACK)

      2             5                  3
   BURGNICH      GUARNERI           FACCHETTI
  (RIGHT BACK)  (CENTRE BACK)      (LEFT BACK)


         4            10              11
       BEDIN        SUAREZ          CORSO
  (RIGHT MIDFIELD) (CENTRE MIDFIELD) (LEFT MIDFIELD)


         7             8                 9
     DOMENGHINI      MAZZOLA         CAPPELLINI
   (OUTSIDE RIGHT) (RIGHT CENTRE FORWARD) (LEFT CENTRE FORWARD)
```

*Diagram 9*

```
                    1
                  BANKS
               (GOALKEEPER)

      2             5             6              3
   COHEN       J. CHARLTON      MOORE         WILSON
  (RIGHT BACK) (RIGHT CENTRE BACK) (LEFT CENTRE BACK) (LEFT BACK)

                    4
                  STILES
             (DEFENSIVE SCREEN)


         7             9              11
       BALL       R. CHARLTON       PETERS
  (RIGHT MIDFIELD) (CENTRE MIDFIELD) (LEFT MIDFIELD)


                    8              10
                  HUNT            HURST
          (RIGHT CENTRE FORWARD) (LEFT CENTRE FORWARD)
```

*Diagram 10*

## *The new playing positions*

season with the names of the players, the numbers they wore and the roles they filled.

Another interesting *shape* has been adopted by England who were said in 1966 to be playing 4-3-3. In reality the *shape* of England's team would be better described as 4-1-3-2 for both Ball and Peters spent most of their time in midfield flanking Bobby Charlton while Stiles was used either to tight-mark a key midfield opponent or as a defensive screen.

The England team which beat West Germany in the World Cup Final would be described in modern terms as outlined in Diagram 10, again with the WM numbers and the respective positions.

# 3 — The tactics of defenders in relation to space, and the relationship between open spaces in midfield with shooting spaces in the penalty area

To the individual player space is important. If he receives the ball in space he has time to control it, for in football, space is time.

Space is equally important in terms of tactics and overall team play for in the modern game defences seek to deny space (and time) to opponents. A defending team cannot hope to deny all space to their opponents, but defenders now have a very clear idea of the relative importance of space in various areas. This was not so in the old game of WM for by the nature of the system defenders were forced to allow one or more attacking players ample space. This stemmed from the covering system in defence which pivoted on the centre-back. When an attack developed on the right flank the opposing left-back would come up close to the outside-right and simultaneously the centre-back moved closer to the left-back (and deeper) in order to provide cover. At the same time the right-back dropped

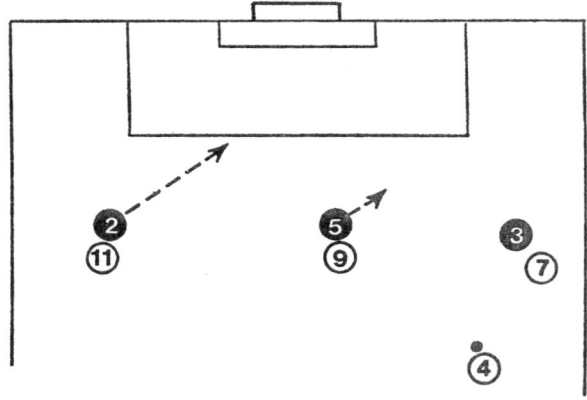

*Diagram 11 (a)*

## The tactics of defenders

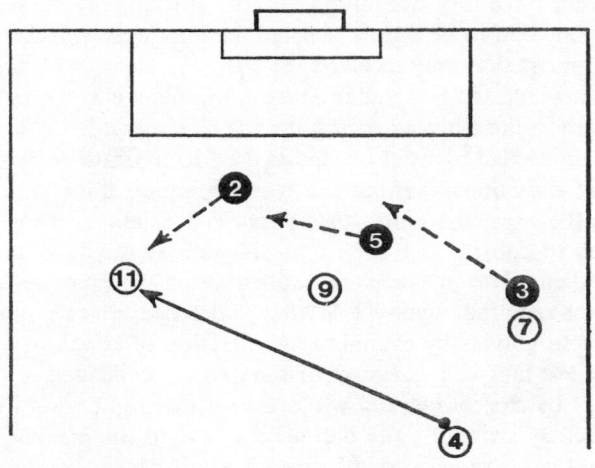

*Diagram 11 (b)*

deep to cover the centre. Diagrams 11 (a) and 11 (b) illustrate the covering system in WM defences which turned on the centre-back. Being short of personnel, defences were forced to choose between marking their individual opponents closely *and* providing cover for each other. In Diagram 11 (a) the attacking right-half (4) has the ball and the defenders move to cover an attack from that flank. If the right-half should make an accurate cross-field pass to his outside-left then all three backs have to sprint to re-position themselves in order to meet this new threat as shown in Diagram 11 (b).

The inherent weakness in this system hinged on the dual role defenders were asked to play. At every moment under pressure, they had to mark opponents *and* provide cover for each other.

The Hungarians finally exposed the tremendous weakness in the centre of the defence but skilful wingers had already been exploiting the same weakness on the flanks for years.

With the full-backs pivoting on the centre-back it is obvious that at any moment at least one winger must be given space. When the winger received a cross-field pass he had ample time to control the ball, turn, and prepare to take on his challenger. Given space and time good wingers created havoc for players like Matthews (Stoke City and later Blackpool) and Finney (Preston N.E.) were almost

## The tactics of defenders

unstoppable once they were in possession. If such players were to be stopped they had to be tightly marked for they were vulnerable only in the moment that they received the ball.

Once they had the ball under control, top-class players had all the advantages in their favour, dribbling the ball towards their challenger the winger had a variety of feints used to indicate an impending change of direction. Turning the trunk, dipping the shoulder and wiggling the hips, the ball artists terrorized defences. They needed only time to control the ball; and allowed by the WM system to position themselves in space they were granted the time they needed.

It will be seen that against a WM-type defence, space can be made for the front players by changing the direction of attack in midfield. With the left-half in possession of the ball his colleague at outside-left would be closely marked while the outside-right would be relatively free. By switching the ball across field to the inside-right the attacking team would send the opposing full-backs sprinting to reposition, pivoting on the centre-back. By using a cross-field pass in midfield, the attacking team could make space for the left-winger—and the inside-right could now find him with a pass. Given space by the cross-field pass the outside-left now has time to control the ball and turn to face his opponent.

Against 4–2–4 or 4–3–3 defences it is not so easy to unbalance the defenders by changing the direction of attack and the space and time so gained is very slight. But against catenaccio type defences a cross-field pass gains not even one millimetre (in space) nor one-tenth of a second (in time).

The covering system in a four-back defence differs considerably from the WM system. In 4–2–4 and 4–3–3 the full-backs give only secondary cover on the centre and are thus allowed greater freedom of action against their personal opponent. If the left centre-back is drawn into a duel for the ball it is the right centre-back who drops to cover him (and vice versa). Cover for the right-back is now provided by the right centre-back while the left-back is covered by the left centre-back.

In the WM game the full-backs might give the wingers as much as twenty-five yards of free space, but in four-back defences this may be reduced to as little as five yards.

The really big problem of modern football is catenaccio and here it is the free-back who provides cover for each defender as necessary. Full-backs and centre-backs in this system are not required to cover

## The tactics of defenders

anyone. They are free to tight-mark their individual opponent. Now there is little or no advantage to be gained from cross-field passing in midfield. In the new game it can be assumed that several enemy players (from midfield) were caught in attacking positions when their move broke down. If a counter-attack can be developed quickly the midfield players may not recover in time to help their defensive colleagues, but cross-field passes waste time—which is on the side of the defenders.

It was the problem of coping with outstanding forwards which sent the Italians off on the road to catenaccio. By tight-marking, the defenders are able to tackle quickly, challenging for the ball before the front player can even get one touch at the ball.

Just how tight the marking can be was illustrated for me in the 1964 European Cup Final, played at the Prater Stadion in Vienna between Real Madrid and FC Internazionale. As the teams lined up for the kick off, the Inter left-wing pair Suarez (10) and Corso (11) were deep in midfield playing respectively at centre-midfield and left-midfield. Though they played as usual to their 1–3–3–3 system I was surprised to see an Inter player standing where the orthodox left-winger would position himself at the kick off and as he turned away from me I saw his number. It was Facchetti the left-back, *tight-marking* Real winger Amancio right from the opening second!

Later in the same game I noted an incident which will underline just how tight the man-for-man marking can be in catenaccio for the benefit of those who have not been able to study the system closely. On the left-wing Real Madrid's Gento had possession; shuffling inside with the ball at his feet and Burgnich the Inter right-back positioned a yard and a half away, backing off. From the right-wing Amancio sprinted across field towards Gento, with his shadow Facchetti right on his heels. As Amancio approached Gento, the right-winger raced across his colleague's back, passing so close to Gento that they almost touched. Facchetti had been following Amancio at around two yards distance (goal-side) and the left-back passed between Gento and Burgnich. Though Facchetti's left foot almost touched the ball he didn't even glance at it. His attention was on Amancio, and Facchetti followed him into space.

Summing up we can say that changing the point of attack brings an advantage to front players against a WM defence but gains nothing and wastes time against catenaccio-type defences. This point is illustrated in Diagram 12 where it will be seen that the only defen-

## The tactics of defenders

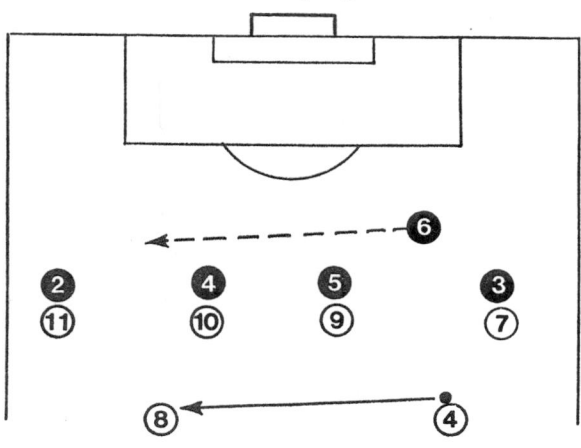

*Diagram 12*

sive player to change position following a square pass in midfield . . . is the *libero*.

In the modern game defensive players are consciously denying space (and time) to front players and this very largely explains why fewer goals are being scored today. It also helps to explain why the standard of wing play seems to have declined and why wingers of outstanding ability are quite rare.

If defenders are now aware of the importance of denying space to their individual opponents it is also apparent that the game as a whole has changed its attitude towards open spaces. Recognizing that the play in midfield is now unimportant in terms of results, midfield players don't even bother to challenge for possession in midfield. Instead they sprint back to reinforce their defensive colleagues when their attacks break down. Once an attacking move has failed and possession of the ball is lost it is far more important for the midfield players to get back into positions where they can *screen* their defensive colleagues. The enemy can keep the ball for the moment—and they are very welcome to the big open spaces in midfield.

If the enemy is foolish enough to waste time by inter-passing in midfield then so much the better. If they choose to run with the ball instead of pushing it forward quickly, then that's good too. More and more it is becoming apparent that the top teams are prepared to concede midfield to their opponents.

## The tactics of defenders

If opponents choose to build up their attack by inter-passing in the *open spaces* the defenders will withdraw in good order. They are happy to do so for two reasons:

1. Midfield players are getting closer to their defensive colleagues with every second that passes.
2. The defenders are knit more closely together on the edge of their penalty area than they are on the halfway line.

A four-back defence on the half-way line is far more vulnerable if a front player should gain possession of the ball and beat his opponent. With twenty-yard spaces between the defenders, cover is not as close as it would be if the four backs were spread across their penalty area. Diagram 13 illustrates quite clearly that when defenders are

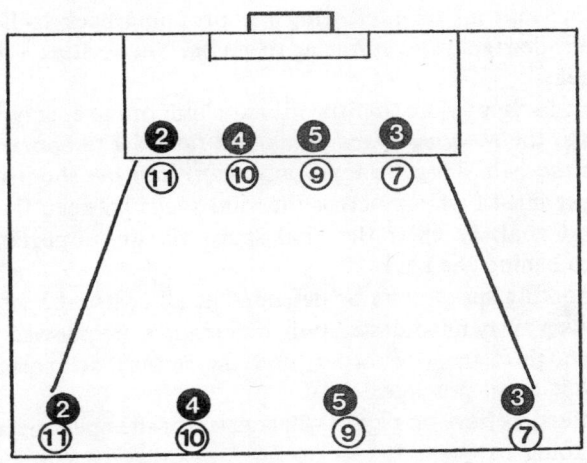

*Diagram 13*

allowed to *funnel* back, the defensive unit becomes more compact. Just as a goalkeeper narrows the shooting angle when he *advances* to meet an oncoming front player, so the defenders narrow the attacking angles when they withdraw.

Underlying all defensive tactics is the fact that while a team might dominate a game in terms of ball possession, it is goals that count—and goals win matches. Goals are not scored in midfield, but in and around the respective penalty areas. When defenders funnel back they are not particularly perturbed as long as they are able to cover

## The tactics of defenders

the shooting area and mark the enemy's front players. To challenge in midfield would be foolish for if a defender were to be beaten out in the loose, it could lead to space and an unmarked front player in the shooting area.

If we really want to worry defensive players let us consider the question of space from their point of view. As the four backs face up to an attack each defender moves close to his particular front player. His aim will be to stay close and thus be able to make a quick challenge if the ball should be passed to his opponent. Consider the position of the left-back in Diagram 14. Close marking his immediate opponent, the enemy outside-right, he does not particularly worry that the inside-right has the ball and is bringing it towards him. He can see that his team-mate 6 is moving to challenge the man in possession; that his own left-winger is dropping back to help, and that the inside-right (8) is sprinting to get back in position—goal-side of the ball.

The left-back is aware that the ultimate aim of the enemy is to put a man into the *shooting space* unmarked (at least temporarily) and give him the ball. To get a man (any man) into the shooting space that player must first run across the vital space between the centre-backs and goal, or enter the vital space via the important space which lies behind the backs.

The shooting space must be defended at all costs; the vital space will be given away uncontested only if defenders are allowed to withdraw through it in good order, and the important space will be defended if at all possible.

The defenders have no regard whatsoever for the open spaces. They are not going to be persuaded to go forward. Given a choice the defenders will retreat, withdrawing towards their penalty area and the shooting space. They will give up the ground that is in front of them as they withdraw, but they will not allow any opponent into the spaces at their backs. If anyone tries to get in there the defenders will withdraw.

This is in fact what happens when a front player suddenly sprints towards goal away from his colleague in possession. If the outside-right sprints forward the left-back will not be caught. Generations of wingers have gone looking for the ball over the full-back's head, and it would be a poor player indeed who let his opponent get free in this manner.

As the inside-right advances in Diagram 14 the conventional right-

## The tactics of defenders

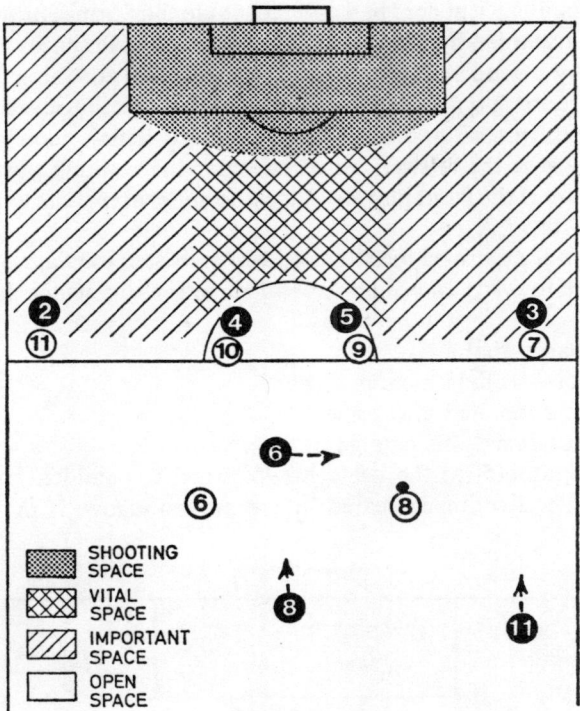

*Diagram 14*

winger will edge away. Rather than let the winger move into the *important space* behind him the left-back will retreat. The important space is now getting smaller and part of that area which was once important space is now in front of the left-back—and transformed into useless *open space*.

If the player in possession continues to advance the defenders will withdraw, marking their opponents tight and ready at any moment to cover each other. Steadily the defenders retreat until by the time they reach their penalty area they are in good order, compact and balanced to meet any challenge. By this time too the three men who were dropping back to help (6, 8 and 11) should all be goal-side of the man with the ball.

To the casual observer the open spaces in midfield appear attractive, and a team using these spaces for inter-passing is considered both intelligent and constructive. In reality, however, the open spaces

## The tactics of defenders

are useless. If such spaces had any real value they would never be left open but occupied by defenders. The really valuable spaces are those covered by defenders and opening them is the art of the game.

Good running *off the ball* (without the ball) is said to be the secret of football, but no one has yet managed to define good running. Assuming it is the answer, let us consider the running possibilities open to one of the front players, taking as our example the left centre-forward (10).

Basing our attack on the situation which existed in Diagram 14 the left centre-forward has four general directions in which he could move.

1. Towards goal.
2. Across the field moving right.
3. Across the field moving left.
4. Back towards his own goal.

In Diagram 15 (a) the left centre-forward has suddenly sprinted away in the direction indicated by the broken arrow. If the man in

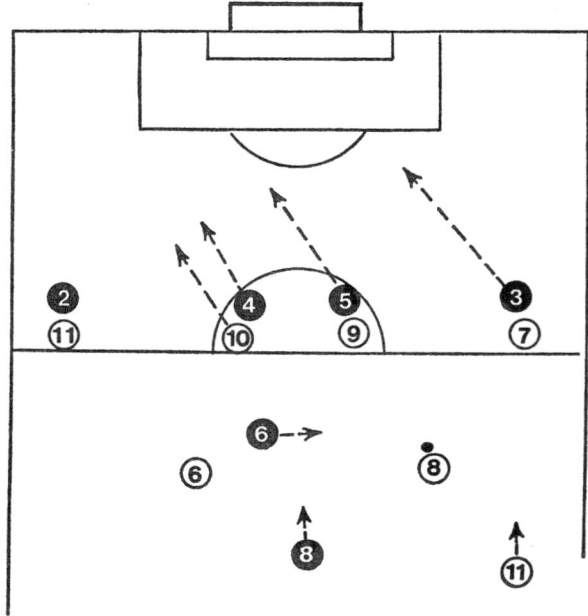

*Diagram 15 (a)*

## The tactics of defenders

possession has seen 10 go it is conceivable that a good pass could be dropped in space ahead of the left centre-forward, but there are two basic reasons why this kind of move breaks down:

1. The left centre-forward is isolating himself from support by running away from his colleagues.
2. The four-back defence might well catch him offside.

We must remember too that the right centre-back was watching 10 closely, and this kind of break is too obvious to catch an alert defender. In all probability the right centre-back would cover 10 at every step and at the same time the left centre-back would drop back to cover.

Finally, against a catenaccio-type defence, such a break is doomed. The *libero* is positioned behind the defensive line and from his deep position ten to fifteen yards behind the centre-backs, the *libero* would be first to the ball. Cutting off this long pass the *libero* can (a) clear the ball upfield, (b) pass the ball back to his goalkeeper, or (c) if under any form of pressure he could put the ball out of play.

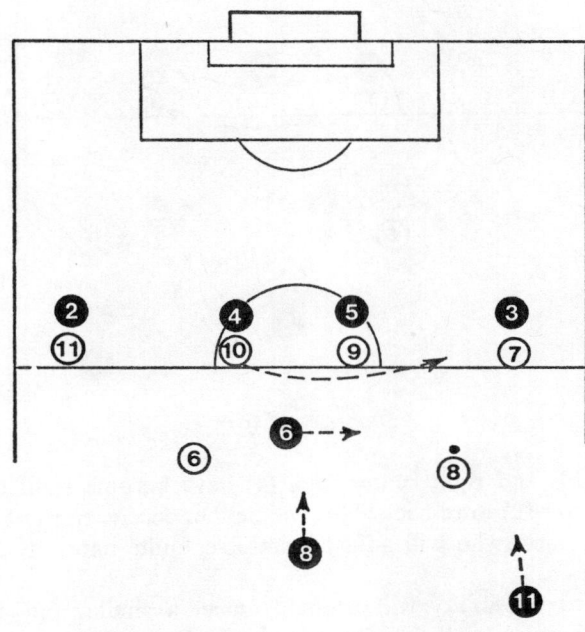

*Diagram 15 (b)*

## The tactics of defenders

If the left centre-forward moves across the pitch towards the right there is a much better possibility that he will get free. In Diagram 15 (b) the left centre-forward has moved to inside-right and if he went quietly—without calling for the ball—it is conceivable that he might escape the attention of an inexperienced pair of centre-backs, and receive a through pass from 8.

It is more likely, however, that an experienced defender would cover 10 at every step and when he has arrived at inside-right the situation would be that shown in Diagram 15 (c). Here the left centre-

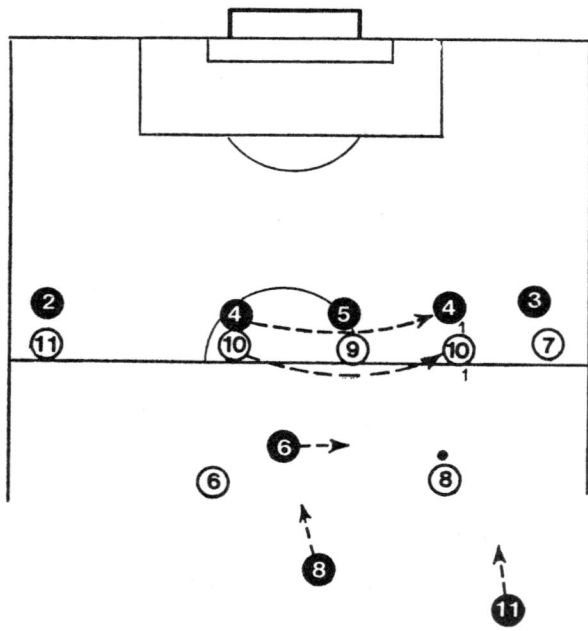

*Diagram 15 (c)*

forward (10) and right centre-back (4) have become right centre-forward and left centre-back. This will neither deceive nor unbalance a good defence, who will adjust themselves quite naturally to this new situation.

The third possibility will probably meet a similar fate but in addition there is very little space to the left of 10. If he moves left as illustrated in Diagram 15 (d) and the outside-left moves inside it is

*The tactics of defenders*

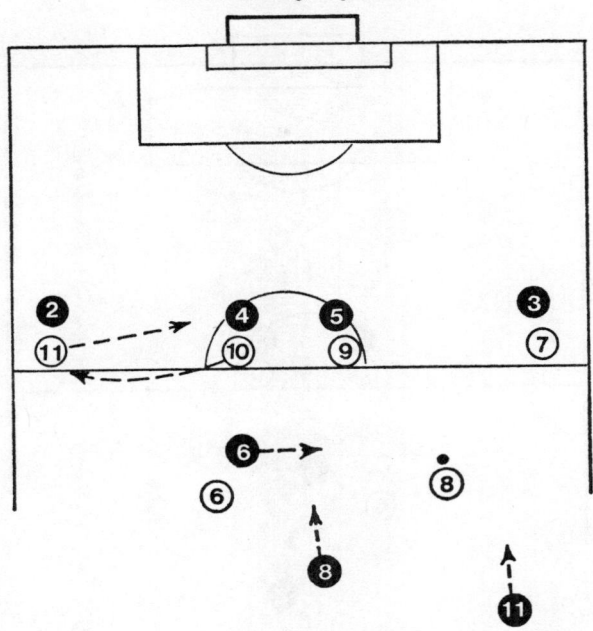

*Diagram 15 (d)*

possible that either 10 or 11 *could* get free but again it must be stressed that this could occur only against gullible defenders. A well-drilled defence would continue to cover their men and the net result would simply be a temporary positional switch as shown in Diagram 15 (e).

Finally, there is the fourth possibility open to the left centre-forward, and for very good players this could be very rewarding. If 10 drops back ten to twelve yards he will find that his opponent has two choices:

1. He can come forward with him but by doing so he makes it impossible for him to cover the left centre-back if the need arises.
2. He can concede to 10 both space and time if he elects to remain in a covering position.

In Diagram 16 (a) we see that the defender marking 10 has followed him deep. It may also be observed that for the first time we have created space *within* the previously impregnable defence. If the man in possession is also a very good player he can help now by turning to

*The tactics of defenders*

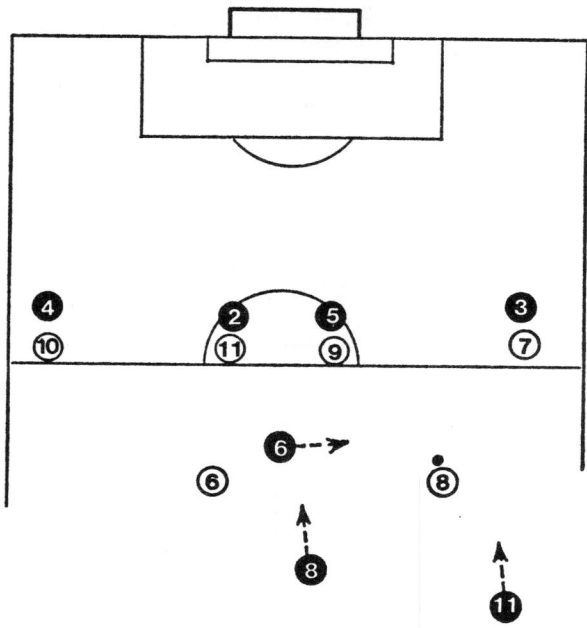

*Diagram 15 (e)*

face his colleague 10, by calling his name and shaping up to make a pass to him. Having committed himself so far it is unlikely that the right centre-back will allow his opponent to receive a pass, control the ball and turn to face the challenge. He will probably press even closer in a bid to beat 10 to the expected pass.

At this moment 10 now also has an opportunity to break away. Surprise will be on his side and if he is quick and his colleague 8 has delayed his pass then 10 might well break through sprinting into the unguarded space he has just created for himself with his opponent on the 'wrong' side of him. A good pass now from 8 and the defence could be in serious trouble as illustrated in Diagram 16 (b).

It should also be noted that breaking away from a relatively deep position there is little or no chance that 10 can be played offside, unless the pass to him is delayed too long.

It must be stressed, however, that only top-class players can be expected to make space for themselves in this way. Any hint from 10

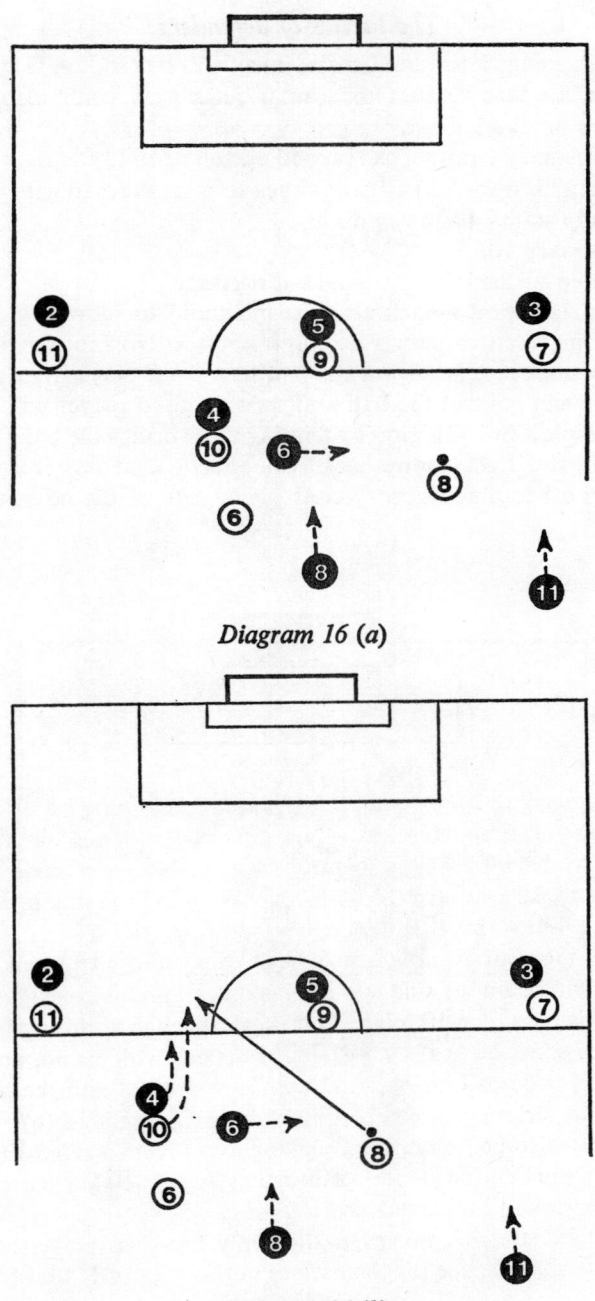

Diagram 16 (a)

Diagram 16 (b)

## The tactics of defenders

that he is going to turn and sprint away will be fatal. A failure by 8 to appreciate that 10 does not want a quick pass would also lead to the move breaking down.

We must now consider the second option open to the right centre-back when his opponent 10 drops back to meet the man with the ball. As already stated 4 has two duties:

1. To mark 10.
2. To cover his left centre-back if needed.

If the right centre-back elects to maintain his covering position then 10 can receive a pass from 8 in free space. Now for the first time we have succeeded in giving the ball to a front player in a position where he can control the ball and turn. A good player will now be able to exploit this situation by feinting as he brings the ball forward. Certainly the right centre-back will offer a challenge but in this situation a Matthews-Finney-class player has all the advantages.

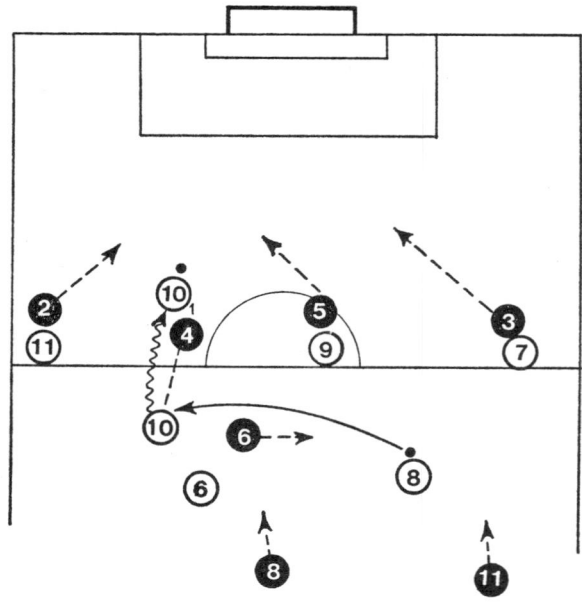

*Diagram 16 (c)*

## The tactics of defenders

It will be seen in Diagram 16 (c) that if 10 can succeed in dribbling past the right centre-back then he can only be cut off if either 2 or 5 leave their man to challenge. Though 10 may not succeed in making a clean break he now presents his colleagues 9 and 11 with an opportunity to get 'free' and receive a pass in an unmarked position. As in the move outlined in Diagram 16 (b) the chances of creating a shooting position for someone look very bright.

It will now be realized that front players can only make space *for themselves* by dropping back to meet the midfield player in possession and it must be understood that only very good players can do this. Later we shall see that ordinary players can *make space* for other players.

It should be realized, however, that the vast majority of front players will not find it easy to drop back. This is particularly true of British players who tend to favour the direct attack; a sprint into space behind the defenders, looking for a long pass over the defensive line.

Finally, this is probably a good point at which to consider the often debated question . . . 'should football be based on the long pass or the short pass?'.

The short answer to this is that it depends entirely on the situation. If a front player is temporarily unmarked perhaps because the man marking him is lying injured then the very long pass may be 'ON' as in Diagram 17. However, this will be very rare indeed in the modern game. It has been argued that while the Hungarians of 1953/54 produced a great deal of pretty short passing, it was their long passes which brought them the majority of their goals. This is true, but if we return for a moment to Diagram 1 (a) it will be seen that the long through pass from 10 to 8 was 'ON' because it had been prepared by two short passes.

In a similar way the left centre-forward prepared the way for 8 to give him a long pass (in Diagram 16 (b) ) . . . by dropping back. Very rarely will it be found that the long pass is 'ON' unless preparatory moves are introduced.

Without adequate preparation the long pass has four major points against it:
1. Tight-marking defenders make it difficult for front players to get 'free' to pick up the long pass.
2. The front player *breaking* in anticipation of a long pass is in danger of running offside.

*The tactics of defenders*

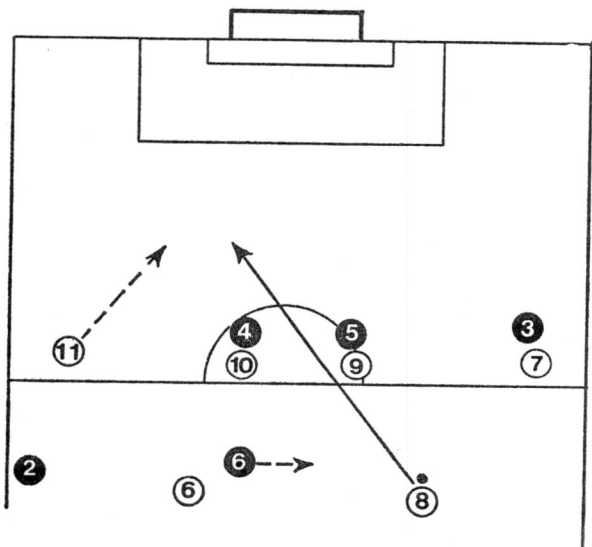

*Diagram 17*

3. The player seeking a long pass isolates himself from support.
4. The presence of a *libero* behind the enemy defence makes it impossible to break through from a direct long pass.

# 4 — Creating space in attack and exploiting this space by coming from behind

Having set the scene in the first three chapters we are now in a position to put the new game—Modern Football—into perspective. We have already seen how difficult it is for a front player to create space for himself but it is another matter entirely for a front player to make space for a colleague. What we must understand very clearly is the simple truth that in the modern defensive game it is impossible to create space for the front players.

In a simple positional switch between an outside-right and a right centre-forward the chances are that well-drilled defenders will simply follow their particular opponents. In Diagram 18, the outside-right has moved inside to right centre-forward while the player wearing 9 has moved to the wing. We have achieved nothing here for while the

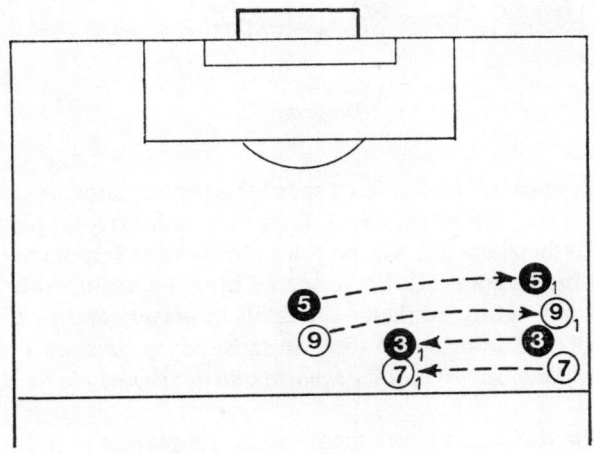

*Diagram 18*

## Creating space in attack

outside-right succeeded in creating space on the wing the player who attempted to exploit this space was another *front player*. In the modern game all front players are tightly marked and will be followed wherever they go. This is particularly true of catenaccio-type defences in which the *libero* accepts responsibility for covering all his defensive colleagues. However, it is clear that in the tight-marking game we can make space at any time and the tighter the marking the easier this is. We can create space anywhere in attack—at any time—by having a *front player* run square across the pitch. The outside-right made space on the wing in Diagram 18, and in Diagram 19 the right

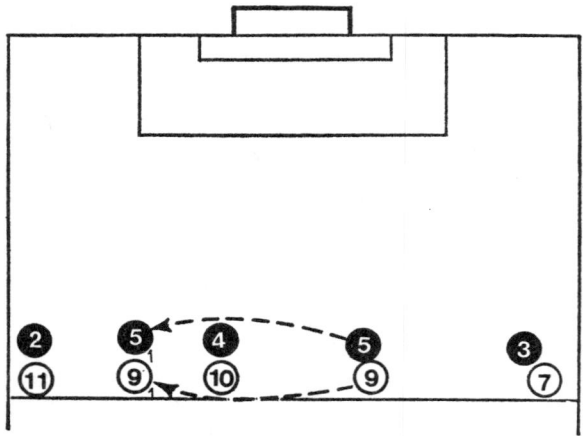

*Diagram 19*

centre-forward has also created space this time by moving left. Either of these spaces can be exploited, but not by other 'front' players who are tightly marked and will be followed by their opponents as were 7 and 9 in Diagram 18. These spaces must be exploited by players who are not tightly marked—the midfield players and/or the defensive players. The principle that we must accept is simply this: *We must exploit space in attack by putting an unmarked player 'IN' from behind.*

In normal circumstances there will be six players in a 4–2–4 team who are not tightly marked by opponents. They are the players marked in a square in Diagram 20 (a).

## Creating space in attack

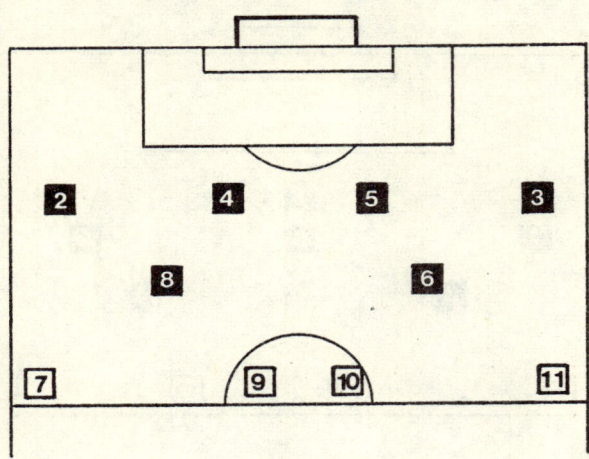

*Diagram 20 (a)*

In a 4-3-3 team there will be seven players who are not tightly marked and could therefore move up to help in attack. These seven are 'squared' in Diagram 20 (b).

In a catenaccio-type team there will be seven players 'free' to attack if the catenaccio is based on the 1-3-3-3 formula and these players are 'squared' in Diagram 20 (c).

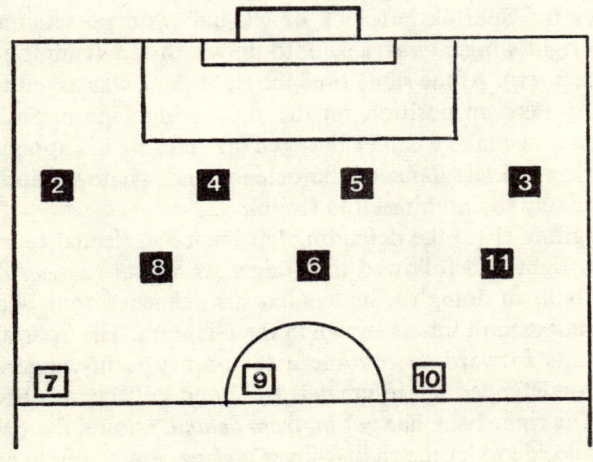

*Diagram 20 (b)*

*Creating space in attack*

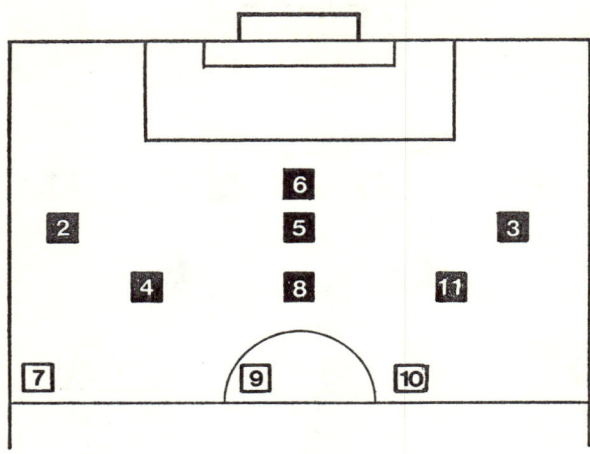

*Diagram 20 (c)*

At any moment when their team is in possession any of the unmarked players could break through *if space can be created for them*.

Let us first consider a move of this type already to be seen in Czechoslovakia, where Spartak Trnava made a tremendous bid for the 1966/67 championship and finally won the Czech F.A. Cup. Whenever the Spartak left-back or left-half won possession of the ball the right-winger was asked to move inside (running square across the pitch). At the same time the right-back was asked to sprint forward to take up position on the right wing. The opposing left-back must now make a choice between (a) marking his opponent and (b) covering the left flank of the defence and whatever decision he makes is likely to find himself in trouble.

In Diagram 21 (a) the defending left-back has elected to mark his opponent tight and followed the winger as he *ran to meet* the man with the ball. In doing so, he has left his defensive zone wide open and Spartak exploit this as shown in the Diagram. The Spartak right-back sprints forward to become a temporary right-winger, racing into the undefended space created by 7 and collects a lobbed pass from 6. The right-back has *got in, from behind*. Should the defending left-back decide to let the right-winger go free, preferring to cover his zone rather than mark his individual opponent, then as seen in

## Creating space in attack

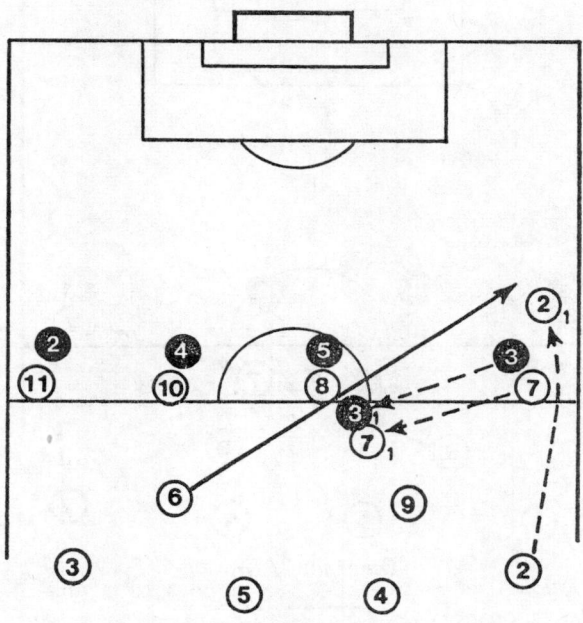

*Diagram 21 (a)*

Diagram 21 (b), 6 will give the ball to the feet of 7, who can control the ball and turn. The right-winger now has possession and the opportunity to effect a break-through in the space between (5) and (3). It is unlikely that (5) will leave his opponent (8) to challenge the right-winger now advancing in possession and in all probability it will be the left-back who moves in to cut off the winger's run to goal. In so doing the left-back now leaves his *zone* open with the attacking right-back (2) *coming from behind*.

As the left-back comes across to challenge, the Spartak attack is often developed at this point by 7 giving the ball to his colleague 2, as shown in Diagram 21 (c). When this happens it is clear that Spartak's right centre-forward (8) must move away towards the left in order to keep his opponent (5) away from a position in which he could intercept the pass 'inside' the left-back.

We can also find examples of this type of move in England where West Ham United have played a great part in developing attacking

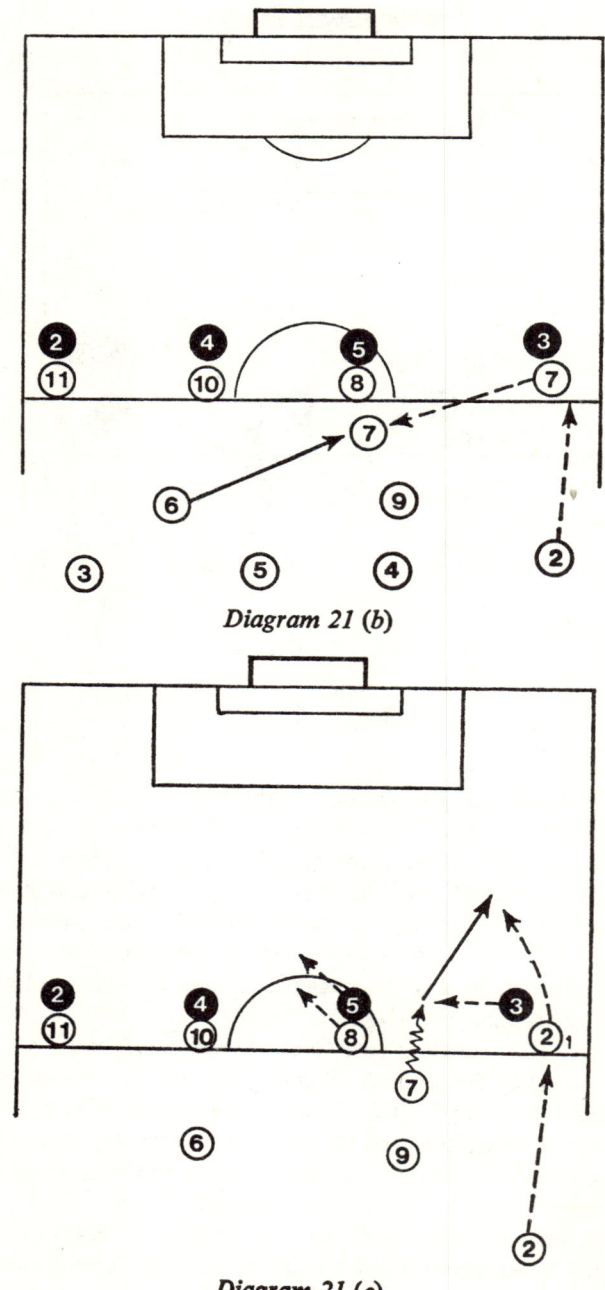

*Diagram 21 (b)*

*Diagram 21 (c)*

## *Creating space in attack*

football in modern defensive conditions. Since 1963 West Ham have been using their full-backs in attack—putting them *in from behind*.

A typical West Ham move involved Moore, Sissons, Boyce and Charles (and others who followed them). On the left-wing Sissons drops back down the touch-line when Moore has possession and the ball is played to the winger's feet. The West Ham back is moving out from his defensive position as the ball travels to Sissons and now the enemy right-back (marking Sissons) has two choices:

1. He can move forward to challenge Sissons in a bid to beat the winger to the ball.
2. He can lay off to cover his defensive zone.

If the defender comes forward to challenge then the West Ham attack is developed as shown in Diagram 22 (a). Sissons plays the ball first-time to Boyce, turns and sprints inside—moving diagonally across the pitch. Charles meanwhile has sprinted forward to become the new left-winger and receive a pass from Boyce.

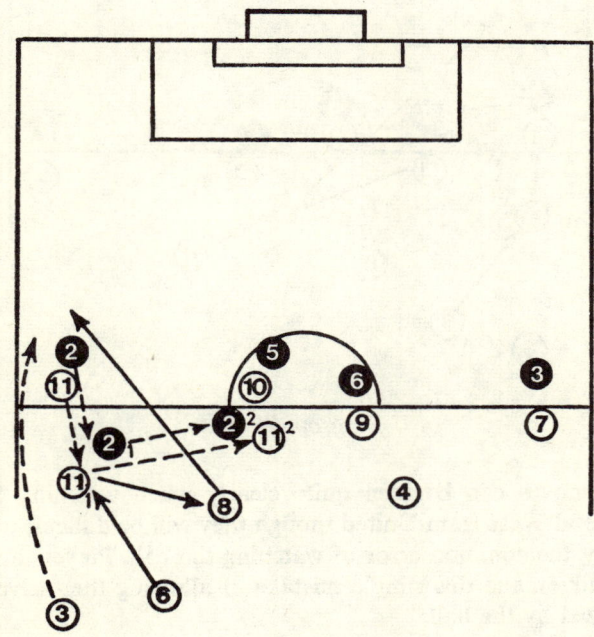

*Diagram 22 (a)*

## *Creating space in attack*

If the right-back decides to lay off as Sissons drops back to receive the pass from Moore then the left-winger controls the ball and turns to face his opponent. Shuffling forward, Sissons inevitably attracts the right-back whose duty it is to mark him and challenge him. Veering inside, Sissons moves across field with the right-back closing in. Having drawn his opponent out of position (ten yards is enough) Sissons then passes to a colleague in right-midfield—perhaps Peters— and from there the ball is played out to Charles—see Diagram 22 (b).

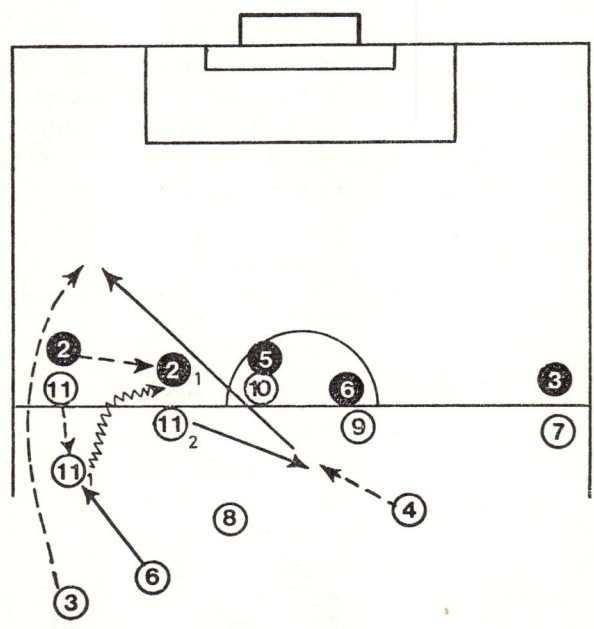

*Diagram 22 (b)*

Such moves can be seen quite clearly when watching Spartak Trnava and West Ham United though they will be difficult to spot if we adopt the common error of watching the ball. Players and spectators alike make this simple mistake of allowing themselves to be hypnotized by the ball.

This is common to all ball games but can be most readily observed in tennis. Watch the spectators at any tennis match—constantly

## Creating space in attack

turning their heads to follow the ball from end to end. Ball watching makes it impossible to see how the crack tennis player moves in anticipation of his opponent's return and the top players seem to be in the right place by accident or chance. Similarly, the ball-watcher at a football match will never see players running *off the ball*, and he will never observe a player *coming from behind*.

It was this factor which prevented the vast majority of spectators—fans and experts alike—from seeing exactly what Bozsik, Kocsis, Hidegkuti and Puskas were doing back in 1953 when they played together in the great Hungarian XI. We all agreed that the Hungarian forwards were superbly skilled; that they demonstrated a brand of football never seen before, but we did not see that they were *coming from behind*. We were all too busy watching the ball and enjoying the game!

Now, however, we are in a position to use the principles observed in Hungary—Spartak—West Ham moves and coach our players in the new game, but first we must explain a simple principle which will *link* the players together mentally.

If we return for a moment to the Spartak and West Ham moves we shall see that everything hinges on the intelligence of the individual players. There is no direct *link* between the players and it will be more easily understood if we begin coaching the new game with the principle of *place-changing*.

If we return for a moment to Diagram 1 (a) we will see that the inside-right (8) is passing the ball to the centre-forward and then *running round the back of the man to whom he has given the ball*. He is now moving to take up a new position *at centre-forward*. The inside-right is changing places with the man to whom he passes. Now study afresh the Spartak Trnava move described in Diagram 21 (a). Although the right-back (2) has not played the ball, he is moving to take up position on the right-wing as his colleague (7) moves across field. The right-back is *changing places* with the right-winger. Finally, look once more at the West Ham move outlined in Diagram 22 (a) and it will be seen that the left-back is not merely attacking but is in fact becoming a temporary left-winger.

Any player coming from behind is changing his position temporarily. Coming from behind, a defender or a midfield player is seeking to exploit space within the enemy defence—a task which was once given exclusively to the *front* players—and the defender temporarily is fulfilling the role of a front player.

## *Creating space in attack*

With certain reservations the new game demands that each of the midfield and defence players should be ready at any moment to race forward to exploit space within the enemy defence. But it will be clear that unless we *link* the players together mentally, unless we introduce a methodical approach, our attempts to attack in the modern manner could well end in disaster. As will be seen from Diagram 23 there are three players who *could* come from behind to exploit space on the right wing created when the winger (7) moves inside. All three players might well move up together and if the move breaks down for any reason the temporary absence of three players with defensive duties will expose their goal to a quick counter-attack. With the left-midfield (6) in possession of the ball, the right-winger runs across the pitch to receive a pass and with his opponent following him, space is created on the right wing. It is clear that if 6 were to lob the ball forward into the space vacated by the right-winger then a player coming from behind could break through. The question is *which player?* And the great danger, in the absence of method, is that 2, 4 and 8 would all *see the space* and *go forward*, as shown in Diagram 23.

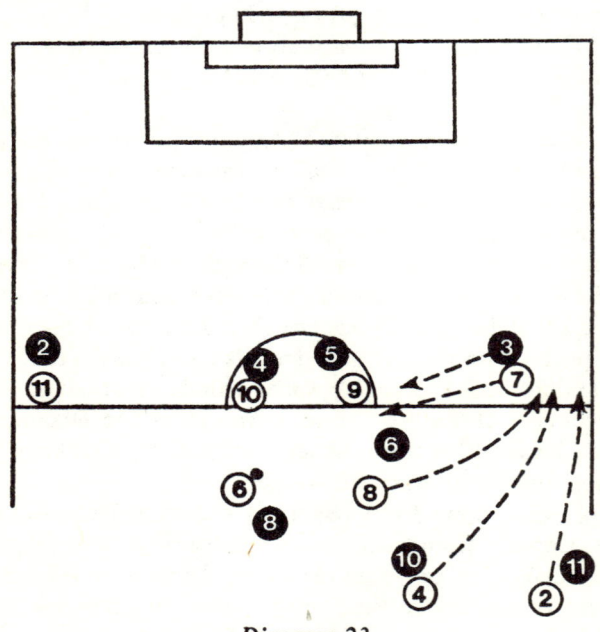

*Diagram 23*

## *Creating space in attack*

If the left-midfield player (6) should give a bad pass—for example a chip that did not gain enough height and was intercepted by his opposite number (6)—then with the enemy in possession our goal is exposed. Two enemy front players are unmarked (10) and (11) while both (6) and (8) are loose in midfield.

Intelligent players, experienced in the new game, will be able to read the situation for themselves and decide which of them is best placed to exploit the opening on the right wing, but when we begin to coach place-changing we must simplify the position. We can do this in several simple ways but before we decide which players to nominate we should consider what risks we are prepared to take and what kind of pass we want to give to the player breaking through.

As far as the risks to our own goal are concerned it is clear that an unmarked opponent in the central region represents a far greater danger than a temporarily unmarked enemy winger. For this reason it is best to restrict the central defenders to purely defensive roles. Full-backs can be thrust forward but the twin stoppers at centre-back should not be encouraged to attack.

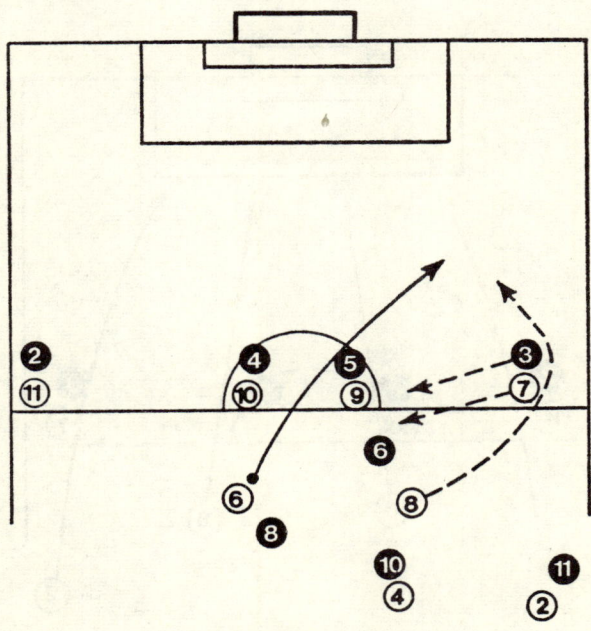

*Diagram 24*

## Creating space in attack

It will be clear that the ideal pass to a player coming from behind will be one which gives that player the opportunity to go straight for goal. Stopping or changing direction will tend to slow the attack and speed is all-important.

Having decided that we can commit to attack both full-backs and/or the midfield players, we should consider the regions in which these players will generally be positioned. From their defending positions the players on the right flank will not be able to burst forward on the left wing without changing direction. The same limitation is placed on the right-midfield player if he attempts to break through on the right wing. Diagram 24 illustrates such a break and it will be seen that as the right-midfield (8) moves forward he must change direction to move in from the wing towards goal.

If we consider the general positioning of the midfield players and the full-backs and imagine them going straight for the enemy goal it will be clear that the full-backs are best placed for a wing attack while the midfield players are generally well placed to sprint through the centre. Diagram 25 illustrates the *straight for goal* path taken by

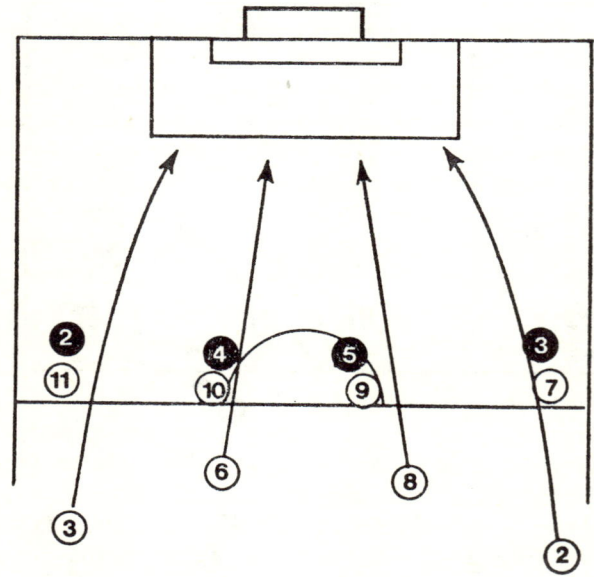

*Diagram 25*

## Creating space in attack

the full-backs and the midfield players and suggests that some players are better placed to change places with particular front players. The full-back coming from his position in defence and running straight for the enemy goal moves directly through the customary zone of his wing-forward colleague. Similarly, the midfield players seem to become right or left centre-forward as they race forward straight for goal. Because it is important that we should go directly towards goal; because turning or changing direction will slow the speed of our attack we can say that the right-back will usually be best placed to break through on the right wing. It follows that the left-back is the ideal choice for left wing 'breaks'; that right-midfield is the man to change places with the right centre-forward and the left-midfield should be the secondary left centre-forward.

Now we can say:
1. If 7 creates space in attack then 2 should come from behind to exploit it.
2. If 9 creates space in attack then 8 should come from behind to exploit it.
3. If 10 creates space in attack then 6 should come from behind to exploit it.
4. If 11 creates space in attack then 3 should come from behind to exploit it.

In this way we ensure that the 'attacking' player coming from a defensive position will be able to press the attack with minimum delay. We also ensure that if the attack breaks down the defender now caught out of position has only to cover the minimum amount of ground (i.e. a straight line) back to his defensive position. Before leaving this theme to move on to methodical place-changing it is worthwhile considering why other players should not attempt to break through in zones other than those allocated to them above. It would seem, perhaps, that although the right-back is the ideal player to exploit space on the right wing, there is no reason why the right-midfield player should not do so. Indeed if at the moment of decision the right-midfield player is temporarily positioned out near the touchline then there is no reason why he should not sprint forward to exploit space on the wing for he would then move in towards goal on the same general line as would the right-back. Usually, however, the right-midfield will be found closer to the position he occupies in Diagram 26 (a).

At any given moment in a fluid game the three colleagues closest to

## Creating space in attack

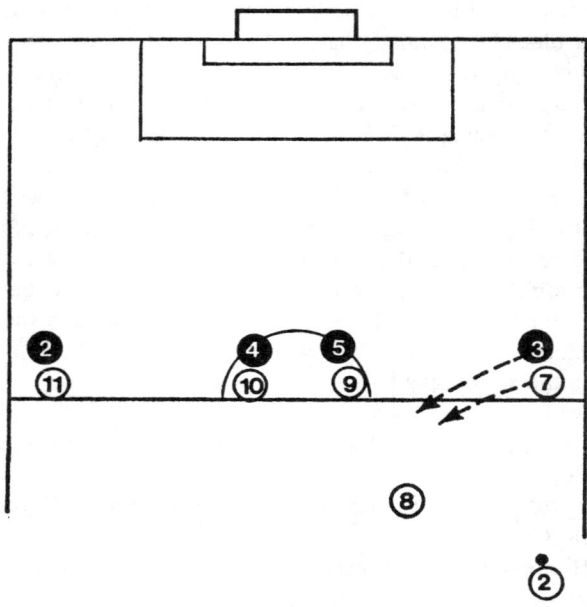

*Diagram 26 (a)*

the right-winger will be the right centre-forward, right-midfield and right-back. Generally they will be positioned roughly according to Diagram 26 (a). Now, with the right-back in possession, consider the advantages and disadvantages facing each of the three players if they attempt to exploit space on the wing.

As the right-winger drops back slightly and moves across the pitch he will normally be closely marked by the enemy left-back. Following his man, the left back concedes space on the wing and each of the three players mentioned above is close enough to exploit this space. In Diagram 26 (b) the right centre-forward (9) is moving to the wing as the right-back makes a long pass down the touchline. In this situation the right centre-forward will probably be followed by the enemy left centre-back and in this case he must:

1. Look right to follow the path of the ball in order to collect the pass.
2. Look left to see where his opponent is in relation to himself.
3. Screen the ball from his opponent and face an immediate tackle as he attempts to control the ball and turn.

*Creating space in attack*

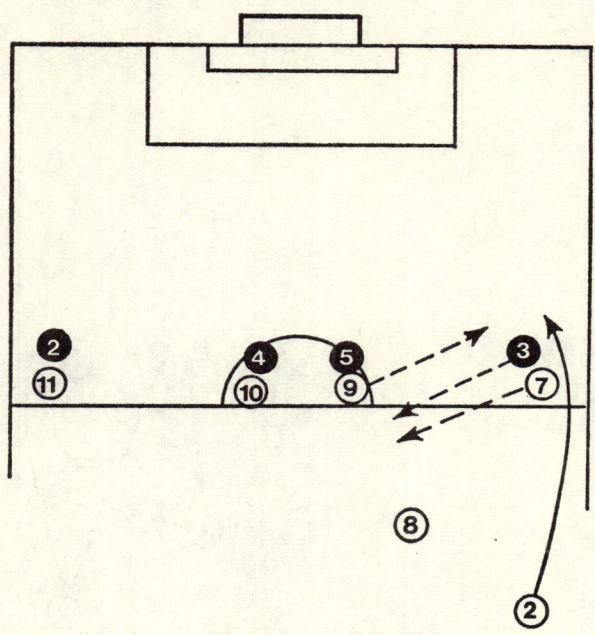

*Diagram 26 (b)*

4. Change direction to move in towards goal.

If by some chance the left centre-back did not follow the right centre-forward to the wing then there is a definite danger of being played offside by astute defenders. Either way the chances are that the right centre-forward will not have much success in his bid to exploit space on the right wing.

The right-midfield player (8) has a better chance for unlike the right centre-forward he is not tightly marked, and he has alternative lines of approach illustrated by Diagram 26 (c). If the right-midfield attempts to pick up a pass from the right-back by following path A he suffers from the same disadvantages which faced the right centre-forward:

1. He must look right to follow the ball in order to collect the pass.
2. He must look left to see if the enemy left centre-back has seen him coming and is moving to intercept the ball.
3. He will almost certainly have to slow down to collect the pass—turning to face his own goal as he received the ball and then

77

## Creating space in attack

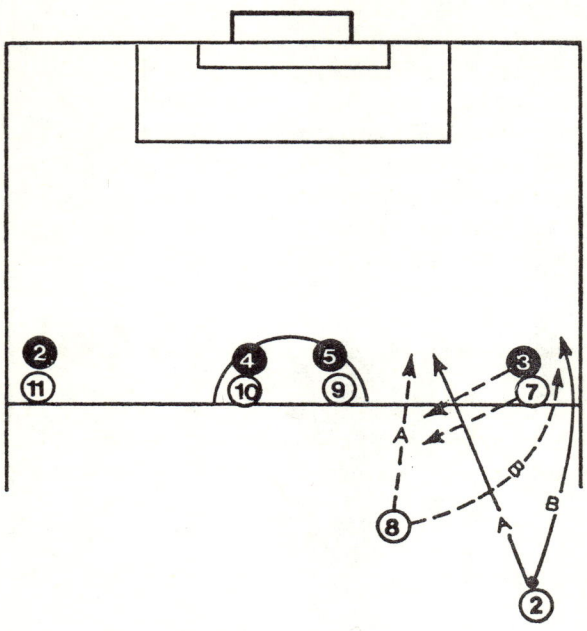

*Diagram 26 (c)*

turn once more (and build up speed) to move on towards the enemy goal.

The right-midfield also runs the risk of being played offside and while he must look back over his right shoulder to follow the ball, he must also look over his left shoulder to see along the line of defenders to note the offside situation. Finally, if the right-midfield follows path A there is a chance that the enemy left-back may see him coming for 8 is moving across the face of the enemy 3. If the enemy left-back does see the right-midfield coming he will almost certainly change his mind about marking the right-winger tight. The wise left-back would break away from 7 in this situation and fall back to close the space.

The best chance for the right-midfield player is certainly to follow path B. As the left-back moves inside (following 7) he is less likely to notice the movement of 8 for the right-midfield is now moving on the 'blind side' of 3 and running round the back of the left-back.

However, the right-midfield moving on path B still has one impor-

## Creating space in attack

tant factor against him. Early on his run he must look right to see the ball but left to see if an opponent is moving across to cover him. Of the three players closest to the right-winger it is the right-back who has most of the advantages in his favour, but of course he cannot hope to *run with the ball* into created space and get in unobserved.

If the right-back pushes the ball forward to his colleague at right-midfield and then immediately sprints forward he has a very good chance of breaking through. Like the spectators the enemy players are attracted by the ball and as it travels to the right-midfield everyone concerned with the game turns to see what he will do with it. With the ball on its way from 2 to 8 and the right-winger moving across to meet the man with the ball, the right-back has everything in his favour.

The right-midfield should make the pass illustrated in Diagram 26 (d) with the 'inside' of his right foot *or* the outside of his left foot. In either case the ball in flight will tend to drift 'in' towards goal. At

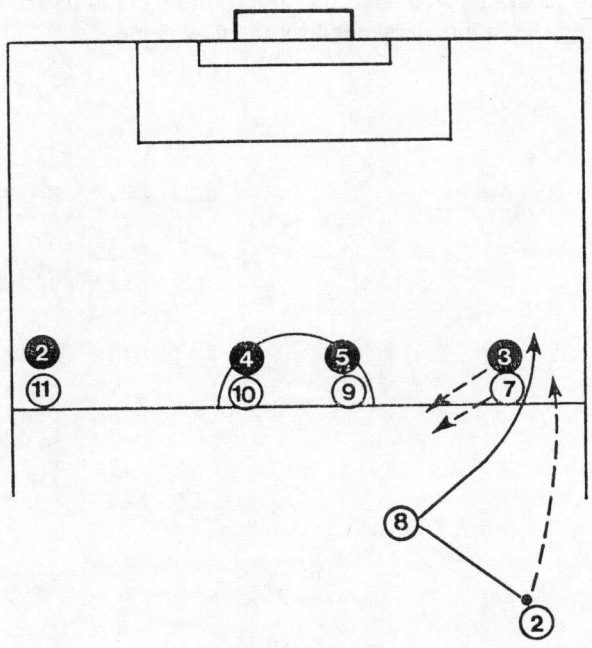

*Diagram 26 (d)*

## *Creating space in attack*

the same time the right-back has only to turn his head slightly to take in the entire scene. With the minimum of difficulty he can:
1. See the offside position (looking along the line of defenders) and adjusting the speed of his approach.
2. Note whether or not he has been *seen*.
3. Move directly towards goal without having to change direction or turn.
4. Ensure that there is no covering defender on his blind side, for they are all in front of him.

It will now be clear that the players generally best situated to exploit created space within the enemy defence are indeed those immediately behind the space as indicated in Diagram 25. Once these players have developed *the habit* of looking for space ahead of them it will not be difficult to get them to move forward. Getting the front players to *run square* in order to create the space, and getting the man in possession *to look for* the man coming from behind will be rather more difficult but by no means impossible. It is all a question of habit and, as will be seen later, modern training methods are aimed at developing the habits demanded by the new game.

## 5 — Push the ball and run spotlights the wall-pass, but tighter marking makes 'push and run' obsolete. With an extra twist it leads directly to the 'Whirl' predicted by Willy Meisl

The examples of modern attacking football provided by Spartak Trnava and West Ham United are both simple and effective, but they depend completely on the intelligence of each player. Under their outstanding coaches Anton Malatinsky (Trnava) and Ron Greenwood (West Ham) the players have already been educated beyond the first grade. But for other players new to place-changing and *coming from behind* the introduction will be best made at a less mature level. What we need is something essentially simple and easily understood which will bring out the general principles of place-changing. We need something that will link the players together mentally so that place-changing occurs naturally and inevitably. Fortunately this link has already been provided by the Hungarians.

If we return once more to Diagrams 1 (a), 1 (b) and 1 (c) we shall see that in every case it is the player who gives the ball to the centre-forward who sprints forward in a bid to exploit the space behind the enemy centre-half. Putting this another way we can say that: the man who makes the pass runs round the back of the player he gives the ball to. *The player giving the pass changes places with the man receiving the ball.*

Nothing could be simpler than this, and suddenly the new game begins to take shape with the maxim: follow the ball. In its very simplest form the principle of *place-changing* can be reduced to the easy training drill described in Diagram 27 (a). Three players: A, B and C stand in Indian file with C having a ball at his feet. Twenty yards away there are three more players: D, E and F. To begin the drill, C pushes the ball to the feet of D and immediately runs to take up position behind F. Meanwhile D controls the ball and then makes

## The 'Whirl'

*Diagram 27 (a)*

his pass to B and immediately runs to his new position behind A. B passes to E and runs; E passes to A and runs, and so on.

With very young players one or two touches of the ball can be allowed to the players receiving the ball before they make their pass, but older and more skilful players should be able to perform this drill with first-time passes. In this exercise we find many of the basic elements demanded by the modern game, and in one drill the players are receiving practice in ball skills (e.g. trapping and passing), training for speed and stamina according to the demands of the coach and the duration of the practice and they are also changing

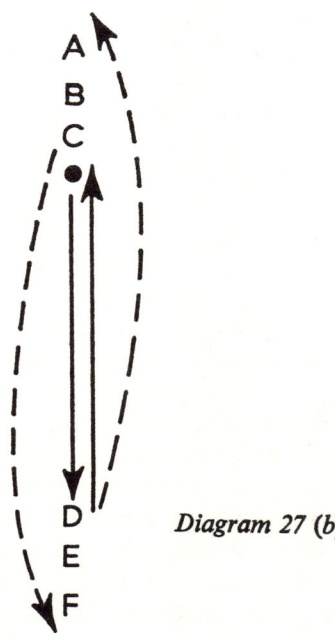

*Diagram 27 (b)*

## The 'Whirl'

places. This exercise is very closely related to the overlapping moves now commonplace in English football. This will become clearer if we turn Diagram 27 (a) so that the ball is passing up and down the page as in Diagram 27 (b). Compare the movements of the players running without the ball with those in Diagram 27 (c). C has become

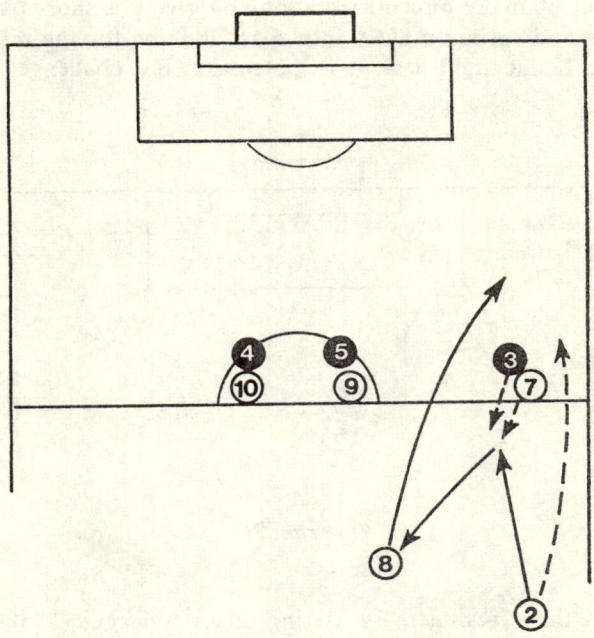

*Diagram 27 (c)*

7 and D is now 2, and here we have the overlapping full-back. The right-back (2) passes to his colleague on the right-wing and immediately runs to change places with him. The pass to the winger is only a preliminary move to draw the enemy left-back forward and thus keep the space clear for the right-back as he comes from behind.

In the early 1950s the Hungarians used this move to destroy the old stopper centre-half. In Diagram 1 (a) Kocsis is overlapping Hidegkuti *and* changing places with him. Comparing the movements of the ball and the player running off the ball, the moves described in Diagrams 1 (a) and 27 (c) are exactly the same.

## The 'Whirl'

The principles behind the Hungarian's *central combinations* and the English *overlap* are directly related to the earliest attempt to develop team play. This was of course the *one-two*, known in Hungary as the *double-pass* and in England as the *wall-pass*. First seen in Central Europe during the thirties, the wall-pass was adopted throughout the world. Used in defence the one-two enabled a player to get out of many difficult situations by giving a short pass to a colleague and sprinting away into space looking for the return. In Diagram 28 the right-back is in possession but challenged by his

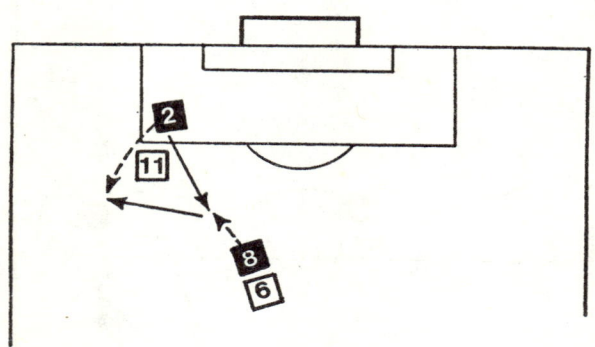

*Diagram 28*

opponent the left-winger. By passing to his colleague (8) the right-back avoids the risk of being caught in possession and losing the ball, and receives the ball back in space.

Used in attack the wall-pass was equally effective in the old WM game for in those days defenders were still attempting to fulfil dual roles. At the same time they were trying to mark their wingers *and* cover the centre-half. Thus when a right-winger played the ball inside, the left-back marking him had to look across-field to ascertain whether or not the centre-half needed cover. Though this required only a quick glance from the back the slight delay enabled the winger to get 'free' and pick up the return pass as in Diagram 29. Today, however, the full-backs are not required to give close support to the centre-half for the 'twin stoppers' in 4-2-4 and 4-3-3 cover each other. Now the full-back is free to mark his opponent tightly, tackle

## The 'Whirl'

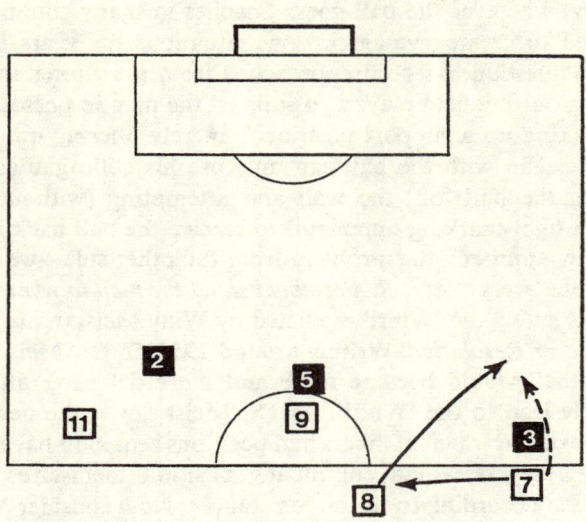

*Diagram 29*

quickly and concentrate solely on blotting his particular opponent out of the game. Free to concentrate, the modern full-back doesn't even look to see where the ball has gone—he turns and sprints away still marking his winger tight. If the return pass does not come then no harm has been done, but if it does then the full-back is still tight-marking his winger and can either beat him to the ball or be close enough to challenge him before he can control the ball.

Up front the one-two has very limited value and cannot be used to effect a clear break for the player making the first pass. Tighter marking has made 'push and run' obsolete. This was already clear to Gustav Sebes around 1950–51 when, assisted by Marton Bukovi, Janos Kalmar and Geza Kalocsai he was in charge of the Hungarian national team. It is not clear whether it was Sebes or Bukovi who gave the extra twist to push and run and produced *push and run to change places with the man receiving the ball* but this was the basic conception behind much of the superb football produced by Puskas, Kocsis, Hidegkuti and Bozsik.

When we take the lengthy step from push and run to place-changing a great many advantages automatically accrue. Perhaps the most important being that now we have two against one (auto-

## The 'Whirl'

matically) wherever the ball goes. Coaches in many countries have attempted to create two-against-one situations for years but until now this question has been approached from the wrong angle.

Asking our midfield players to support the man in possession, the player taking up a support position is merely offering himself as a wall. The man with the ball can now use his colleague as a wall, bouncing the ball 'off' the wall and attempting (without success against a tight-marking opponent) to receive the ball back in space. If we now approach this problem from the other side—we get two-against-one everywhere. *Run around behind the man to whom we pass the ball* is surely the 'Whirl' predicted by Willy Meisl in his very fine book *Soccer Revolution*. Writing around 1955–56 Dr. Meisl forecast that football would become more and more defensive and would ultimately lead to the 'Whirl'. As Dr. Meisl saw it the new system would be one in which numbers and positions ceased to have any real meaning. Players would continually position themselves as they judged best according to the circumstances. Now consider *'push and run to take the place of the man to whom we give the ball'* in general terms. Armed with this simple idea the players would constantly be changing position—positional-switching on a scale as yet undreamed of.

When the right-back tackles an opponent and wins possession of the ball he would probably find his right wing colleague dropping back looking for a pass. This has been demanded for years in many professional clubs as an easy way of turning defence into attack. Now, however, with our new conception something extraordinary occurs. The right-back pushes the ball up the touchline to his right-winger and then immediately sprints upfield, running to change places. The right-winger plays the ball inside to the right centre-forward, who turns it back to the right-midfield and from there the ball goes out once more to the right wing.

Follow the move outlined above in Diagram 30 (a) and it will be seen that with 2 *coming from behind* 7 and 2 give a two-against-one on the left-back. When the winger plays the ball inside to the right centre-forward, 7 then runs to make another two-against-one on the enemy left centre-back. Everywhere the ball goes we have two against one.

Look at Diagram 30 (a) once more, this time from the viewpoint of the defending left-back. When his opponent plays the ball inside and runs, the left-back is faced with a clear choice between marking

## The 'Whirl'

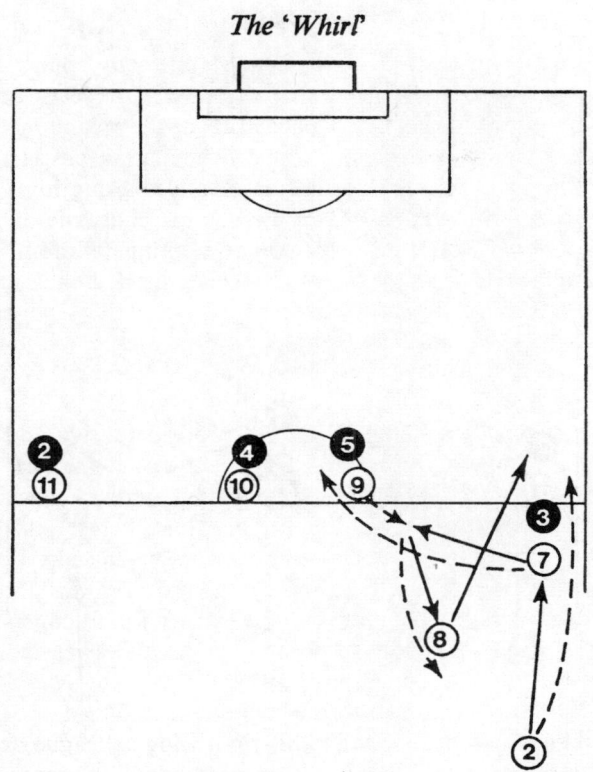

*Diagram 30 (a)*

his man and covering his defensive zone. The left-back has two choices:
1. He can follow 7, marking him tight.
2. He can let 7 run free and cover his zone.

If the left-back elects to follow his opponent (7) then the attacking team would break off 'whirling' when the ball reached the right centre-forward and develop their move as described in Diagram 30 (b). With the right-back unmarked it is a simple matter to exploit the space created by the right-winger. The right-back breaking through on the right-wing from his position at $2_1$ has made a major break-through.

Should the left-back opt for his second choice he will naturally pick up the right-back who is temporarily positioning himself as a right-winger but if the team in possession continues to 'Whirl' for

## The 'Whirl'

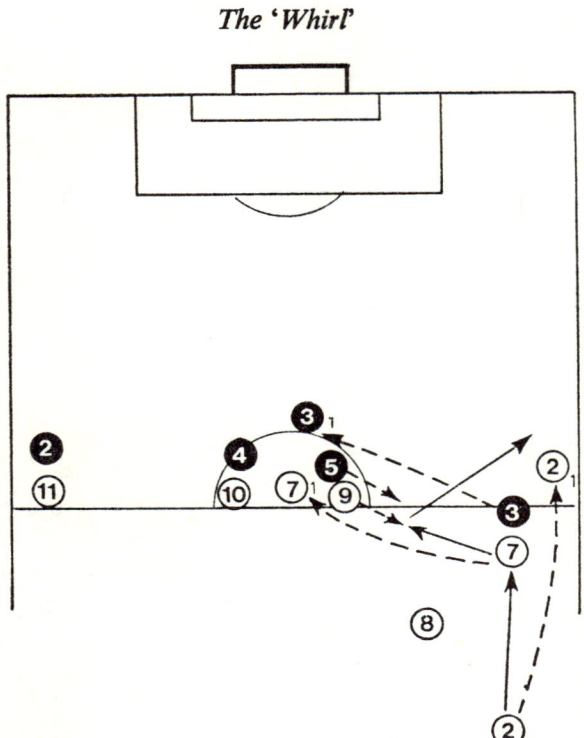

*Diagram 30 (b)*

one more pass then another major break-through can be effected. In Diagram 30 (c) the 'Whirl' has been given its final spin and this time the 'break' comes through the centre where the attacking team now has three-against-two.

Moving to meet the pass from the right-winger, the right centre-forward has the enemy left centre-back right on his heels challenging for the ball. Playing the ball back to the right-midfield as the right-winger sprints to become the temporary right centre-forward, the way is now clear for a through pass from 8 to 7.

From the defenders' point of view, whirling forwards leads to chaos on the grand scale, and in the long run defenders will be forced to return to zonal-defence. This in turn will make life easier for the front players who until now have been tightly marked and tackled quickly. If zonal-defence is not the answer to whirling forwards then

## The 'Whirl'

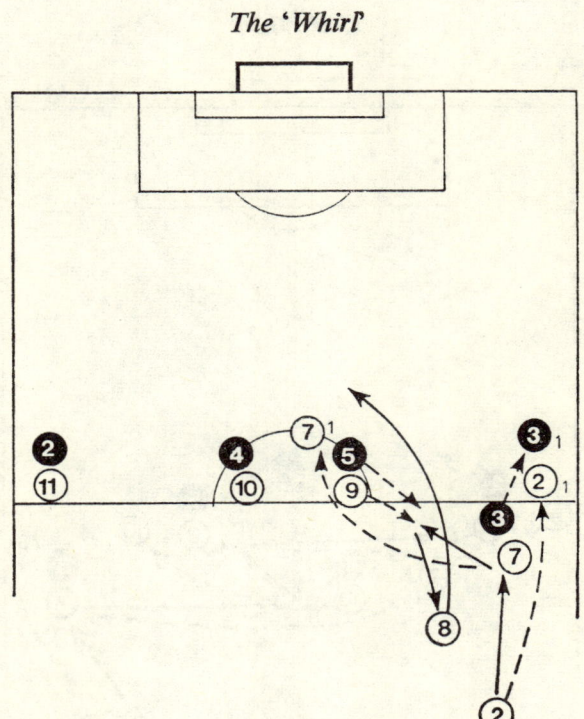

*Diagram 30 (c)*

the only alternative will be to call even more players back into defence. If a fifth or sixth player is pulled back permanently into defence to supplement the 4-2-4 or 4-3-3 defensive system then this will seriously limit the attacking possibilities of a team playing 5-2-3 or 6-2-2. It will not, however, preclude a well-prepared team, skilled in the modern approach, from scoring goals.

To gain an appreciation of the problems facing tight-marking defenders when their opponents begin to 'Whirl', consider the effect of a three-pass move amongst whirling forwards. The right-winger receives a pass from his colleague at right-midfield, plays the ball across-field to the left centre-forward and runs. From 10 the ball is pushed on to 9 and finally to 11 and after making his pass each of the front players has run to take up his new position. In Diagram 31 this move is described and in a bid to avoid confusion the halfway line and the centre circle have been omitted. In addition the relative

## The 'Whirl'

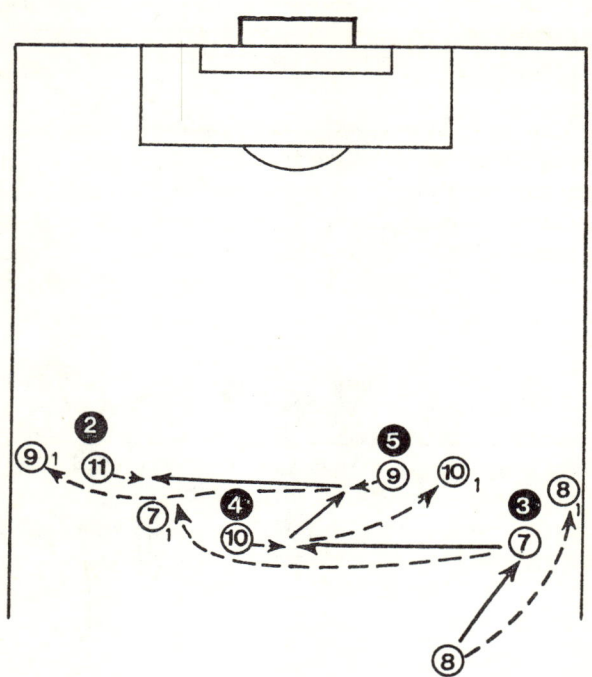

*Diagram 31*

positions of the front players and their individual opponents have been staggered solely to avoid having a maze of crossed lines. This move may well appear to be very complicated but in fact it involves only four passes. To each of the attacking players it is very simple—run to take the place of the man to whom he gives the ball.

The defenders, however, are caught in a terrible dilemma. Should the left-back follow his winger to inside-left? If he does then who will cover 8 as the right-midfield *comes from behind*? Should the right centre-back (4) follow his man (10) to right centre-forward and if he does then who will cover the new left centre-forward?

Should the left centre-back follow 9 out to the left wing . . . or not?

At the very least the defence will be a shambles. As the left-winger receives the ball, moving in-field to meet the pass, 8 is now on the

## The 'Whirl'

right wing; 10 is at right centre-forward and 7 at left centre-forward, while 9 is on his way to the left wing!

Well-organized defences can cope with a situation like this in two ways:
1. They can stay in position within their zones and pick up their new opponent as he moves into their territory.
2. They can rigidly stick to man-for-man marking.

If the defenders react according to 1 (above): if they *all* stay in position then 9 must be running free on the left wing. If the defenders react as one and stick determinedly to their allotted man, following their opponent to his new position, then 8 will be running free on the right wing.

At the very least there must be one attacking player 'free' but the chances are that some of the defenders will follow their man while others will cover space. If that happens there will be two or possibly three attacking players free. Obviously a 'Whirl' involving all four front players is a complicated affair and certainly not a point at which to commence coaching the new game. This theme has been developed only to illustrate that place-changing leads to the 'Whirl' predicted by Dr. Willy Meisl and to begin our approach to modern football we must deal with the players in small groups.

## 6 — The overlap developed in England, or place-changing on the wings.
## The method of coaching wing combinations and some of the problems we meet when coaching modern football

The simplest way to introduce players to place-changing is via the overlap in which a full-back and the winger on his flank change places. To have given this move a specific name is misleading for many people have come to believe that overlaps can only be made on the wings. This is not true and it will soon become clear that in the Hungarian's Central Combinations Kocsis, Bozsik and Puskas were simply 'overlapping' the centre-forward.

To avoid confusion it is better to refer to the various forms of overlapping (on the wings) as Wing Combinations. Whatever we call them the place-changes effected on the wings are easier than similar moves in the centre. Out on the flanks there is more space and when players have space they also have time.

Initially it is very important that the players should be successful for if this is lacking then they will have no confidence in place-changing. If they are successful then enthusiasm will grow with every training session and when the moves they practice begin to show in match play a new confidence will emerge.

In the early stages all the advantages lie with the defenders for the attacking players cannot possibly acquire complete understanding after a few minutes. Certainly they will understand the simple basic moves but reacting to live opposition in match conditions is quite a problem. For this reason it is important that in training the opposition be restricted at first and if we consider the alternatives open to a defender we shall see how this can best be done.

In general terms each full-time defender has two basic responsibilities; he has to mark an opponent and cover a zone in the defensive area. Full-backs will always attempt to position themselves in such a

## Place-changing on the wings

way that they can fulfil both these duties, but with the right approach attacking players can force the full-back to make a choice between man and space. Whenever an unmarked opponent has possession and brings the ball towards a full-back, the defender always prefers to lay off. Knowing that his colleagues are sprinting back (a) to challenge the man in possession and (b) to cover the approach to goal—the defender knows that time is on his side. In addition he is facing a two-against-one situation and any attempt to challenge will almost certainly be disastrous.

## WING COMBINATION (1)

In Diagram 32 we have this situation with the attacking right-back in possession and here the defending left-back knows exactly what he wants to do. With time on his side he wants to lay off, back-pedalling towards goal. Meanwhile generations of wingers have been en-

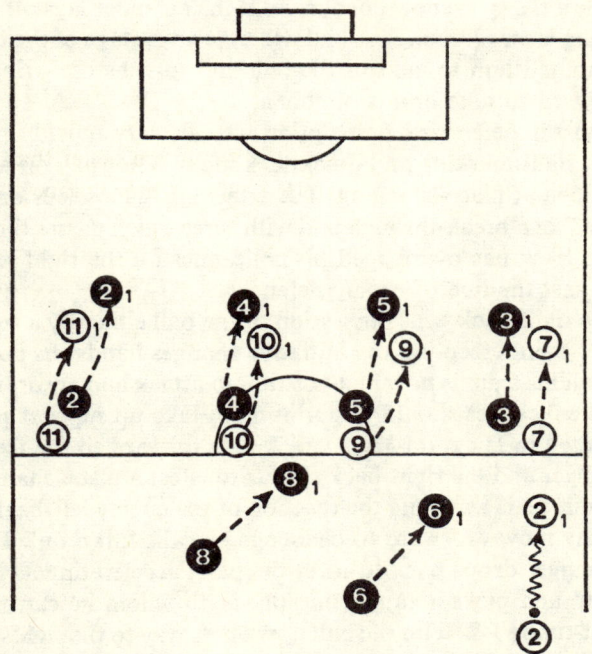

*Diagram 32*

## Place-changing on the wings

couraged to run away from the man with the ball—seeking a long pass over the left-back's head. The defender would indeed be a real novice if he allowed such a pass to elude him and aware of the danger he wants to run away, to lay off. As the winger advances he plays right into the defender's hands for now the full-back can fulfil both his defensive duties—he can mark his man *and* cover his defensive zone.

If the attacking right-back were to push the ball forward towards his colleague on the right wing then the defender must make a choice between marking his man and covering the space at his back. When the ball is played forward quickly *to feet* the defender has two basic options:
1. He can advance to challenge for the ball.
2. He can lay off to cover space.

When the attacking players are conversant with the possibilities of place-changing they will leave the defender helpless. If the defender comes forward to challenge for the ball then the attacking players will exploit the space now uncovered. If the defender lays off to cover space the player receiving the ball will take advantage of the time and space granted him to control the ball and turn before bringing the ball forward to take on his opponent.

Taking the defender's first option we can very quickly persuade him that tight-marking and quick-tackling will not pay off against a team skilled at place-changing. The attacking team needs only three men to effect a break-through and with three quick passes the attacking right-back has overlapped his colleagues on the right wing and broken past the line of enemy defenders.

As the right-back wins possession of the ball either by a successful tackle or by interception the initiative changes hands. In possession of the ball his team is now in a position to attack and accordingly his midfield colleagues should be sprinting to take up support positions as indicated in Diagram 33. A quick pass forward to the feet of the right-winger and the right-back sprints to effect a place-change at $2_1$. Meanwhile he is watching the reaction of the enemy left-back and as the enemy moves forward to challenge he calls 'Man on'.

The winger drops back to meet the pass, accelerating as he hears 'Man on' and picks a supporting player to whom he can make an easy first-time pass. With the ball now on its way to the right-midfield player (8) there is an obvious, first-time pass 'on' to the right-back and when this pass had been made the place-change is completed.

## Place-changing on the wings

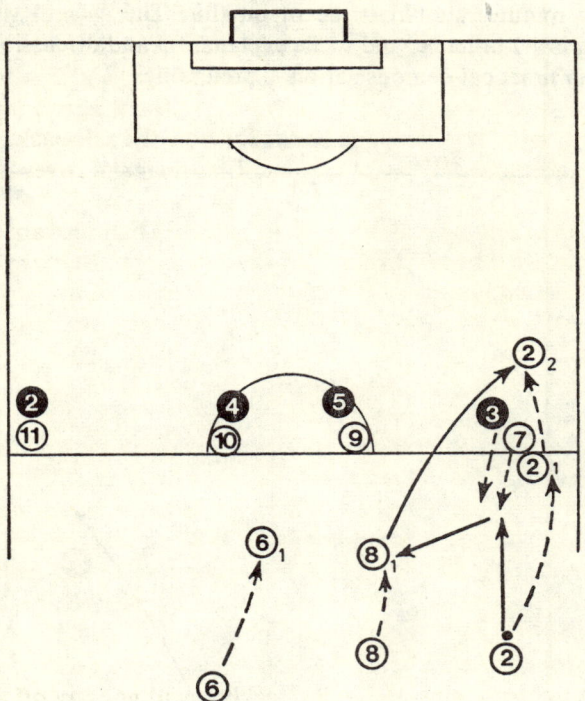

*Diagram 33*

We now have an unmarked player on the right-wing at $2_2$ in possession of the ball, and he has broken past the line of defenders.

To familiarize the players with this simple but effective *Wing Combination* we need only four players. Later we shall see that we can use ten or more players but four is the absolute minimum. If we add a fifth (a goalkeeper) then each practice will have an extra value for we can add practice for the goalkeeper and by pressing each combination to a shooting position we can also have shooting practice in match-like conditions.

Setting up this combination in practice is a simple matter. We need only one ball and five players; a goalkeeper, right-back, left-back, right-winger and right-midfield. If we explain to the players what is involved, illustrating the explanation by sketching the move on a blackboard, this will help clarify the idea in their minds but only a

## *Place-changing on the wings*

very few minutes should be spent on this. The way to success in coaching is via practice, and while explanation and discussion can be of value a practical demonstration is preferable.

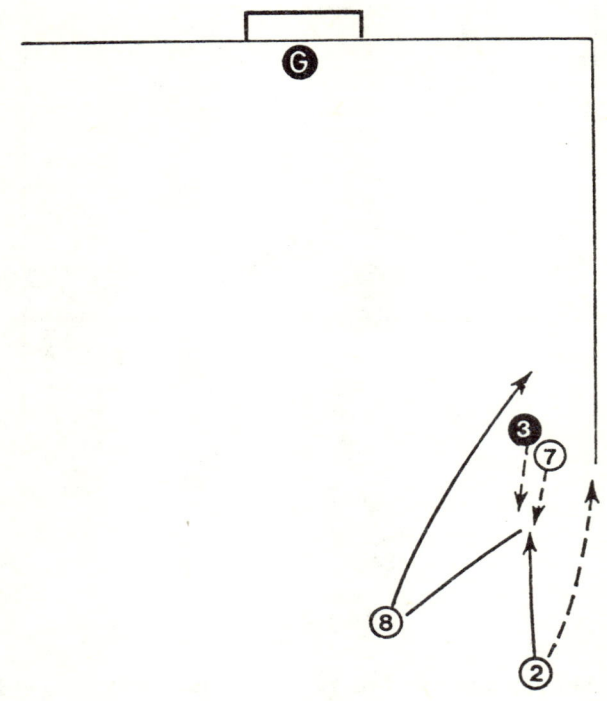

*Diagram 34 (a)*

Position the players as in Diagram 34 (a) with the right-back in possession. Preferably the distance between 2 and 7 should be at least twenty yards with another forty yards between 7 and the goalkeeper. Begin with a slow-motion demonstration carefully explaining each step and pay particular attention to the left-back who represents the opposition. He must understand that until the other three players become skilled at this move it will be useless if he is too successful. The left-back may be persuaded to co-operate by not tackling energetically with the promise that after fifteen minutes he will be given the chance to play the attacking full-back role in a left-wing

## Place-changing on the wings

combination. At all events the opposition must not intervene too vigorously in the early stages and if the left-back cannot be persuaded there are two alternatives:

1. Replace the left-back with another, more co-operative player.
2. Position the left-back further away from his opponent so that his intervention will come too late.

Once the right-back has broken away with the ball he should be encouraged to sprint towards the near post. Simultaneously the right-winger should turn once more and race towards goal while the left-back should be exhorted to try and overhaul the man in possession. The final stage is reached when the player who has broken through reaches a shooting position as in Diagram 34 (b) (and shoots at goal) or pulls the ball into the path of the right-midfield who should follow up in a supporting position as in Diagram 34 (c) some twenty yards behind the ball. From there he can sprint forward to shoot at goal himself.

At the first training session fifteen minutes work on this wing

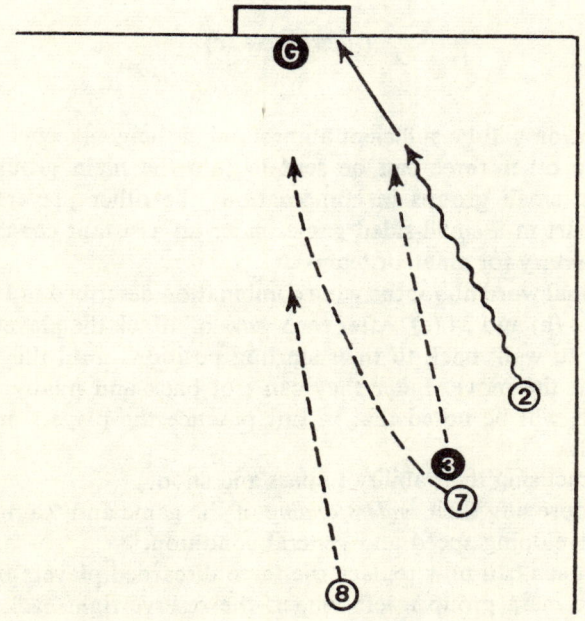

*Diagram 34 (b)*

*Place-changing on the wings*

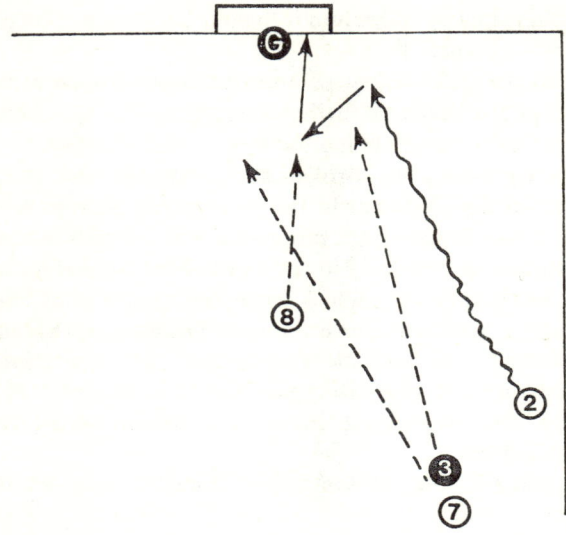

*Diagram 34 (c)*

combination will be sufficient and retaining the goalkeeper and left-back the other three can be sent to join the main group. While coaching small groups in combinations the other players can be taking part in a small-sided game under an assistant coach (or the club secretary for amateur teams).

One final word about the wing combination described in Diagrams 34 (a), 34 (b) and 34 (c). After each *wave* of attack the players can be allowed to walk back to their starting positions until they become skilled at the move. Later they can trot back and finally they can sprint. It will be noted that in this practice the players are simultaneously:

(a) practising their ability to pass and shoot;
(b) improving their *understanding* of the game and team play;
(c) developing speed and general condition.

The coach can now replace the three discarded players by taking from the main group a left-winger, the reserve right-back and the left-midfield. With the goalkeeper and left-back retained from the first practice a left-wing combination can be set up.

*Place-changing on the wings*

## WING COMBINATION (2)

With time and practice the players should soon be able to deal effectively with a full-back who comes forward to challenge the winger when he drops back to receive a pass (to feet) from the full-back. Now we must consider the second option which is open to every defender when his immediate opponent drops back to receive a pass. If the defending left-back elects to lay off—and he certainly will when he has been beaten a few times by the wing combination already described—we must have another combination ready for him. At the second training session we can introduce the same five players: goal-keeper, left-back, right-back, right-winger and right-midfield to another combination. This time our aim will be to defeat the full-back who allows the right-winger to drop back and receive a pass unhindered.

Commencing once more with the right-back in possession he will make a pass towards the feet of his colleague on the right wing. Immediately the pass has been made the winger will sprint back to meet the ball, while the right-back moves up and watches for the reaction of the defender. This time, noting that the winger is unopposed, the right-back will call 'Turn'. Hearing the advice to turn the winger will ease up on his fast approach to the ball and turn ... by extending his left foot to meet the ball and *withdrawing* his foot on contact. Turning on the ball is described in many coaching books (concentrating on technique) but is dealt with later in the chapter headed—Drills and exercises aimed at developing the techniques required in place-changing. Having elected to cover space and let his opponent run free temporarily, the defending full-back cannot lay off indefinitely. If he were to do so then a good winger would advance towards goal threatening other defenders (who will not want to leave their opponents to offer a challenge) and if completely unopposed the winger could reach a shooting position—and shoot at goal.

Like it or not, the defending full-back must now make at least a token challenge by cutting off the winger's direct approach to goal. The defender will be forced to commit himself to the winger though not necessarily be forced to tackle. In this situation full-backs usually position themselves 'inside' the winger—inviting the winger to go past the back on the outside.

Facing the second *wing combination* the defending left-back should

## *Place-changing on the wings*

be instructed to lay off initially but then cut off the winger's path to goal and position himself 'inside'. In Diagram 35 (a) the right-back has made his pass to the right-winger and while running to change places he calls 'Turn'. The winger turns and in Diagram 35 (b) the defender positions 'inside'.

By inviting the winger to beat him on the outside the full-back is inevitably offering space on the outside, and this space can be exploited with a pass to the right-back as he sprints forward 'overlapping' his colleague on the wing. Coming from behind, the right-back is already moving at top speed and cannot possibly be offside if the winger's pass is made just before the attacking back sprints past the ball.

With a firmly-laid pass hit some twenty yards and played into the right-back's direct path towards the near post the defender has been left standing and helpless.

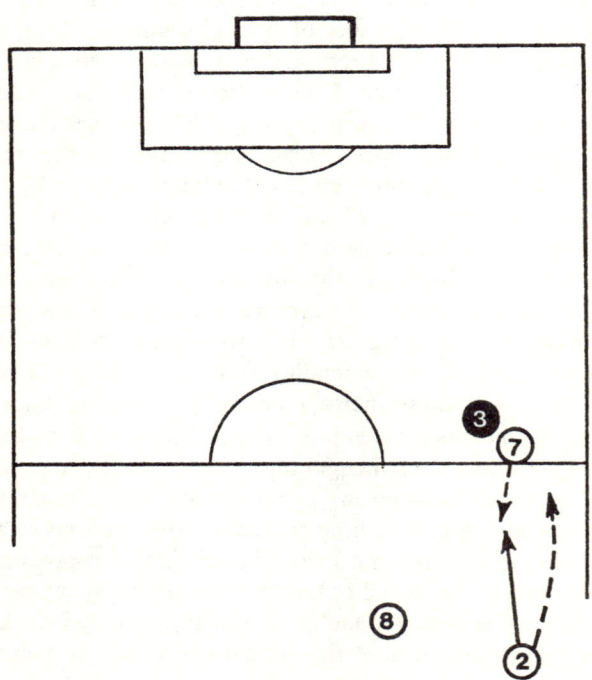

*Diagram 35 (a)*

## *Place-changing on the wings*

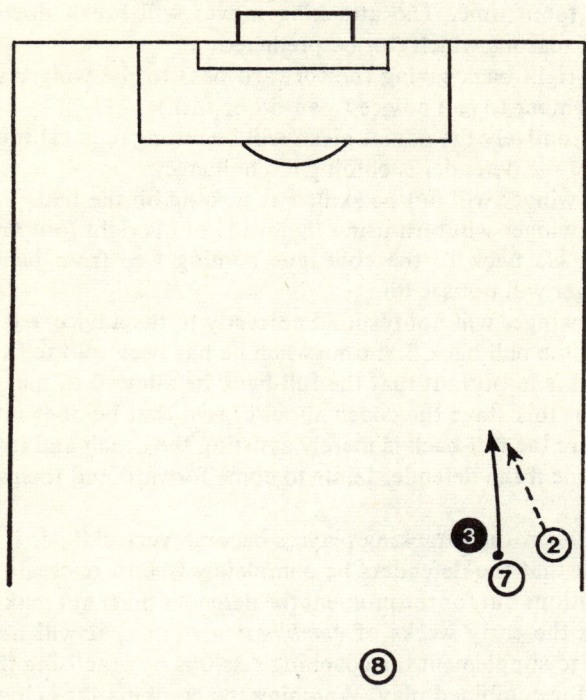

*Diagram 35 (b)*

At this point we have succeeded in breaking past the full-back whether he comes forward to challenge or lays off to cover the winger's approach to goal. While these themes have to be developed further and supplemented by more *wing combinations* it will be wise to remember that to almost every player this will be entirely new. With exceptionally intelligent and talented players or with full-time professionals it may be possible to go further but while the coach in charge is obviously the best judge it will be best in most cases to pause at this point.

The players should now be in a position where they can go past a full-back almost as if he didn't exist, but to date the defender has been restricted by the coach. At first he was ordered to challenge and later he was instructed to lay off and cover the winger's path to goal. Now we must set the defender free.

In all probability the defender will now be in command of the

## *Place-changing on the wings*

situation for a time. The attacking moves will break down for a variety of reasons which can be predicted.
1. The right-back giving the forward pass to the winger will not remember to call advice (man-on or turn).
2. Alternatively the advice given will be wrong (e.g. calling 'Turn' when the defender is coming to challenge).
3. The winger will not be skilled at turning on the ball.
4. The winger will turn using the inside of his right foot and thus, with his back to the colleague coming free from behind the winger will not see him.
5. The winger will not respond correctly to the advice, e.g. he will play the ball back first time when he has been told to turn.

While it is important that the full-back be allowed to make a free decision at this stage the coach should insist that he does not make feints. Here the full-back is merely assisting the coach and it will not help anyone if the defender feints to come forward and then stops to lay off.

Later, when the attacking players become very skilled, it will be important that the defenders be completely free to re-create match-like conditions but for the moment the defender must not make feints.

During the early weeks of *combination training* it will help considerably to supplement the coaching sessions by practising the skills required for combined play. Watching the combinations closely, the coach will see why they break down and reference to the chapter headed—Drills and exercises aimed at developing the techniques required in place-changing—will be useful.

Rehearsing the wing combinations time after time, and practising the various skills required the players will soon reach the point where they can go past a free defender almost faultlessly.

The players will now be ready to be introduced to more combinations which will allow the defenders greater freedom of action.


## **WING COMBINATION (3)**

It is reasonable to suppose that in match play the enemy defenders will not lack intelligence. It is also reasonable to suppose that when the first time the ball is played to the feet of the winger the defender will come forward to challenge. Having been out-flanked in his first encounter the more intelligent defenders will lay off 'goal-side' when he faces the next attack. Now he will be shown the second wing

## Place-changing on the wings

combination and if all goes well for the attacking trio the defender will be beaten just as easily. The defender will now want to try a different approach.

Not all opponents will be aware of what is happening but clearly we must prepare the players for all eventualities. Even the best defenders will make errors of judgment—for example, they will come forward to challenge for a pass which they *think* they can win, but many full-backs will want to experiment in a bid to find answers to their problems. One alternative which may appeal to some full-backs is to mark their winger tighter than ever and thus be in a position to win the 'man-on' pass. If the defender could do this then all his problems will be solved (temporarily) when he clears the ball upfield.

Now we can set up our coaching situation for *wing combinations* and instruct the defending full-back to stay really tight on the winger. In match play the winger would begin to drop back down the touchline as the right-back wins possession but now the defender is right on his heels. To give the winger a pass now would lay him open to serious injury against a completely ruthless defender and the attack might well break down if the winger was asked to fight for an unnecessary pass.

If we cannot give the winger a man-on pass against a really tight-marking defender we can still use the winger to create space. Indeed, the tighter the marking, the easier it is to make space.

As the winger drops back in the third *wing combination* the coach demands that the defender follows him closely. Now the full-back ignores the winger and pushes the ball to his colleague at right-midfield (and calls 'Turn'). Right-midfield receives the ball and turns to face the enemy goal and meanwhile two things are happening.

1. The right-winger is sprinting diagonally across the face of the right-midfield apparently 'looking for a pass' but in reality, using himself as a decoy.
2. The right-back is once more moving out to become the temporary right-winger.

Diagram 36 (a) illustrates this basic move which could hardly be simpler. With the right-winger having reached a withdrawn position at $7_1$, and still very tightly marked the right-back passes the ball to 8, and immediately sprints forward. With the ball on its way to the right-midfield this is the signal for the winger to make his decoy run. With two players moving across in front of the right-midfield it will be useful if he is instructed to chip or lob his forward pass to the

## Place-changing on the wings

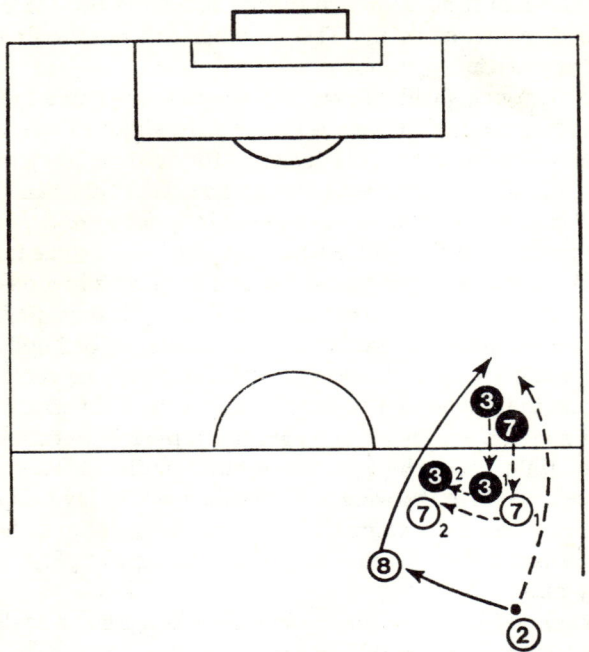

*Diagram 36 (a)*

temporary right-winger, thus eliminating the risk of the ball hitting his colleague or the enemy (3).

Because of its simplicity and the lack of real opposition this will soon become the most effective *wing combination* (in training) and it therefore offers an opportunity to introduce a basic follow-up to all the *wing combinations*.

At this stage the winger should be instructed to watch his tight-marking opponent (3) closely. If he should break away in a late bid to cover space then somehow, someone must go to help the right-back.

Now that this particular *combination* is going well, the coach can instruct the defending full-back to break off his attempt at tight-marking and sprint back to cover space. At first, however, the coach should restrain the defending full-back from leaving the winger until the right-midfield player has made his first contact with the ball. As the left-back breaks away from 7, the positions of the right-back and right-winger are now almost reversed for 2 is well in advance of

## *Place-changing on the wings*

7 and either in possession or about to receive a pass. The right-back is a temporary right-winger. Now 7 must sprint to support his colleague 2—by overlapping the right-back—as illustrated in Diagram 36 (b). Presumably the defender changed his mind about tight-mark-

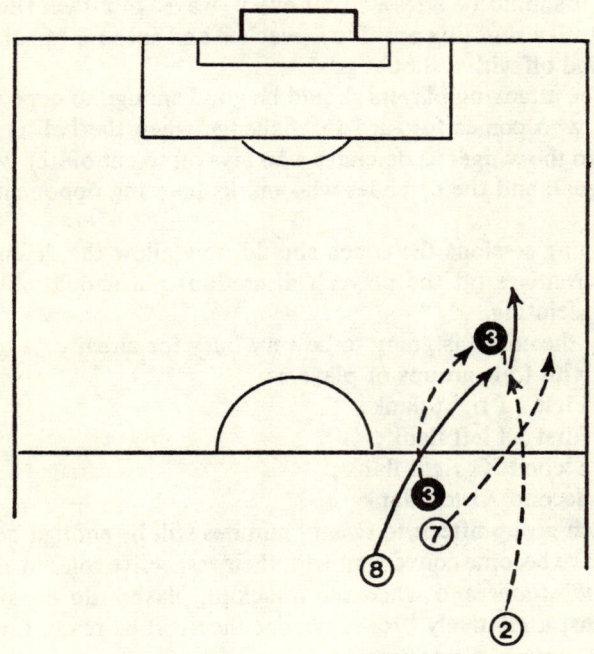

*Diagram 36 (b)*

ing when he realized he had been forced to concede space. Seeing that 2 was about to exploit this space, the defender would turn away in a bid to cut off the new winger. Concentrating on the right-back, the defender will temporarily forget his winger in his bid to cut off what appears to be the greater danger, and if the defender is successful he will turn away from his own goal to face 2 who is now in possession. By turning to challenge the right-back, the defender stops running and this gives 7 the opportunity to *come from behind* at top speed. With the right-winger a pace or two behind the ball (and therefore on-side) this is the moment for the right-back to give the winger a pass—laid firmly into the winger's path to goal.

## *Place-changing on the wings*

As with the first two *wing combinations* the coach must restrain the defender from 'reading the situation' until the attacking players are thoroughly conversant with their roles. When this point has been reached the emphasis should be changed once more and a greater degree of freedom granted to everyone.

Again it should be stressed that every 'wave' of attack should be pressed until a shooting position is reached and each rehearsal should be rounded off with a shot at goal.

Now the attacking players should be good enough to cope with: a defender who comes forward to challenge when the ball is played forward to the winger; a defender who lays off to cut off the winger's path to goal, and the defender who marks his wing opponent really tight.

In training sessions the coach should now allow the defender all three alternatives (at the player's discretion) but should still deter him from feinting.

Clearly the coach is going to be very busy for already he must be working with four groups of players:
1. the First XI right flank;
2. the First XI left flank;
3. the Second XI right flank;
4. the Second XI left flank.

For each group fifteen to twenty minutes will be enough once the players have become conversant with their respective roles in all three *wing combinations* and when the attacking players do consistently well against a relatively 'free' defender they will be ready for introduction to another *combination*.

## WING COMBINATION (4)

The fourth *wing combination* is probably the most difficult and while it would have been a natural follow-on to the second combination it is better left for a time.

Now for a moment we must return to *wing combination* (2) in which the defender lays off and positions himself to cut off the winger's direct path to goal. Positioning himself 'inside' the defender gives his opponent space on the 'outside' which is exploited in the second *wing combination* by a pass laid in front of the attacking right-back as he comes from behind. Once the astute defender has been beaten a few times he will want to experiment in a bid to thwart

## Place-changing on the wings

his opponents. The most logical thing for the defender to try in these circumstances would be to position himself 'outside' in a bid to prevent the winger's pass to the overlapping right-back. In the old WM days this would have been disastrous for the one thing that full-backs always fear is to allow their winger to get 'goal-side'. Now, however, the threat represented by the player *coming from behind* is the greater danger and many defenders will be tempted to 'invite' the winger inside. In the fourth *wing combination* this is exactly what the coach must instruct the defending full-back to do. As the right-back plays the ball forward to his colleague on the right wing the defender lays off—close enough to maintain contact and prevent the winger going off on a solo dribble to goal, but not close enough to be caught in a 'man-on' situation. Varying his approach, the defending full-back now positions himself (very slightly) on the 'outside' and by so doing he will attain his immediate objective; he will prevent the forward pass to the player coming from behind.

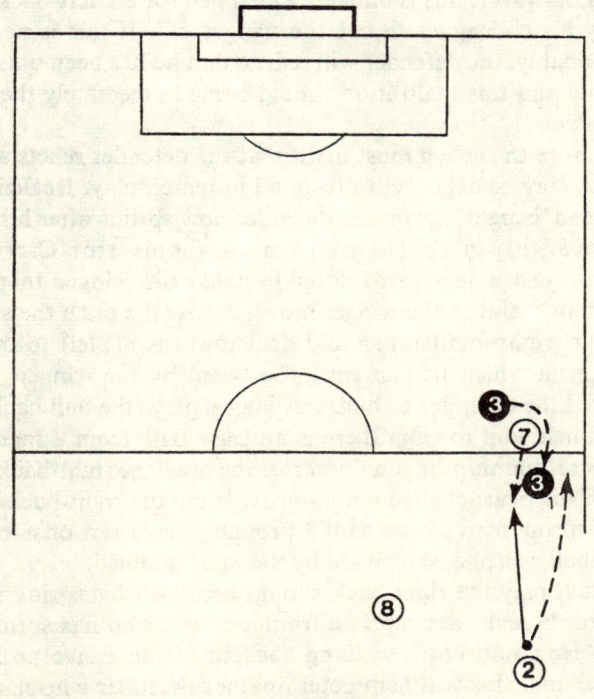

*Diagram 37 (a)*

## Place-changing on the wings

In Diagram 37 (a) we see again the basic situation on the right flank when the right-back gains possession of the ball. Again the right-winger comes back down the line to *meet the man with the ball* and once more the ball is played to him. Having laid his pass, the right-back moves up to effect a *place-change* and watching for the reaction of the defender he calls 'Turn'. The winger turns on the ball, again using the inside of his left foot and with the ball under control he confronts his opponent.

This time the defender is laying off 'outside' to prevent the pass down the line which previously enabled the right-back to leave the defender behind the play, and recognizing this the winger turns away. Running with the ball, diagonally across the pitch, the right-winger has beaten the defender and if he is unchallenged he can go in towards goal. Sooner or later he will either draw another defender 'off' the man he is marking or alternatively if all the defenders lay off, then the winger will reach a shooting position.

In fact, however, this is unlikely to happen for the left-back will be urged by his colleagues to cut the winger off—if this is necessary. More probably, the defender will realize that he has been outsmarted once more and this realization should come immediately the winger turns inside.

Once more the coach must insist that the defender reacts as a live opponent may be expected to respond in match play. Realizing that he has been 'caught' again, the defender now sprints after his winger (Diagram 37 (b) ) in a bid to make amends for his error. Carrying the ball inside just a few yards should enable the winger to pull the defender 'out' and as the winger moves across the pitch the supporting player (right-midfield) should drift towards his left to maintain a position in which he can easily be 'seen' by the winger. Having committed the defender to him, the winger plays the ball back to the right-midfield and for him there is an 'easy ball' from 8 to 2. While the winger is running diagonally across the pitch the right-back should break off his place-change temporarily. Were the right-back to continue to spring forward he would probably have run offside by the time the ball was played forward by the right-midfield.

In match play the right-back should break off his sprint and display open disgust—appropriate from a player who has sprinted for nothing. He could begin walking back to his defensive position at right-back and this will help deter another defender who had 'seen' the place-change coming and was moving across behind the left-back

## Place-changing on the wings

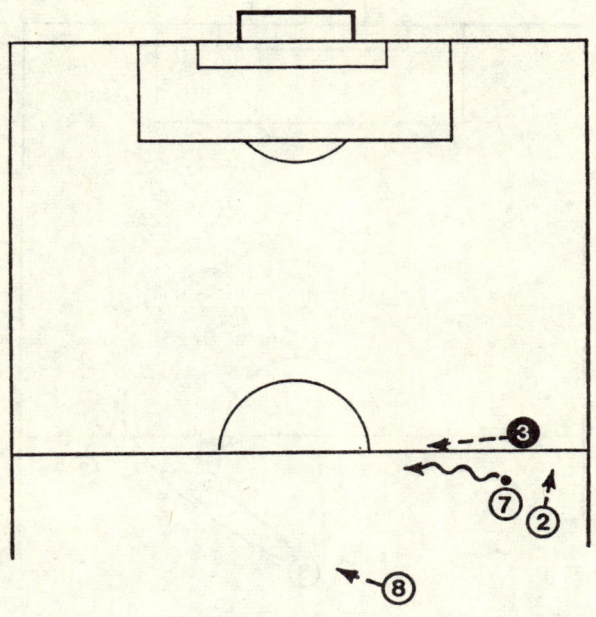

*Diagram 37 (b)*

to cover. With the ball on its way to the right-midfield and checking (looking across-field, along the line of defenders) that he is safely on-side, the right-back should prepare once more to break through on the wing. For the purpose of this coaching session it will be enough if the right-back breaks off his sprint and if necessary adjusts his position so that he remains on-side (relative to the defending back). Then with the pass from right-midfield being played, the right-back sprints down the wing once more as in Diagram 37 (c) to effect the break-through.

As before, the attack is pressed to a shooting position and rounded off with a shot at goal. Once more the players will soon become skilled at facing the defender who responds according to the instructions of the coach. When the attacking players are familiar with the possibilities of *wing combination* (4) the coach should again introduce a degree of freedom into the practice. Now the attacking players can use any of the four wing combinations while the defender can respond as he wishes, except that he should not be allowed to make feints.

## *Place-changing on the wings*

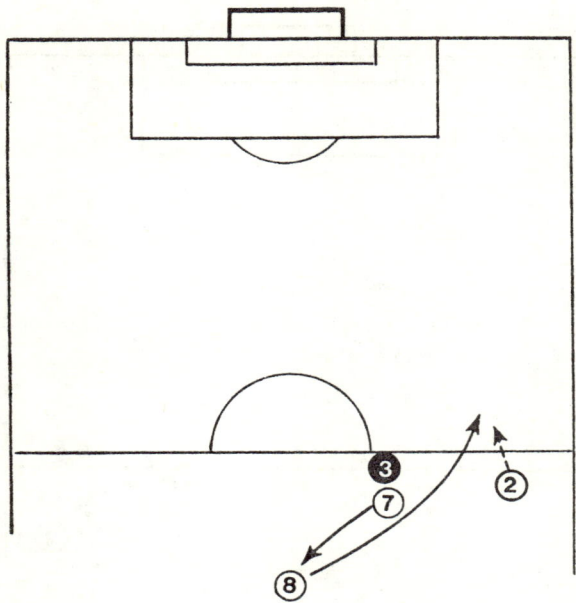

*Diagram 37 (c)*

Only when the attacking players have developed a high degree of understanding will the coach allow the defender complete freedom of action. When this point has been reached it will be possible for the coach to work with two separate groups at the same time. Diagram 38 (a) illustrates how this can be done with two goals and two goalkeepers.

The practices outlined in Diagrams 38 (a) and 38 (b) will save a considerable amount of time previously lost while the players walked/trotted back to their starting positions. Now the *game* becomes more realistic. Each attack commences with a throw from the goalkeeper to his colleague at right-back and is developed from there according to the reaction of the defender. It will be an additional advantage if an extra ball is given to the goalkeeper at each end. Although only one ball will normally be used by both waves of attacking players, time would otherwise be lost when a shot goes wide of the goal. The goalkeeper would then have to retrieve the ball while the other players stand around.

## Place-changing on the wings

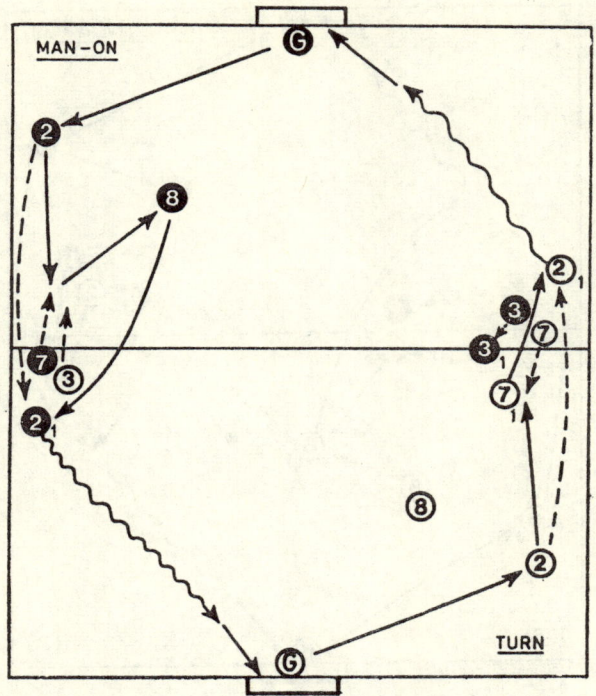

*Diagram 38 (a)*

If the goalkeeper saves the shot he will throw the ball out to his colleague at right-back and return to his goal to await the next attack. If the ball is sent wide of the goal then the goalkeeper will begin the second wave of attack by throwing the spare ball to his colleague, then retrieving the first ball and placing it in reserve. As one attack develops, the players who took part in the previous attack resume their starting positions.

In Diagram 38 (b) we see the practice of the left flank from the First XI and the Second XI. Each wave of attack has the freedom to try any of the *combinations* they have rehearsed according to the reactions of the defending full-back.

This method of 'two-way attacks' may also be introduced earlier if the players are skilled enough at any of their combinations, as long

## Place-changing on the wings

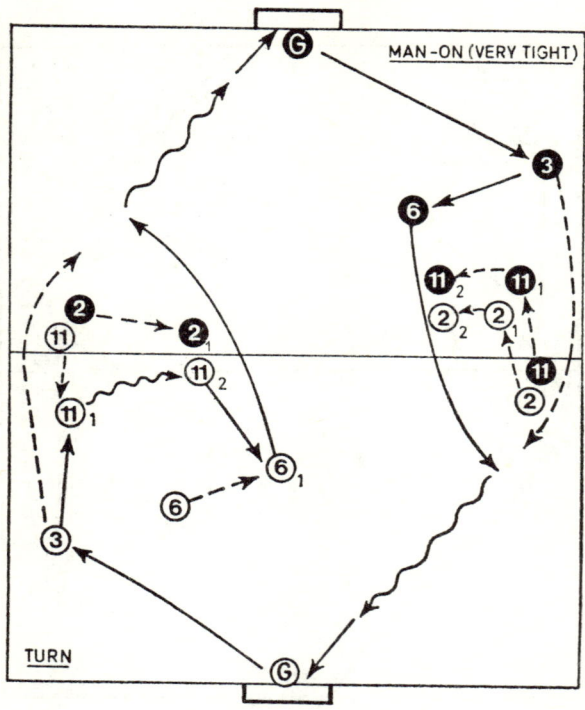

*Diagram 38 (b)*

as the coach insists that the attacking players plug away at the combination he nominates and the defender responds to orders. The disadvantage here lies in the fact that if explanation is required to rectify a basic mistake the coach must necessarily halt the practice for both groups.

Only when players have been coached in *combinations* for some time will the waves of attack flow from end to end without the need for lengthy explanations and analysis by the coach.

Finally, it must be emphasized that in the relatively 'free' two-way coaching sessions the particular combination used by the attacking trio will be dictated by the responses of the defending players.

# 7— Variations of wing combinations and further development after the initial break-through

In each of the *wing combinations* described in the previous chapter it was the full-back who began the move and the same player who made the break-through. This is consistent with the place-changing combinations first developed by the Hungarians (see Diagrams 1 (a), 1 (b) and 1 (c) ) but it is clear that this does give a perceptive opponent an indication of what is to follow. It must be stressed that surprise is an important feature of attacking play and it is not the intention to allow place-changing to become stereotyped. We must begin somewhere, however, and because it will be completely new to the players it must of necessity be kept as simple as possible in the early stages. We shall return to this theme later. Now, however, an attempt must be made to add an extra degree of variety to our wing combinations. If we now approach all the *wing combinations* from another starting point we shall add this extra degree of variety to the moves without further complications for the players.

Once the players have become familiar with the principles of place-changing it will often be seen that in match play the full-backs will move out of defence to act as support-players. This will happen naturally when it is the right-midfield who overlaps the right-winger, but for the moment it will be better to add another player to the practice group. In a 4-2-4 team this extra man should be the left-midfield and in a 4-3-3 team the centre-midfield but for the moment it is only important that we add another support-player. We shall refer to this extra player as the centre-midfield and number him 6.

The coach should now set up the man-on *wing combination* already dealt with (see Diagram 39) and begin the exercise with the right-midfield (8) in possession. The rule until now has been that when a player gives a forward pass he immediately runs to change places with the man receiving the ball. This should be re-emphasized before commencing this second round of wing combinations. Now we find

## *Variations of wing combinations*

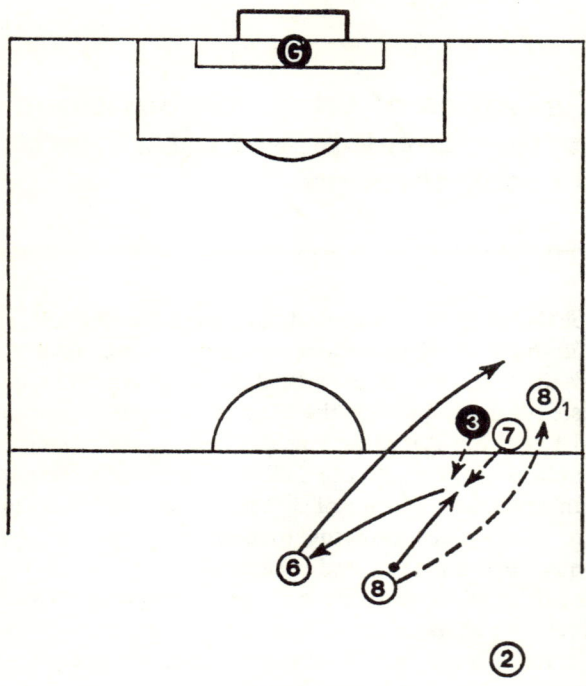

*Diagram 39*

that it is the right-midfield who plays the ball forward to the feet of the winger and will be he who overlaps his colleague on the wing. As the ball travels from 8 to 7, 8 must watch for the reaction of the defender and call advice as he moves to change places. 'Man-on' the right-midfield calls to the winger who sprints to meet the ball. While 8 is moving to take up his new position on the wing the centre-midfield moves closer to support the winger. It should be stressed that the centre-midfield must not get too close for the closer he is then the less time he will have to adjust himself to receive a slightly inaccurate pass. More than twenty yards will be too far, but less than fifteen yards could lead to a breakdown if the winger's pass is not inch-perfect and the centre-midfield is moving at speed.

The simple man-on and turn *combinations* should be no more complicated with 8 starting the move than they were when 2 had possession. The variation to *wing combination* (3) will depend on the

## Variations of wing combinations

*Diagram 40*

ability of the right-back to 'see' that the very tight-marking defender is inviting him to exploit space on the wing. If the right-back does not realize that he is being offered space the coach can suggest that the right-midfield should prompt him. Diagram 41 illustrates this variation although it will be clear that the moves are not carried out simultaneously. As the winger drops back the defender marking him has the two basic options already referred to: he can mark tight or lay off to cover space. Here the defender has elected to mark tight in a bid to win the man-on pass and there comes a moment as he races forward when it will be impossible for him to recover. Seeing the defender staying really tight on the winger the right-back edges forward awaiting the moment when the defender reaches the point of no return. At exactly the right time the right-midfield releases his pass with the right-back taking this as his cue to race forward.

## Variations of wing combinations

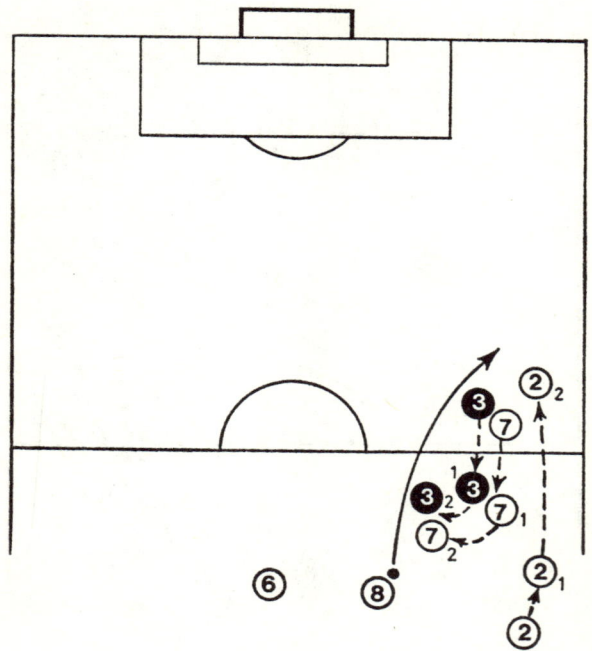

*Diagram 41*

The variation to *wing combination* (4) will be understood very readily by players already familiar with the basic move. In Diagram 42 the winger drops back to meet the right-midfield (the man in possession) and the defender elects to lay off; 8 pushes the ball forward to 7 and runs to change places and the defender 'seeing' the right-midfield on his way to overlap, decides to lay off on the outside. Again the winger turns inside with the ball and with the defender now being drawn away from the touch-line the ball goes back to the centre-midfield who chips the ball forward to the 'new' winger.

Until each of the variations are fully understood the coach must again restrict the defender to a stereotyped response. Time after time the defender *must* come forward to challenge for the first pass in Diagram 39. Time after time the defender must lay off 'inside' while the attacking players release the move in Diagram 40 and he must stay really close to the winger for the practice based on Diagram 41.

## Variations of wing combinations

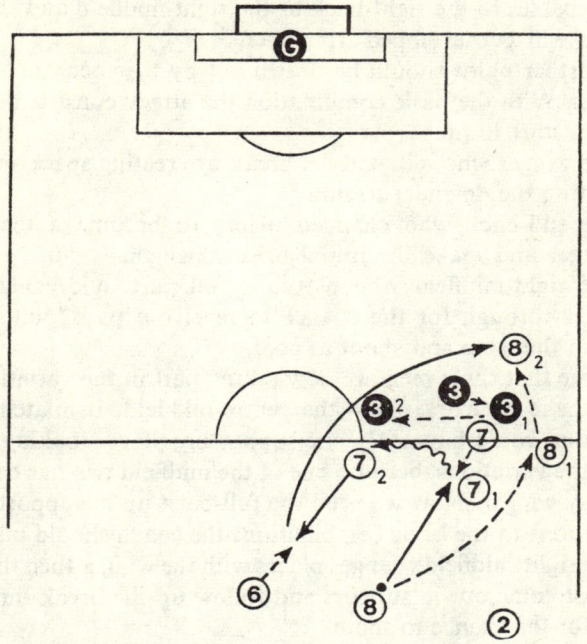

*Diagram 42*

Again, for the drill described in Diagram 42, the defender must always lay off 'outside' until the winger turns but when 7 moves across the field with the ball the defender must follow him. When the attacking players are completely familiar with their roles the coach should ease the restrictions on the defender who can now be allowed greater freedom. The defender now has the option of (a) going forward to challenge the winger, (b) marking the winger so tight that a pass to the winger would be dangerous, (c) laying off 'inside' and (d) laying off 'outside'. The defender must still be restrained from making feints but now the practice sessions will more closely resemble match play and the attacking players will be forced to note the varied reactions of the defender and develop their break-through according to his response.

Now the coach can once more introduce the two-way drill with two goalkeepers and two groups of players familiar with wing combinations. The goalkeepers will now have the option of throwing

## Variations of wing combinations

out their passes to the right-back or the right-midfield and the combinations will be developed from there.

One further point should be drawn out by the coach in all these variations. With the basic combination the attack consisted of three men from start to finish:

1. The winger who initiated the break by creating space and committing the defender to him.
2. The full-back who changed places to become a temporary winger and make the initial break-through.
3. The right-midfield who played a full part in organizing the break-through for the chance to receive a pass 'pulled' back from the wing and shoot at goal.

It is true that three men are now taking part in the variations but now we have an extra man—the centre-midfield. In match play a 4–2–4 team would have only one supporting player looking for the 'pull' in the variations, because one of the midfield two has become a temporary winger. Now we need the full-back up in support and in the variations to the basic combinations the coach should insist that when the right-midfield changes places with the winger then the right-back must come out in support and follow up the break-through—looking for the chance to shoot.

When coaching players in *combination-play* at any level there will inevitably be a whole series of misplaced passes. At first the coach will do well to stop the practice and send everyone back to their respective starting positions but when the players have become familiar with the four basic combinations and the variations, this will be a convenient point to approach the overall problems from a new angle.

The ideal situation to use as a starting point will be one in which a 'man-on' pass is given to the winger. Whether the winger receives his 'man-on' pass from the right-back or right-midfield makes no difference for whoever it was should be running to become a temporary winger. The winger successfully plays the ball back to the supporting player in midfield but from there an inaccurate pass is often dropped behind the overlapping player. This will happen quite frequently and when the players have fully mastered all that they have been shown to date, the coach should take advantage of this opportunity to develop the *wing combinations* as a step further.

The example I have taken is the 'man-on' situation in Diagram 34 (a). The right-back pushes the ball forward and runs; the winger

## Variations of wing combinations

drops back and plays the ball on to the right-midfield and his pass is dropped behind the moving right-back. It will be clear that in match play the defender would have time to recover and get back into a position goal-side before the attacking back could stop, turn and collect the ball. In Diagram 43 (a) the attacking right-back has

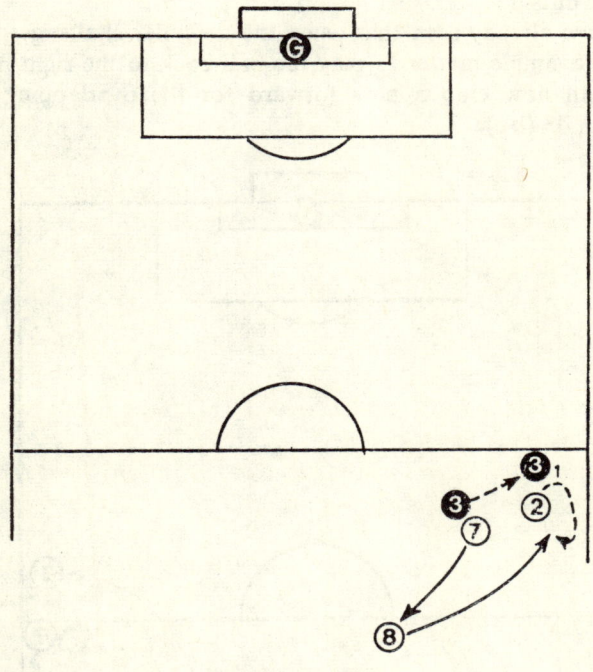

*Diagram 43 (a)*

managed to prevent the ball going out of play but the time wasted while he retrieved the ball has been used by the defender and he has recovered. The defender is now blocking the route usually taken by the attacking right-back. At this point the coach should stress the fact that in the fullest sense number 2 *is the right-winger*. He is in fact the most advanced attacking player on the right-flank and recognizing this his colleagues should support him as they would run to support the player wearing 7.

In the basic move (*wing combination (1)*) the right-back moved round behind the right-winger while the right-midfield stood off in

## Variations of wing combinations

support. Now it is 2 who is the effective right-winger and the coach should instruct the winger to 'overlap' his right-back colleague. The defender still has precisely the same alternatives that he had before:
1. he can move forward to tackle the right-back;
2. he can lay off to cover space:
   (*a*) 'inside';
   (*b*) 'outside'.

We have already seen that when the defender challenges for the ball it is a simple matter to play the ball back to the right-midfield and 8 can now chip a pass forward for the overlapping player (Diagram 43 (b) ).

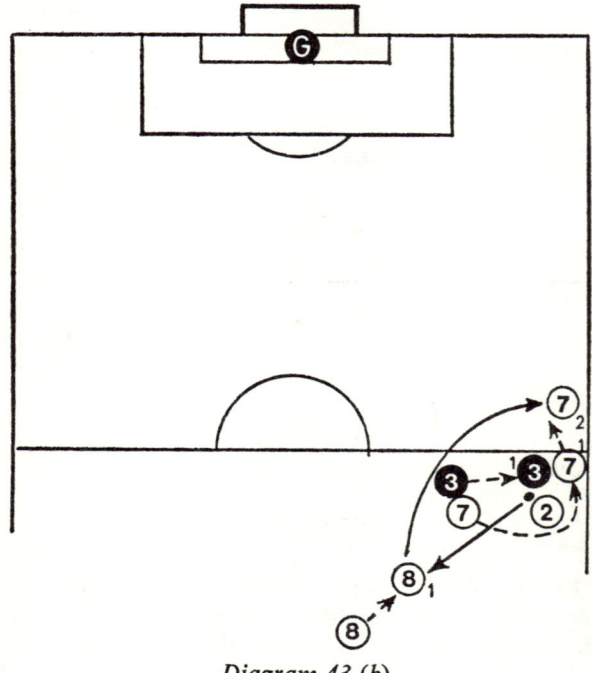

*Diagram 43 (b)*

If the defender lays off 'inside' then the right-back can give a pass down the line to the player overlapping him as in Diagram 43 (c). When the defender lays off 'outside' the right-back should carry the ball inside to draw the defender away from the touchline and then having committed the defender to himself he should now play the

## Variations of wing combinations

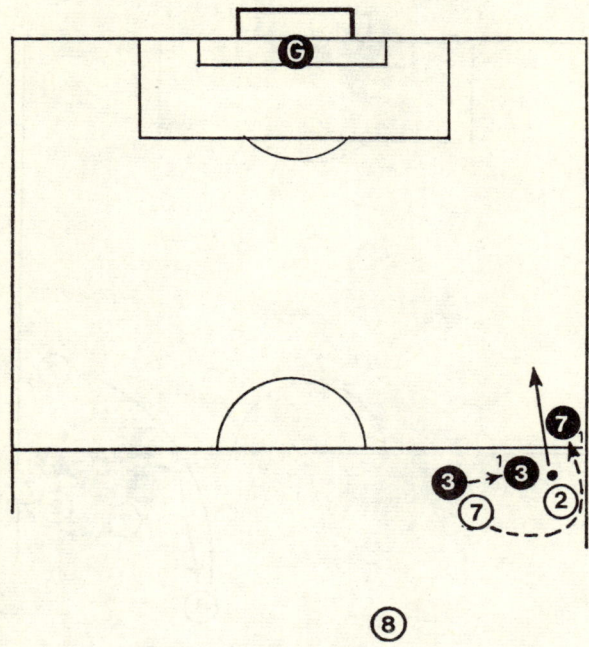

*Diagram 43 (c)*

ball back to the right-midfield (or centre-midfield) and from there the ball goes forward to the overlapping player (Diagram 43 (d) ).

All these variations have already been rehearsed by the players though the roles of the right-back and right-winger have been reversed. Until now it has always been 2 that overlapped 7 but now it is 7 that overlaps 2. When the move has apparently broken down following a misplaced pass to the overlapping player, it will now be possible to start it all off again.

Again it will be necessary for the coach to insist that the defender now regards the right-back (who is in possession) as the greater danger. The defender must treat the right-back as if he were the winger. Starting positions should now be those allocated to the players in Diagram 44 and the practice begins with a 'bad' pass to the right-back.

In the first rehearsal the defender *must* come to challenge the right-back; in the second he *must* lay off 'inside' and the third time he

## Variations of wing combinations

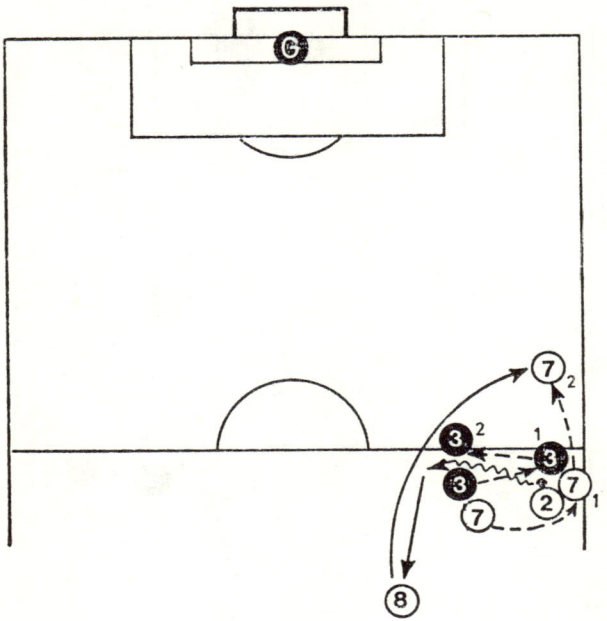

*Diagram 43 (d)*

*must* lay off 'outside'. On each occasion the right-winger overlaps the right-back and the attack is developed according to the response of the defender as in Diagrams 43 (b), 43 (c) and 43 (d). Once more it should be emphasized that every attack should be pressed to a shot at goal and if the moves break down now the players should be encouraged to get one of the combinations going again.

Leaving the question of combinations for a moment we should now consider the defensive reaction when a player breaks through on the flank and is in possession. Sooner or later another defender will have to come across, leaving his particular opponent in order to present a challenge. In all probability it will be the left centre-back who attempts to cover for the left-back and when his challenge comes the attacking players must be ready for it.

We have already seen a logical answer to this problem in Diagrams 43 (b), 43 (c) and 43 (d). In each case it was the right-back who attempted a break-through and being thwarted by a bad pass from

## Variations of wing combinations

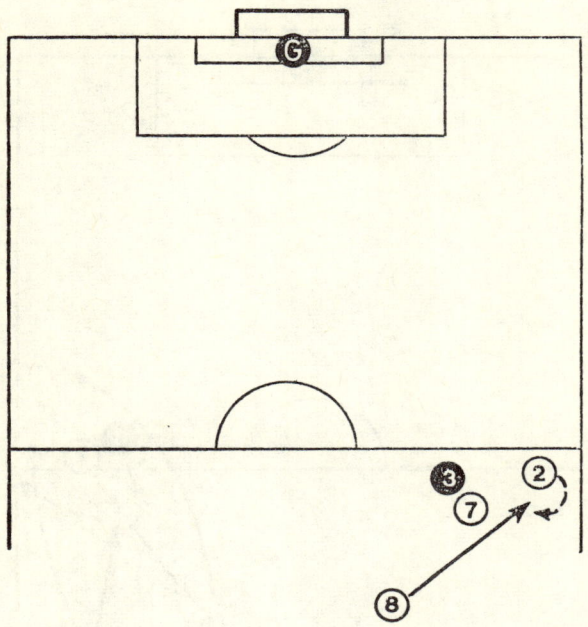

*Diagram 44*

8 he was then overlapped by 7 to get the attack going again. Imagine the situation in match play. The attacking trio has succeeded in putting the right-back through on the right wing by means of one of the *wing combinations*. Now a defender is coming across to challenge. What is required here is another overlapping player—coming up fast —outside the right-back.

The ideal answer to this problem would be to have the right-winger (who has been overlapped) sprinting to take part in a second overlap—or as we may call it—a double overlap.

Later on we can go on to produce treble-overlaps with 2 overlapping 7—followed by 7 overlapping 2—followed by 2 overlapping 7.

To develop the *wing combinations* further the coach should set up a 'man-on' situation as in Diagram 34 (a) and add an additional defender. This should preferably be a left centre-back (5) positioned according to Diagram 45 (a) and he should be instructed to lay off initially, as if he were marking the right centre-forward. Once the

## Variations of wing combinations

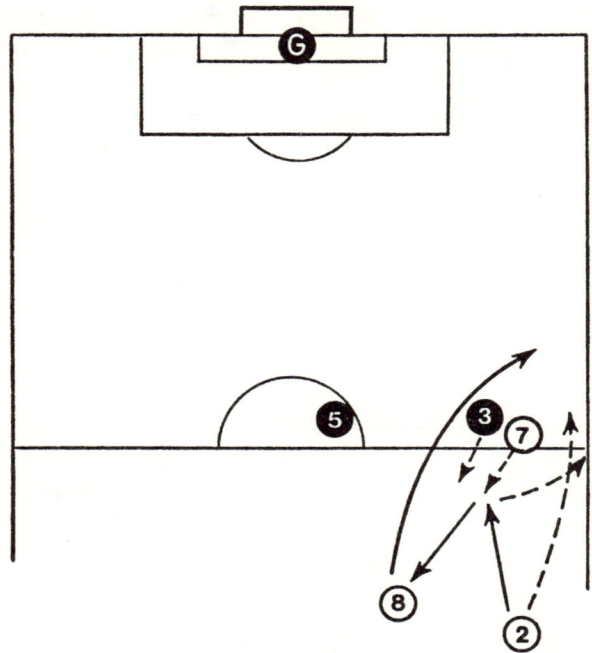

*Diagram 45 (a)*

player *coming from behind* has received the pass from 8 then the left centre-back is free to intervene. In this case it will be 2 who is to be challenged by (5) and as soon as 8 has given his pass to 2, the right-winger must turn and sprint to overlap his colleague at right-back.

With the left centre-back moving across to challenge him the right-back (Diagram 45 (b)) should drop well below his maximum speed—enabling him to have closer control of the ball and also allowing his right-wing colleague to catch him. As the second defender closes in, the right-back should push the ball on and then sprint to overlap his right-wing colleague once more—in case he should be needed.

In match play the left-back would have two options after he had been caught out of position by the pass from 8 to 2 (in Diagram 45 (b)). He could conform to the present covering system in defence and sprint for the penalty spot where he would usually be able to

## Variations of wing combinations

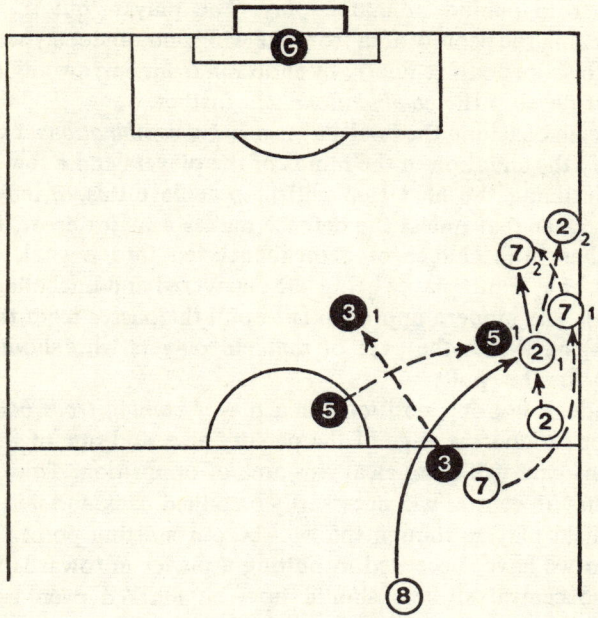

*Diagram 45 (b)*

pick up the 'front' player left free by the colleague who covered the left flank or—he could attempt to get round behind his colleague at (5) in Diagram 45 (b) in case the attacking players produced a double-overlap. In a match the left-back would almost certainly sprint for the penalty spot and the coach should instruct the player to do this as soon as the ball is played from 8 to 2. From this point on, a new twist can be added to all the wing combinations which by now should have reached the stage at which the coach can put on relatively free two-way drills. When a player is overlapped and the ball has gone to the overlapping player, the first player *must* always sprint round behind the player in possession. Now we should always have a 'pair' on each of the wings—overlapping each other—and more often than not because of the nature of the wing combinations, the 'pairs' will be the right-winger and the right-back and the left-winger and the left-back.

Given regular practice at the place-changing combinations on the wings the players on both flanks should soon be able to put some-

## Variations of wing combinations

one in from behind in match play. The player 'put in' will be approaching the penalty area from the wing and obviously we cannot expect to score goals regularly by shooting from narrow angles. Now we must develop the *combinations* still further.

To begin coaching the final stages of *wing combinations* it will help to clarify the situation in the minds of the players and a few minutes spent outlining the next step will help achieve this. Briefly, it has become clear that unless the defence makes a major error, the high centre has little chance of being converted into a goal, and the chances of a 'front' player being left uncovered and unchallenged are minimal. The modern approach is to pull the passes from the wings (centres) back into the path of midfield players who should all be looking for the 'pull'.

The ideal shooting position for a player *coming from behind* will be on or around the edge of the penalty area and one of the major problems here will be to clear this area of opposition. This does not mean that all centres will necessarily be pulled back and laid in front of midfield players though this will be our starting point.

When we have succeeded in putting a player in towards the near post the central strikers should now be marked even tighter in anticipation that the final pass will be an attempt to present one of them with a scoring chance.

As always, the tightly-marked front player is in a very advantageous position. Though the front men may be so tightly marked that they seem to have been played out of the game, they have only to move to create chaos.

Consider the situation which exists in Diagram 46. The right attacking trio—right-back, right-midfield and right-wing—have broken through, finally putting the right-winger in towards the near post at $7_1$. With the defending left-midfield attempting to cover and closing in on the right-winger all the 'front' players are tightly marked.

The key to this situation rests with the central strikers 9 and 10 for if they remain stationary they are not only marked tight but are enabling the men marking them to cover the 'shooting-space' as well. As always when a front player moves, the defender marking him must either continue to mark and concede space *or* alternatively he can let his opponent go free.

It should now be suggested to the central strikers that they should 'move'. If the right centre-forward goes left (to the far post) then 5

## Variations of wing combinations

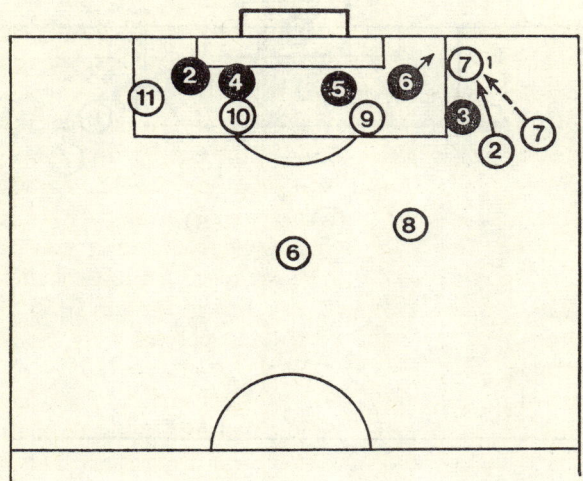

*Diagram 46*

must either go with his opponent or concede space. Simultaneously the left centre-forward should move right (to the near post) and here again (4) must decide whether to go with his man (and concede space) *or* continue to cover space and allow his opponent to get free at the near post.

Moving in this way it is possible that one or both of the central strikers may temporarily get free but even if they are followed by their individual opponents they have a better chance of turning a pass into a goal if it comes. By moving away from their opponents the front players have earned at least a slight advantage in time and space for they were free to choose the moment to go. If the centre-back declines to follow his opponent 9, then the winger in possession has a target at the far post. If the right centre-back does not follow his opponent 10, then the winger now has a target at the near post. If on the other hand the centre-backs elect to follow their opponents then space has been cleared for the midfield players to advance looking for the ball pulled back into space by the winger.

The coach should now set up the situation described in Diagram 47 (a). The right-back has possession and is challenged by the defending left-back. So close to goal the defender would always position 'inside' because if the player in possession were to beat the defender

## Variations of wing combinations

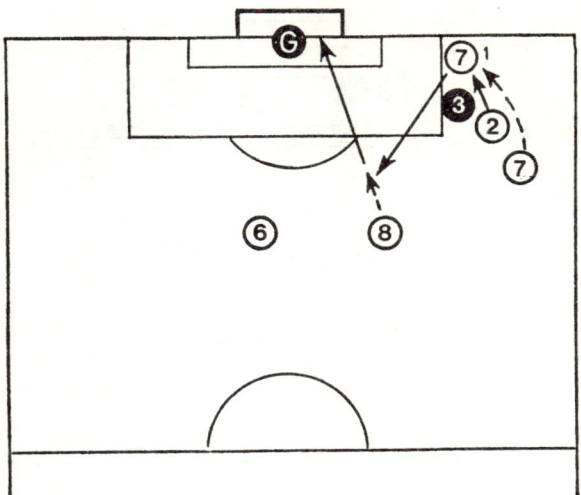

*Diagram 47 (a)*

on the inside (even momentarily) he could shoot for goal himself.

The defender challenges from the inside and at first the coach demands that he does so only half-heartedly. Meanwhile the right-winger is coming from behind on a second overlapping run and the right-back gives his pass forward for the winger to collect the ball at $7_1$. Now the winger *must* pull the ball back, aiming for one of his midfield colleagues who shoots first time.

After the shot at goal the players return to their starting positions and after a few rehearsals the coach can allow the defending left-back more freedom. If the left-back lays off or tends to drift back to cover the overlapping player the right-back should be encouraged to step 'inside' the back and shoot—*or* pull the ball back for a midfield player himself.

These are only further variations, however, and the major purpose here is to get the man who finally gets 'in' from the flanks to look for the midfield players coming on for the pass pulled back. With this in mind the coach should insist on this approach if the players stray too often with their variations based on individual ability.

Finally, it should be noted that it will not only be the winger who overlaps at this point in match play but also the right-back and the right-midfield. Changing the roles of 2, 7 and 8 for the exercise

## Variations of wing combinations

described in Diagram 47 (a) will familiarize them all with the possibilities of the 'pulled' pass when coming 'in' from the flanks.

Now the coach should develop the situation in Diagram 47 (a) on another line by adding the two central strikers 9 and 10 and also an extra defender. He can temporarily send the midfield players off to join the main group.

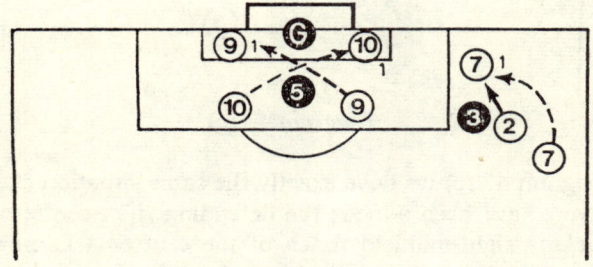

*Diagram 47 (b)*

In Diagram 47 (b) we are once more putting a man 'in' from the flanks but this time his only targets are the right centre-forward and left centre-forward. The defender in this situation we can describe as the old-fashioned stopper centre-half (and number him (5)) for he really has no chance. With the overlapping player about to reach the ball pushed forward by his colleague, the players in the goalmouth must 'move'. The left centre-forward sprints to the near post; the right centre-forward to the far post; while the stopper can decide for himself:

(a) to follow 10;
(b) to follow 9.

The player in possession now has to seek the uncovered 'front' player and get the ball to him while the goalkeeper is free to save the situation if he can. Time after time the players return to the starting positions in Diagram 47 (b) to begin again. Again the coach should see to it that all the players who might 'overlap' on the wings—2, 7 and 8—should all become familiar with this exercise and all should be drilled in the role of 7 in Diagram 47 (b). Finally the coach must ensure that the stopper does not 'feint' to go with one opponent and then race to cover the other. He should be free to decide which of the front players he should mark but not to make feints.

## Variations of wing combinations

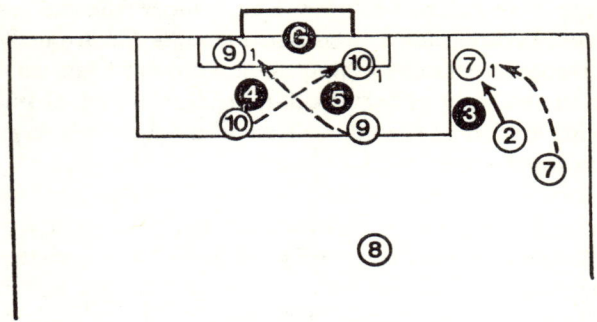

*Diagram 47 (c)*

In Diagram 47 (c) we have exactly the same situation except that two players have been added: the defending right centre-back and the attacking right-midfield. Each of the centre-backs now marks his centre-forward and follows him when the two 'front' players scissor. Now, however, the coach should nominate one of the centre-backs prior to each attack. The nominated defender then has two options:

1. he can follow his centre-forward;
2. he can move out, away from goal, anticipating the pass pulled back to the right-midfield.

The nominated defender must make the move of his choice as soon as the ball is played from 2 to 7 (in Diagram 47 (c)). He must not make feints.

Now the player coming in from the flank has two options:

1. he can play the ball to the 'free' centre-forward who may be at the near post or the far post;
2. he can pull the ball back for the right-midfield to come on, and shoot first time.

Clearly the player in possession is expected to seek and find the colleague who has been left free and he *must* do so. Again it is clear that 2, 7 and 8 will all need to be drilled in the possibilities open to them when they find themselves in possession close to the position of $7_1$ in Diagram 47 (c).

After a few training sessions the coach should now be in a position to add a degree of freedom to the penalty area exercises described in Diagrams 47 (a), 47 (b) and 47 (c). Starting with the right-back (or right-winger) in possession and challenged by the defending full-back

## Variations of wing combinations

the player with the ball is overlapped. Meanwhile the two central defenders can decide for themselves whether to follow their opponent *or* to advance to cut out the 'pull'. Whatever the defenders do, a pass to 9 or 10 or 8 must be 'on' and it should be played.

Another variation can be rehearsed by taking the basic players required for the *wing combinations* (see Diagram 34 (a) ), adding a centre-forward to the attacking trio and including a centre-back to cover him. For right-wing combinations the two new players should be right centre-forward and left centre-back; for left-wing combinations they should be the left centre-forward and right centre-back.

For a right-wing combination the players should be positioned as in Diagram 48 (a). The coach should instruct the left-back to lay off 'outside' to prevent the winger giving an overlapping pass to his colleague coming from behind. The ball goes forward from 2 to 7 and with the defending full-back declining to challenge the winger is

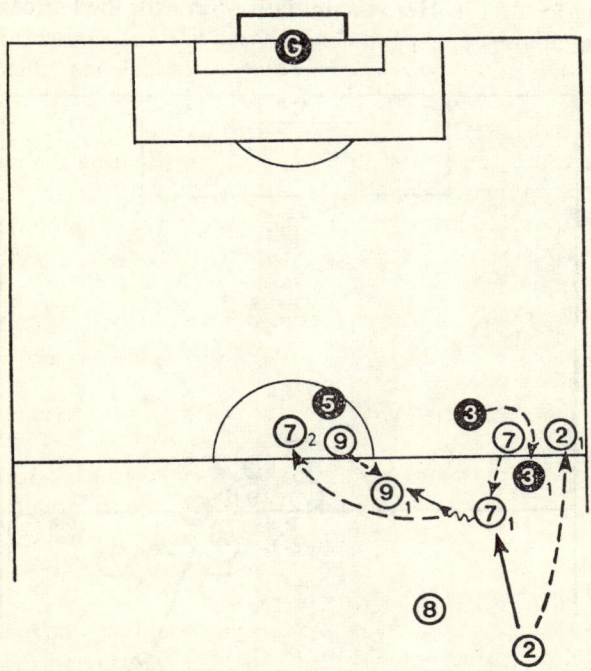

*Diagram 48 (a)*

## Variations of wing combinations

told to 'turn'. The winger turns and with the defender laying off 'outside' the winger moves inside with the ball. So far, this move is exactly the same as the exercise outlined in Diagrams 37 (a), 37 (b) and 37 (c) except that we now have two additional players. With the right-winger moving inside with the ball, the defending full-back would almost certainly be persuaded away from the touchline and once more the coach should insist that he attempts to catch the winger. Now the winger plays the ball towards the right centre-forward—not to him—but towards him. Having given his pass the winger now sprints to change places with the right centre-forward.

The coach should note that once the winger has made his pass, the defending full-back is immediately free to use his discretion. He can, as always when 'front' players move:

(a) attempt to catch and mark his winger;
(b) lay off to cover the space on the left flank.

Now the ball is travelling towards the right centre-forward who is sprinting to meet it. Here the initiative lies with the left centre-back who can choose:

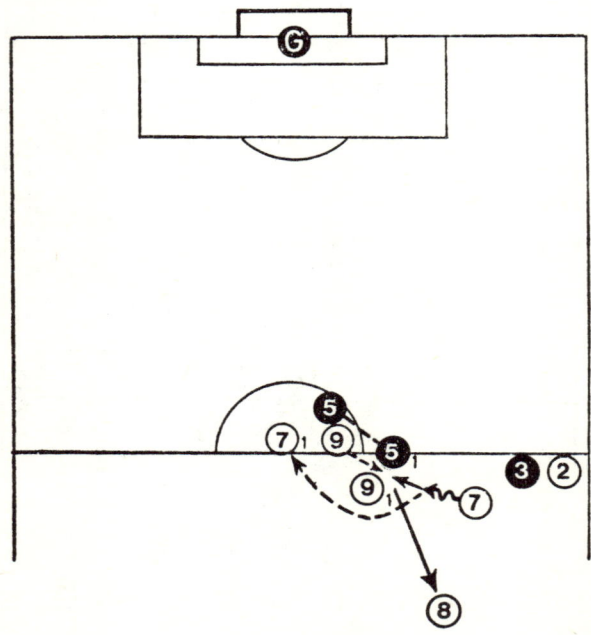

*Diagram 48 (b)*

## Variations of wing combinations

(a) to come forward and challenge his opponent;
(b) to lay off and cover space.

If the left centre-back comes to challenge then the winger (who gave the pass) calls 'man-on' and the right centre-forward plays the ball back first time to the right-midfield (Diagram 48 (b) ). The right-midfield now has two possibilities. If the defending left-back is attempting to catch the right-winger, then the right-back must be free to break through on the wing and in Diagram 48 (c) this move is illustrated.

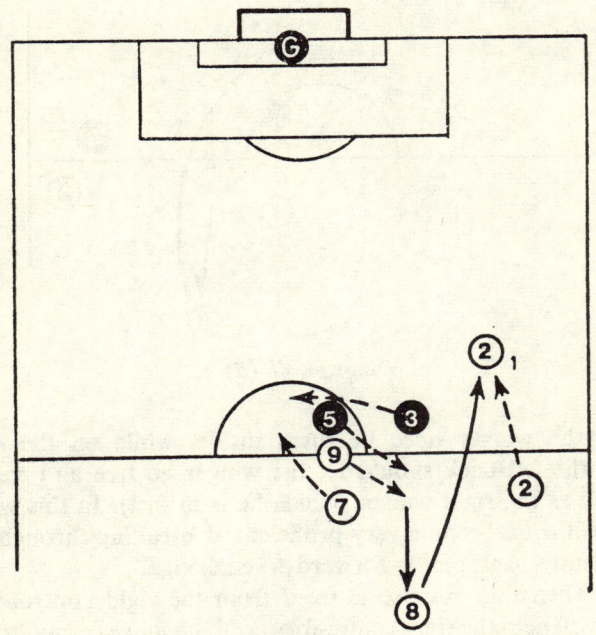

*Diagram 48 (c)*

If the defending left-back has preferred to cover his zone on the left flank, then the right-winger must be free to break-through the centre (Diagram 48 (d) ) with a pass from the right-midfield. When this combination is set up for the first time the coach should instruct the left-back to lay off and position 'outside' every time. He should also instruct the left centre-back to come forward to challenge 9 for the pass from 7. On the first occasion, the left-back should attempt

*Variations of wing combinations*

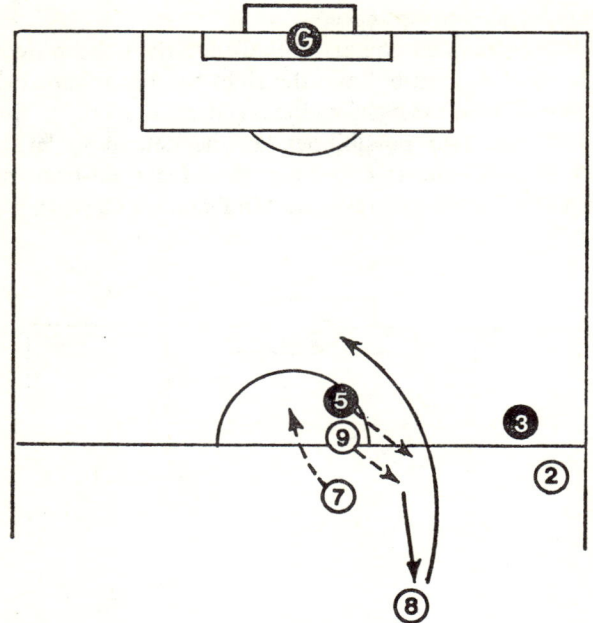

*Diagram 48 (d)*

to catch the winger once he turns inside, while on the second occasion the left-back should let the winger go free and treat the right-back as the right-winger (which he is in fact). In this way the players will soon become very proficient at breaking through when the left centre-back comes forward to challenge.

Later, when this exercise is freed from the rigid control of the coach, it will help the right centre-forward if he moves away (towards goal) in the moment that the winger turns inside with the ball. In this way he will force the left centre-back to move away (in order to mark him goal-side) and then he can choose the moment to turn away and sprint back for the winger's pass.

Over and over again as this exercise is rehearsed the left centre-back must come forward to challenge and alternatively the left-back (a) chases the winger and (b) covers the overlapping right-back.

When the attacking players are familiar with their rules in this new combination the coach should then give new instructions to the left

## Variations of wing combinations

centre-back. Now when the winger gives the pass to 9, the left centre-back must hold off—covering 9 and his direct path to goal, but not allowing himself to be tempted forward. Alternately, the left-back continues:

(a) to chase after his winger;
(b) to cover space and pick up the right-back.

With the left centre-back now holding off, the winger will call 'Turn' to the right centre-forward, and 9 turns as he controls the ball. The left centre-back is now committed to challenging 9 but laying

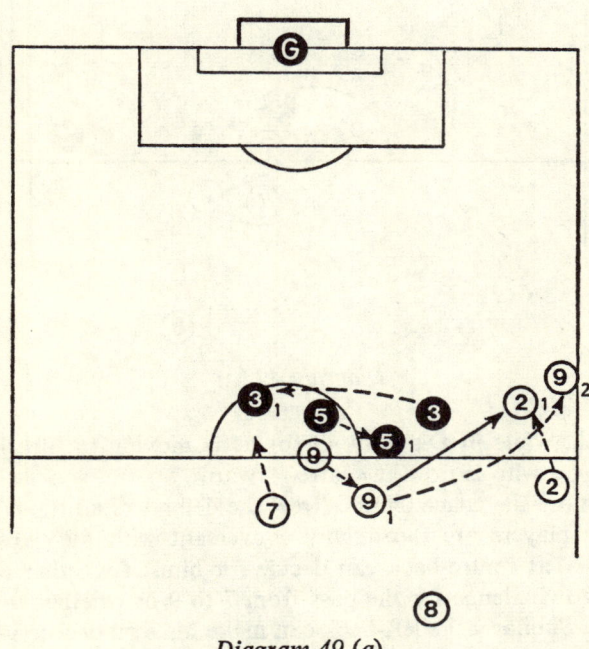

*Diagram 49 (a)*

off goal-side while the defending left-back alternately (a) chases his winger and (b) covers the left flank. Diagrams 49 (a) and 49 (b) show the alternatives open to the right centre-forward and note in each case where 9 should run immediately after giving his pass. The right centre-forward gives his pass and follows the path the ball takes—*he runs to change places with the colleague to whom he gives the ball.* In Diagram 49 (a) the right centre-forward is running to overlap the

## Variations of wing combinations

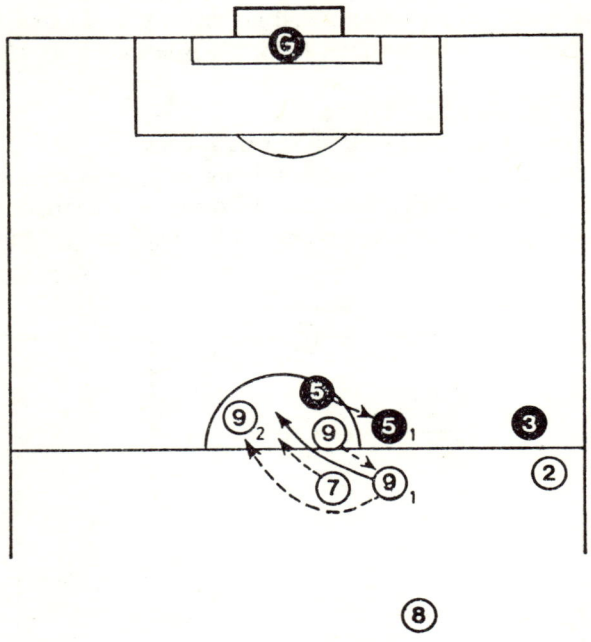

*Diagram 49 (b)*

right-back, while in Diagram 49 (b) he is moving to 'overlap' the right-winger who is now at centre-forward.

Once more the coach should 'free' the defenders a little when the attacking players are thoroughly conversant with their respective roles. The left centre-back can decide for himself whether to come forward to challenge for the pass from 7 to 9 or whether to lay off goal-side. Similarly the left-back can make his own decision—to lay off and cover the left flank *or* to follow his winger once he runs inside.

It should by now be wasting time to limit the practice to small groups who have to walk or trot back to their starting positions after each rehearsal. When the coach has reason to believe that the attacking players are responding correctly to the decisions of the defenders he can again set up the two-way drill. The attacking players are now familiar with so many variations of wing combinations there is **no** telling what they may produce. Diagrams 50 (a) and 50 (b) give some idea of what can be expected.

## Variations of wing combinations

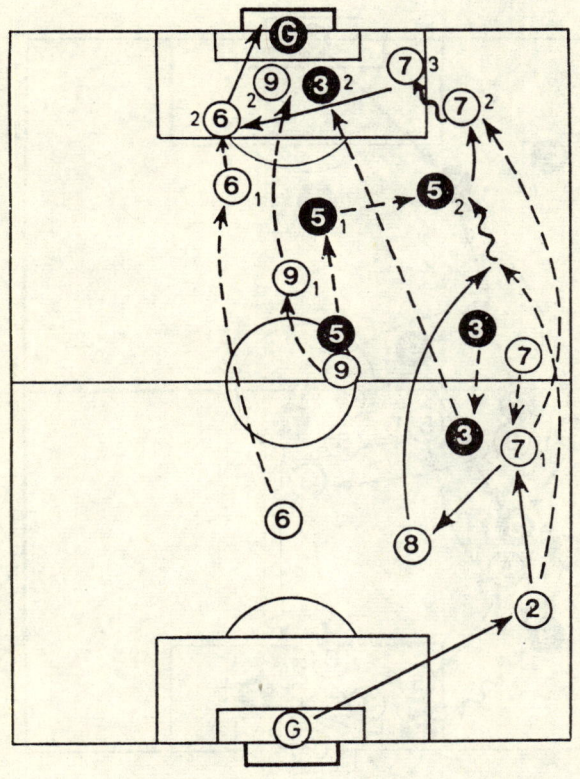

*Diagram 50 (a)*

## *Variations of wing combinations*

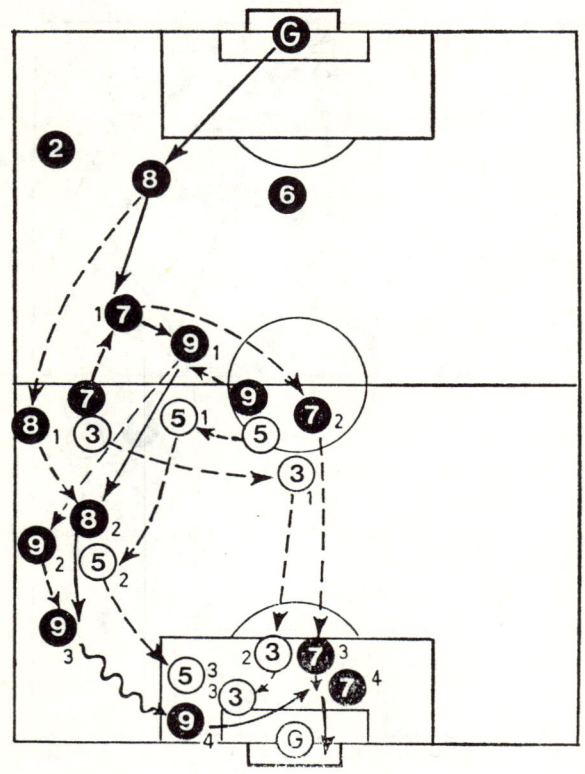

*Diagram 50 (b)*

# 8 — Central combinations

It has taken some time to explain the various way in which place-changing can be effected on the wings. Being realistic it must be anticipated that it will take the players a considerably longer period to adjust themselves to the new playing patterns, but the coach would be well advised to introduce *wing combinations* and *central combinations* in the same training period.

For each group of players working on combinations, twenty minutes will be enough, particularly in the early stages. Assuming that the coach must work with the reserve team as well as the first XI he will have around twenty-two players to cope with. Single-handed this presents a problem but it will be pointless to attempt to coach place-changing in large groups. If the coach has no assistant then the main group of players can be left in charge of the club secretary, the trainer or one of the senior players can be nominated to settle disputed points in a small-side game.

Although lectures and discussions may be of interest and perhaps helpful they should never be lengthy. There is an incredible difference between being able to understand the principles of place-changing and being able to carry them out. All the available time should be devoted to practice.

In a two-hour training session the coach should be able to work with six different groups of players if twenty minutes per training session is made the standard. It will be advisable to begin with *wing combinations* but in the same training session a start should also be made on the *central combinations*.

Perhaps the following programme will serve as a guide in planning the session.

**1st 20-minute period**
Right-wing combination—with 1st XI right-back, right-midfield, right-winger and the reserve left-back as the defender.

## Central combinations

### 2nd 20-minute period
Left-wing combination—with 1st XI right-back acting as opposition for the reserve left-back, left-midfield and left-winger.

### 3rd 20-minute period
Right-wing combination—with the reserve right-winger, right-midfield and right-back opposed by the 1st XI left-back.

### 4th 20-minute period
Left-wing combination—with the 1st XI left-winger, left-midfield and left-back and the reserve right-back providing the opposition.

### 5th 20-minute period
Central combination—for the 1st XI right centre-forward, left centre-forward, right-midfield and left-midfield. Opposition will be provided by the two centre-backs from the 1st XI.

### 6th 20-minute period
Central combination—for the reserve right centre-forward, left centre-forward, right-midfield and left-midfield. The reserve centre-backs act as defenders.

Central combinations are based on the same principles as place-changes on the wings. Centre-backs (right and left) are still playing dual roles if one assumes that their opponents are playing to a system which gives them two central strikers. Against two centre-forwards, each of the centre-backs is responsible for marking an opponent closely. He has also to cover the space at his back and when required, to give close support to the full-back and centre-back on either side of him.

To be nicely placed so that he can cope with all eventualities the centre-back wants to withdraw towards his goal whenever an attack develops. If his immediate opponent moves towards goal whenever a midfield colleague has possession then the centre-back is happy. He is allowed to fall back, cover space, and yet at the same time he can be close-marking his personal opponent. Central combinations are aimed initially at forcing the centre-backs to choose between marking their opponents *or* covering space. Then, if the defender has elected to cover space, we gain time for the centre-forward to control

## *Central combinations*

the ball and turn. If the defender chooses to mark his opponent tightly then one of the midfield players moves to exploit the space.

Starting positions for coaching *central combinations* are described in Diagram 51 with the right-midfield in possession. The next attack

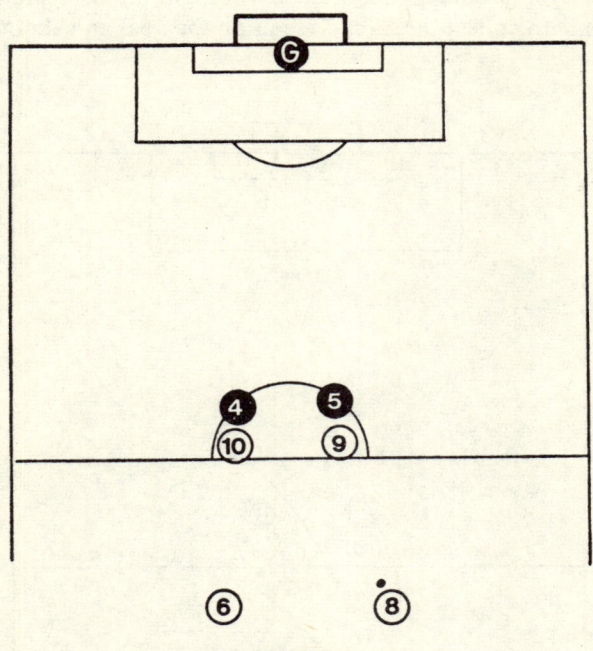

*Diagram 51*

should begin with the left-midfield in possession and each attack should be finished off with a shot at goal. Before the session begins, the coach should re-state the principle that immediately after giving his pass the player should run to change places with the man to whom he gives the ball.

When the situation arises in match play the centre-backs have a choice between challenging for a pass given to their opponent *or* laying off goal-side. For the moment the coach should insist that the defenders challenge for every pass.

Right-midfield begins by pushing the ball forward to his colleague at right centre-forward and immediately runs to effect a place-change.

## *Central combinations*

With the ball on its way to 9, the right-midfield must note the reaction of the left centre-back and call advice to the man receiving the ball. 'Man-on' calls the right-midfield and 9 sprints to meet the ball, pushing it back first-time to 6. With the right-midfield breaking through on the blind-side of the left centre-back, the left-midfield has an easy target (see Diagram 52 (a) ). The right-midfield should have ample time to collect the ball, close in on the goal and shoot.

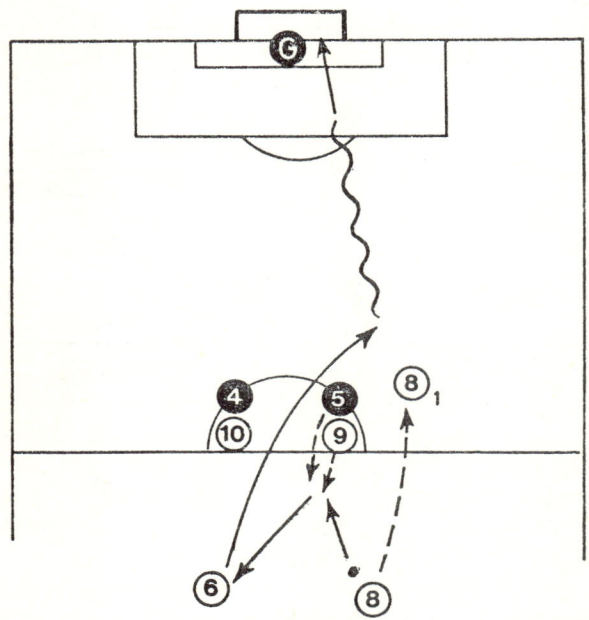

*Diagram 52 (a)*

The players should walk or trot back to their starting positions for the next attack. This time it is the left-midfield who has possession and he starts with a pass aimed at the feet of his colleague at left centre-forward. Now the left-midfield runs to change places and calls 'Man-on' to his colleague. The left centre-forward sprints to the ball, plays it first-time to 8 and from there the ball is chipped forward to 6 as in Diagram 52 (b).

## Central combinations

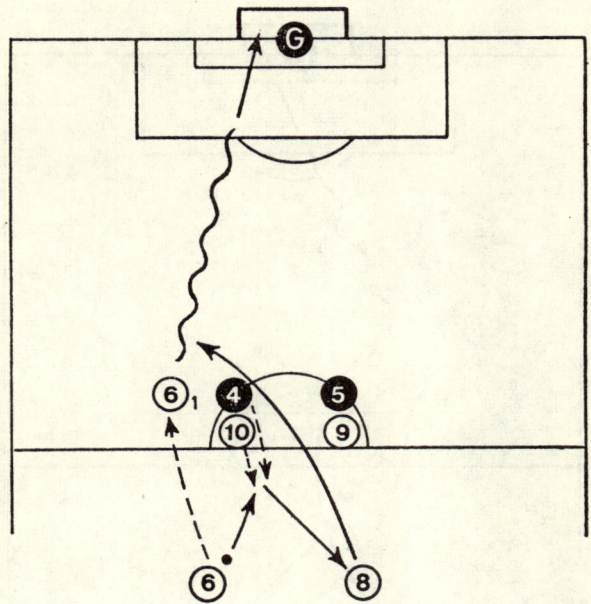

*Diagram 52 (b)*

For the moment the coach should still insist that the defenders must come forward to challenge for every pass but by now they will be very much aware of what is going on. The coach should restrain them from challenging too vigorously for the moment.

To begin the next attack the right-midfield pushes the ball diagonally forward towards the left centre-forward, calls advice ('Man-on') and runs as in Diagram 52 (c). Moving to meet the ball 10 plays it first-time back to 6 and from there the ball goes forward. Attention should be drawn to the fact that in the more crowded central areas, the pass aimed at the place-changing midfield player should always be chipped or lobbed. A ground pass may 'look' better but while a low pass may be intercepted, a high pass—over eight feet above ground—cannot even be handled.

For the last of the basic 'man-on' central combinations the left-midfield should begin the move with a pass given diagonally forward to the right centre-forward. 'Man-on' calls 6 as he makes his run to

## Central combinations

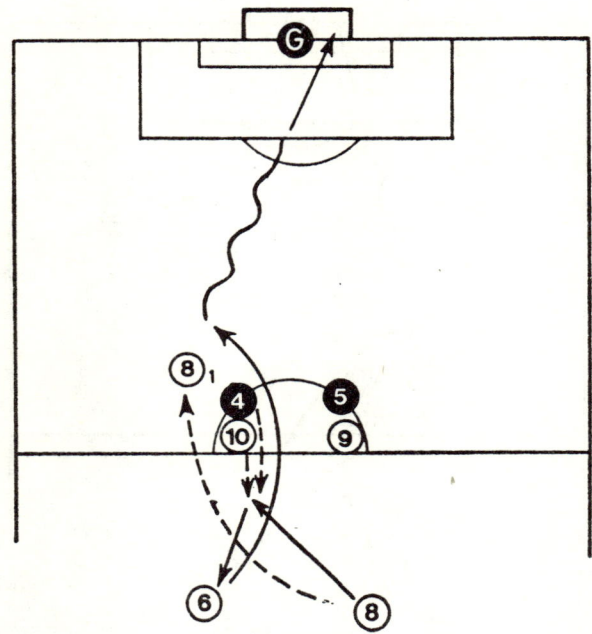

*Diagram 52 (c)*

break-through while the ball goes back, first-time from 9 to 8 and on to 6 as in Diagram 52 (d).

It will be clear that in match play the 'free' centre-back will not continue to blindly mark his man indefinitely. If we take the move outlined in Diagram 52 (a) as an example we can expect an intelligent right centre-back to leave his man in order to cover the space behind his colleague (5). He would then be in a good position to intercept the pass aimed at the right-midfield who is overlapping the right centre-forward—but he is also leaving the left centre-forward wide open.

The coach should explain this to the group and give the 'free' centre-back the option to cover when his colleague challenges for a pass from midfield. When the right centre-back exercises this option the pass from 6 should go to 10 (Diagram 52 (e) ). If it is the left

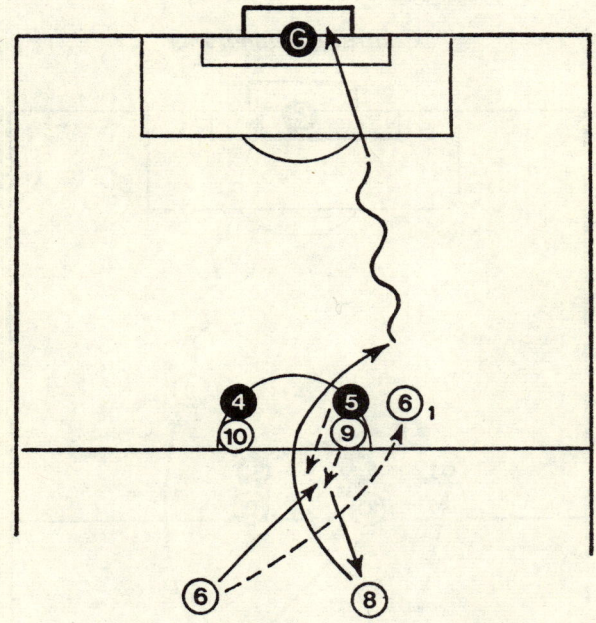

*Diagram 52 (d)*

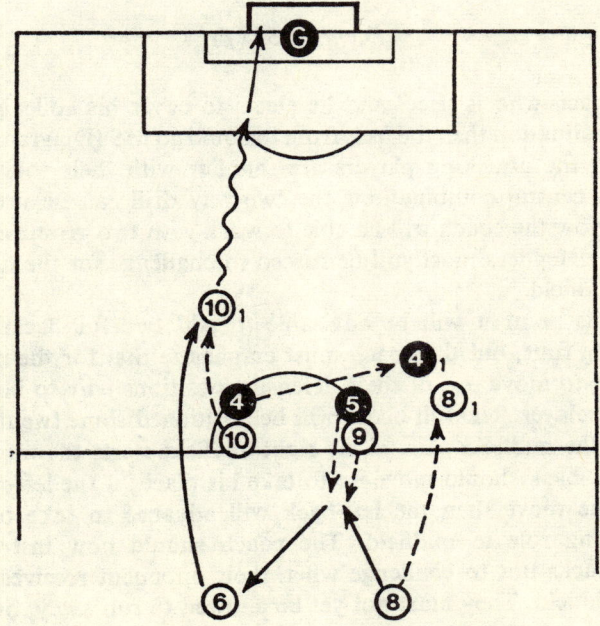

*Diagram 52 (e)*

## Central combinations

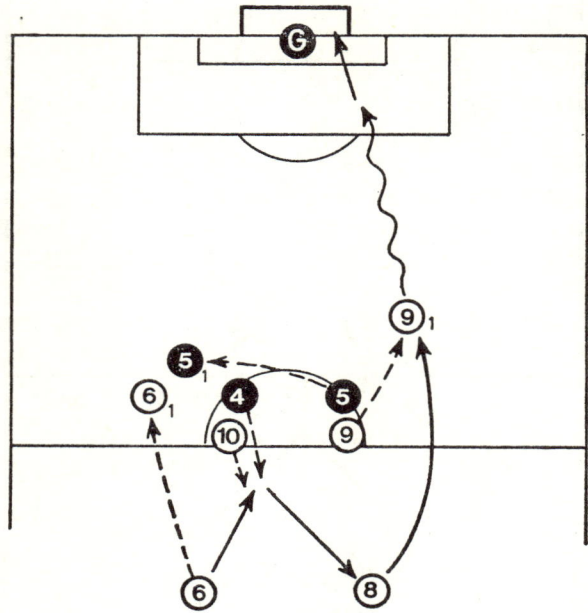

*Diagram 52 (f)*

centre-back who is 'free' and he elects to cover his colleague in a man-on situation then the pass from 8 should go to 9 (Diagram 52 (f)).

When the attacking players are familiar with their roles in the man-on central combinations the two-way drill can be used once more. Now the coach will be able to work with two groups at once, but the defenders must still be forced to challenge for the first pass from midfield.

At this point it will be advisable to add two full-backs to the attacking four, but the coach must emphasize that for the moment they are to move out of their defensive positions *only* to become a support player. The full-backs will be positioned some twenty yards behind the midfield pair. If the right-midfield starts the move then the right-back should move up to take his place; if the left-midfield starts the move then the left-back will advance to take over the supporting role in midfield. The coach should now instruct the centre-backs not to challenge when their opponent receives a pass from midfield. They must not yet be allowed to run away, but must

## Central combinations

stand their ground loosely covering their opponent and blocking his path to goal.

With the central defenders now laying-off the player giving the pass from midfield will call 'turn' and the player receiving the ball will control the ball and turn.

Right-midfield starts the next move (Diagram 53 (a) ) with a pass to the right centre-forward—and runs. Turning on the ball, the right centre-forward should play the ball on to the right-midfield and follow the ball to make another place-change. The left centre-back now moves across to cut off 8 (if he can). If the defender is successful then 8 has an easy pass to 9 (overlapping him) but if the ball was played 'through towards goal' from 9 the chances are that 8 will break-through for a shot at goal.

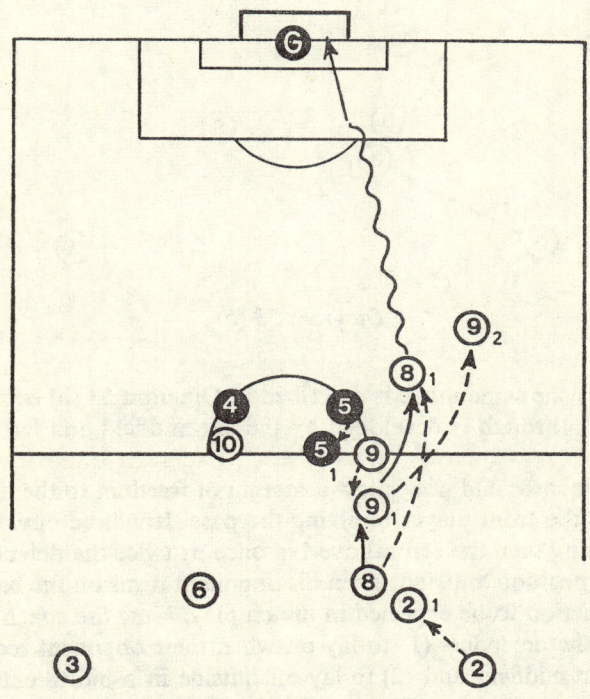

*Diagram 53 (a)*

## Central combinations

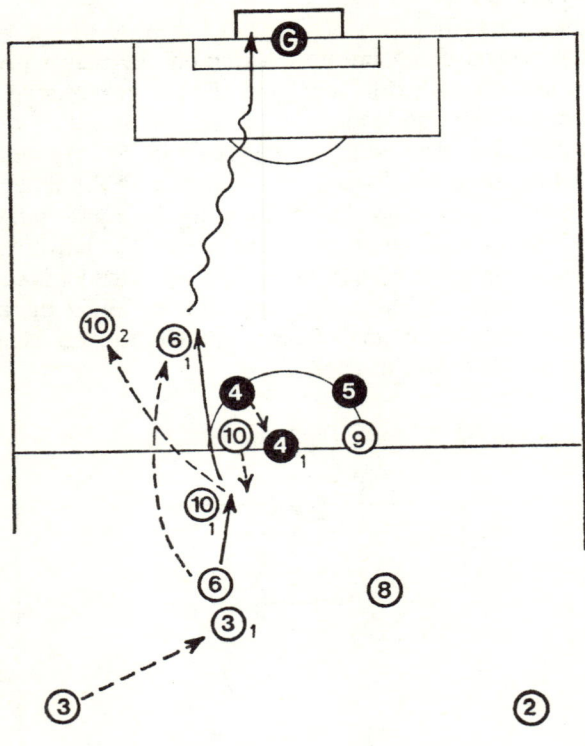

*Diagram 53 (b)*

Exactly the same move is described in Diagram 53 (b) except that the break-through is developed by the left-midfield and left centre-forward.

The coach should now allow a margin of freedom to the defender covering the front player receiving the pass. It will be obvious that after having seen the central overlap once or twice the defender will begin to position 'outside' when his opponent turns on the ball. This is the reaction to be expected in match play. Now the coach should instruct the defenders (1) to lay-off when their opponent receives a pass from midfield and (2) to lay-off outside in a bid to cut off the pass to the overlapping player. This time (Diagram 54 (a)) the right-midfield pushes the ball to the right centre-forward, runs to change

## Central combinations

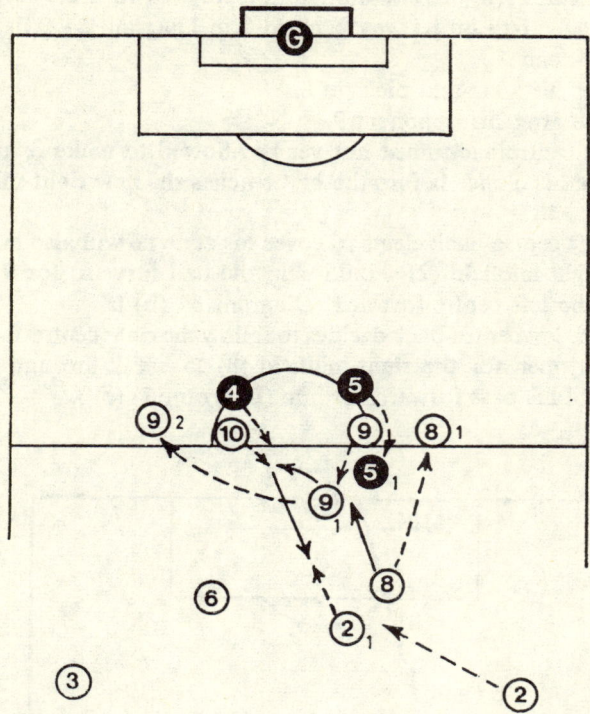

*Diagram 54 (a)*

place and calls 'Turn'. Receiving the pass, 9 turns and with his opponent cutting off the pass to his overlapping colleague, 9 moves to the left with the ball. The left centre-forward should be advised to edge away—left— when 9 receives a 'turn' ball, but when the right centre-forward moves towards him with the ball then 10 should run to meet him. 9 now pushes a pass towards the feet of 10 and runs to change places.

The coach should now insist that the right centre-back challenges the left centre-forward for the pass from his colleague 9, and told 'Man-on' the left centre-forward plays the ball back to the right-back who has moved up to right-midfield. Here the new right-midfield (2) has two possible moves but the final pass depends on the reaction of the left centre-back. The coach should allow the left centre-back to

## Central combinations

use his discretion (in this situation) and there are two courses open to him. With the ball on its way back to 2 in Diagram 54 (a) the left centre-back can:

1. Cover his zone and pick up 8.
2. Chase after his opponent 9.

The left centre-back must not yet be allowed to make feints. He must make his choice before the ball reaches the new right-midfield and stick to it.

If the left centre-back elects to cover his zone he will also cover 8, and the right-midfield (2) should chip the ball forward for 9 as he overlaps the left centre-forward (Diagram 54 (b)).

When the left centre-back decides to follow the right centre-forward the way is open for the right-midfield (8) to break-through and 2 should send his pass forward for him (Diagram 54 (c)).

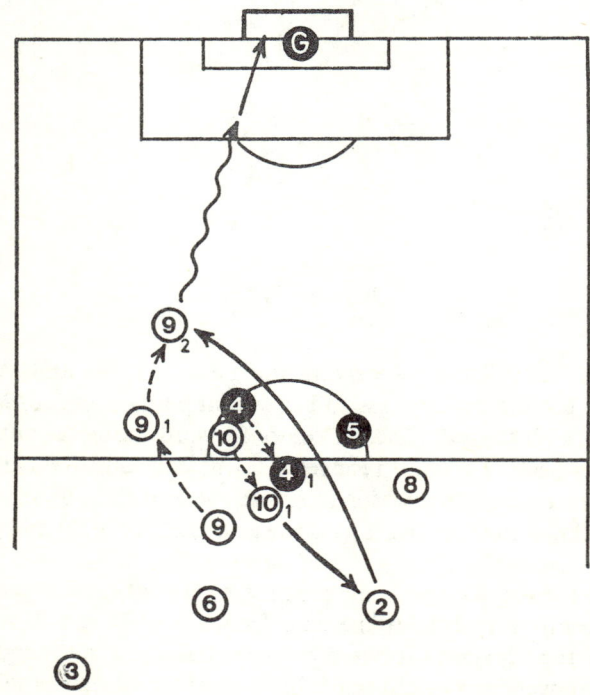

*Diagram 54 (b)*

## Central combinations

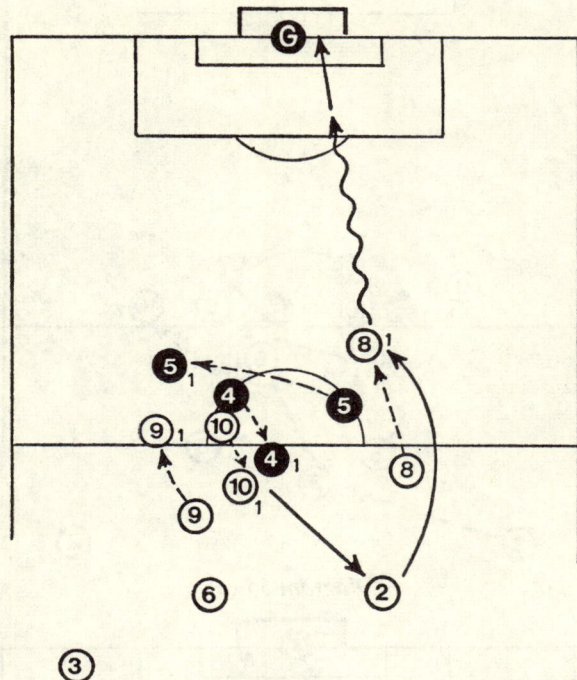

*Diagram 54 (c)*

Exactly the same move should now be set up with the first pass from 6 to 10 (Diagram 55 (a) ). The coach instructs the right centre-back to lay off 'outside' and given space inside the left centre-forward turns towards his colleague 9. Again the coach insists that the left centre-back comes to challenge the pass from 10 to 9 and told 'man-on' the right centre-forward plays the ball back first time to the left-back who has replaced the left-midfield. With the ball on its way back from 9 to 3, the right centre-back has two choices:
1. He can cover his zone and pick up the left-midfield.
2. He can follow his opponent who is overlapping 9.

The coach must insist that the right centre-back makes his decision early and alternately (a) marks his man, and (b) covers his zone. In this way the left-midfield (3) learns to make the correct decision (see Diagrams 55 (b) and 55 (c) ).

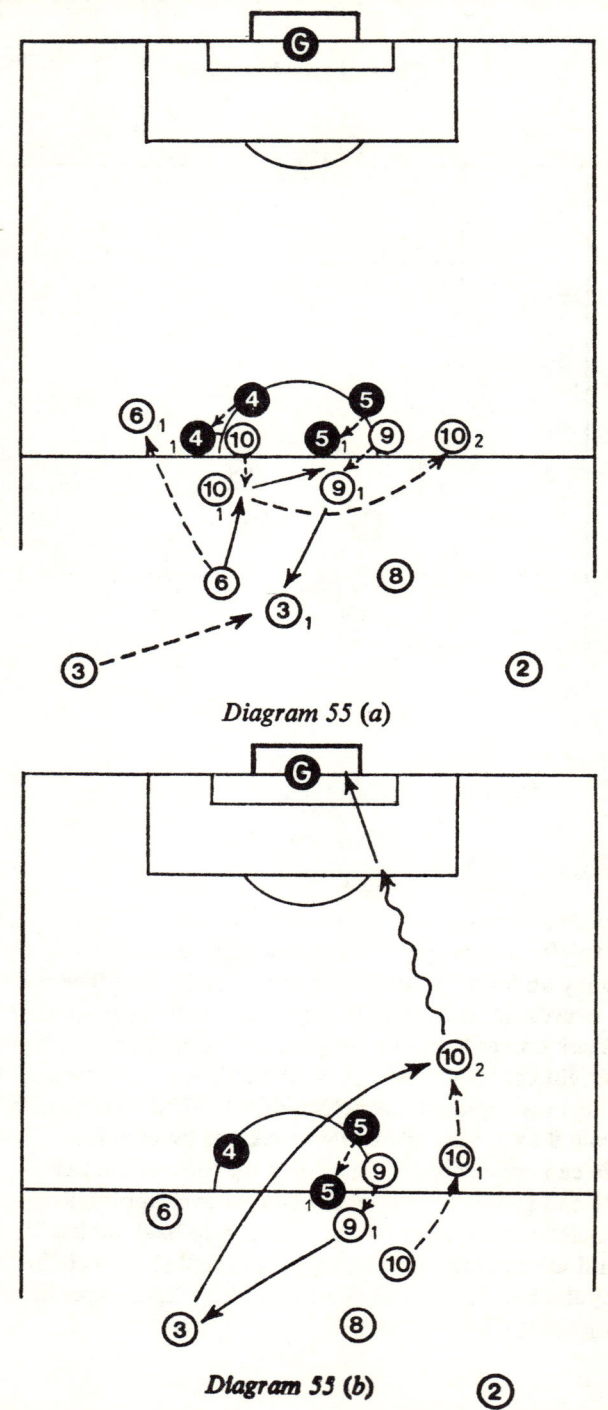

*Diagram 55 (a)*

*Diagram 55 (b)*

## Central combinations

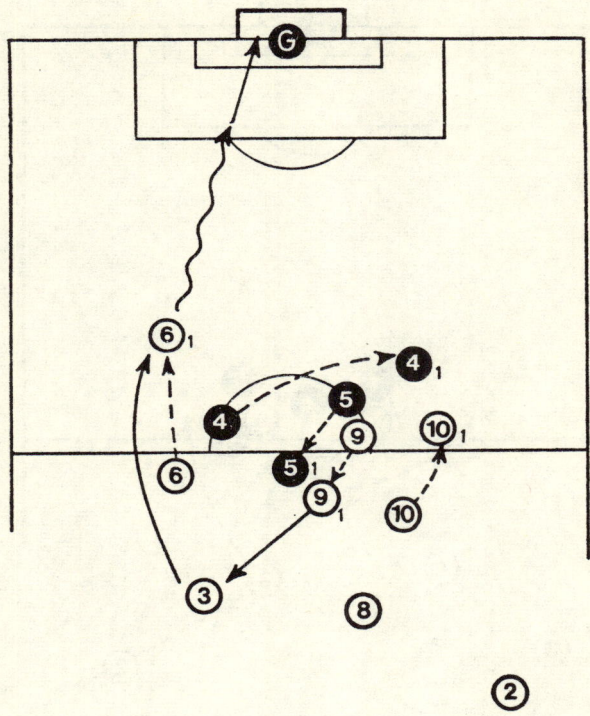

*Diagram 55 (c)*

Until now the coach has insisted that when one of the centre-forwards receives a 'turn' pass and plays the ball to the other centre-forward, the man marking the second centre-forward . . . comes 'man-on'. Now the coach should instruct the second centre-back to lay off.

In Diagram 54 (a), 9 has turned, played the ball to his colleague 10 and then run to overlap him. Now the right centre-back (4) lays off and noting this reaction by the defender, 9 calls 'Turn' to his colleague. The left centre-forward turns with the ball and the situation facing him is that described in Diagram 56 (a). At this point the coach should stop everyone exactly where they are as the left centre-forward turns. Analysing this situation for the players the coach should explain the alternatives open to the defenders.

## Central combinations

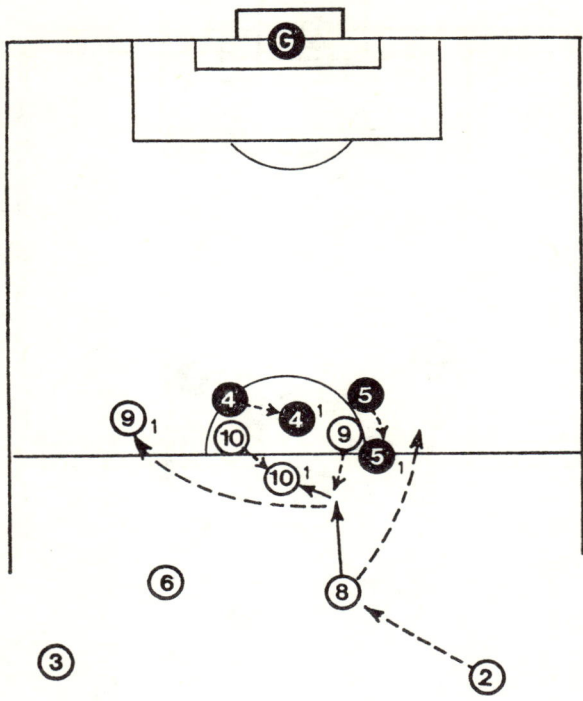

*Diagram 56 (a)*

The left centre-back can continue to cover his zone *or* sprint after his opponent who is overlapping 10. The right centre-back can lay off 'outside' to cut out the pass from 10 to 9 *or* he can lay off 'inside' to bar the direct path to goal of 10.

If the left centre-back chooses to follow his opponent (9) then 10 has an easy pass to 8 who was overlapping 9 (Diagram 56 (b) ). After passing to his colleague 8 the left centre-forward must immediately sprint after the ball (to change places with 8) and if (4) succeeds in catching the right-midfield, thus preventing him from shooting, then 8 now has 10 overlapping him. In that case 8 passes to 10 and the latter goes in to shoot.

If the left centre-back elects to cover his zone he naturally picks up the right-midfield who has become in effect the right centre-forward, but leaves 9 as he runs to overlap 10. Diagram 56 (c) describes the

## Central combinations

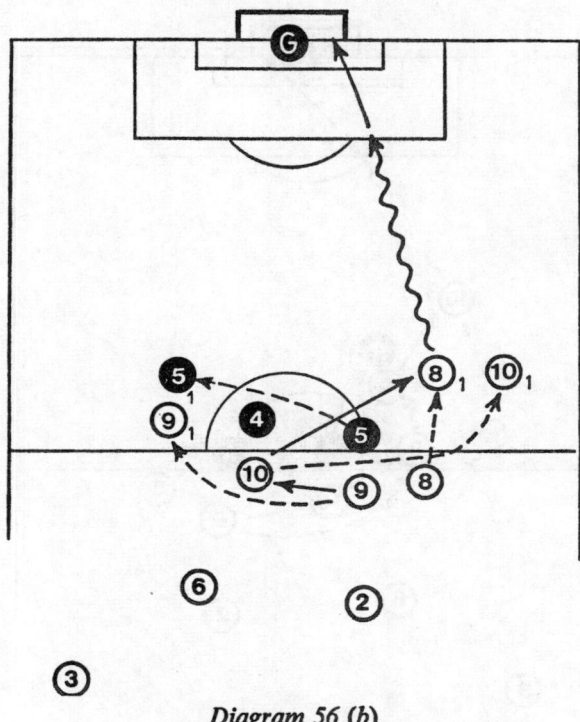

*Diagram 56 (b)*

move which follows this decision: 10 plays the ball to 9 and immediately runs to look for a second overlapping pass—a double overlap. Here again 9 should attempt to break in and shoot but if the right centre-back recovers in time and cuts him off then 9 has an easy pass to 10 (overlapping) and 10 goes in to shoot.

In match play it may be found that experienced defenders will anticipate the impossible situation which will develop as opponents come from behind. At any moment the defenders may decide to break off the action and sprint towards goal. When this happens the man in possession should head straight for goal at top speed—constantly looking right and left for the first sign that someone is coming to challenge.

If the defenders continue to fall back then the man in possession will reach a shooting position (and shoot) but in fact the defenders are unlikely to allow this to happen. Before this possibility arises, one

## Central combinations

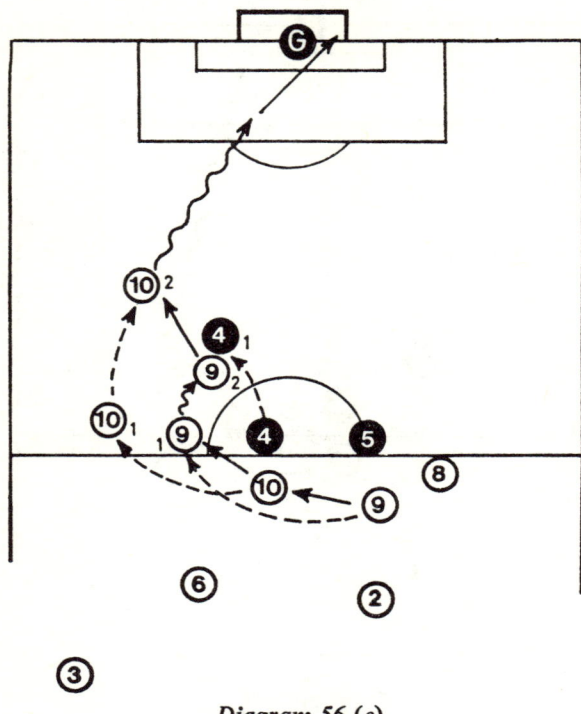

*Diagram 56 (c)*

of the defenders will be forced to challenge. Assume for the moment that the defenders elect to fall back after 9 has received a 'turn' pass from 8, turned and played the ball onto 10, (Diagram 56 (a) ). With 8 advancing on the right and 9 sprinting behind 10 to advance on the left, the right centre-back decides to retreat. Turning, he moves away towards goal and the left centre-back drops back—taking his cue from his colleague (Diagram 57 (a) ).

The left centre-forward now dribbles forward with the ball and, sooner or later, one of the defenders will come to challenge. If this challenge comes from the right centre-back (Diagram 57 (b) ) then 10 passes to 9 and runs to change places. If the challenge comes from the left centre-back (Diagram 57 (c) ) then 10 passes to 8 . . . and runs to change places. Either 9 or 8 should now be able to reach a shooting position but if anything should go wrong—a fumbled pass,

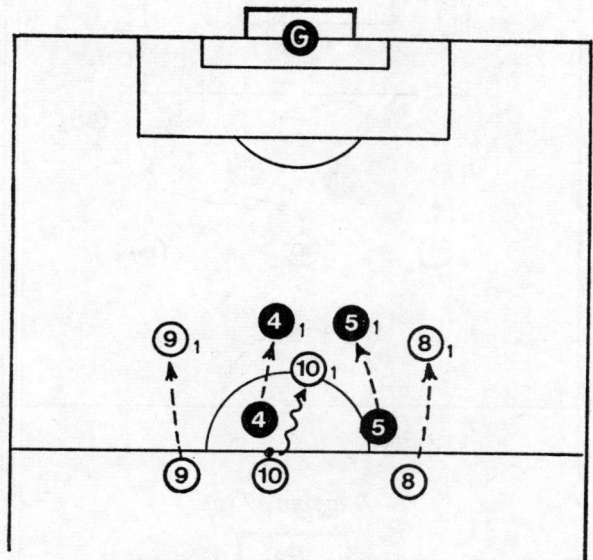

*Diagram 57 (a)*

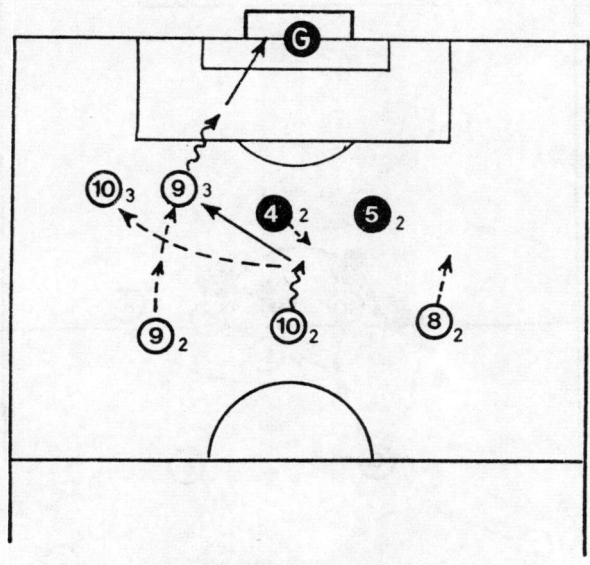

*Diagram 57 (b)*

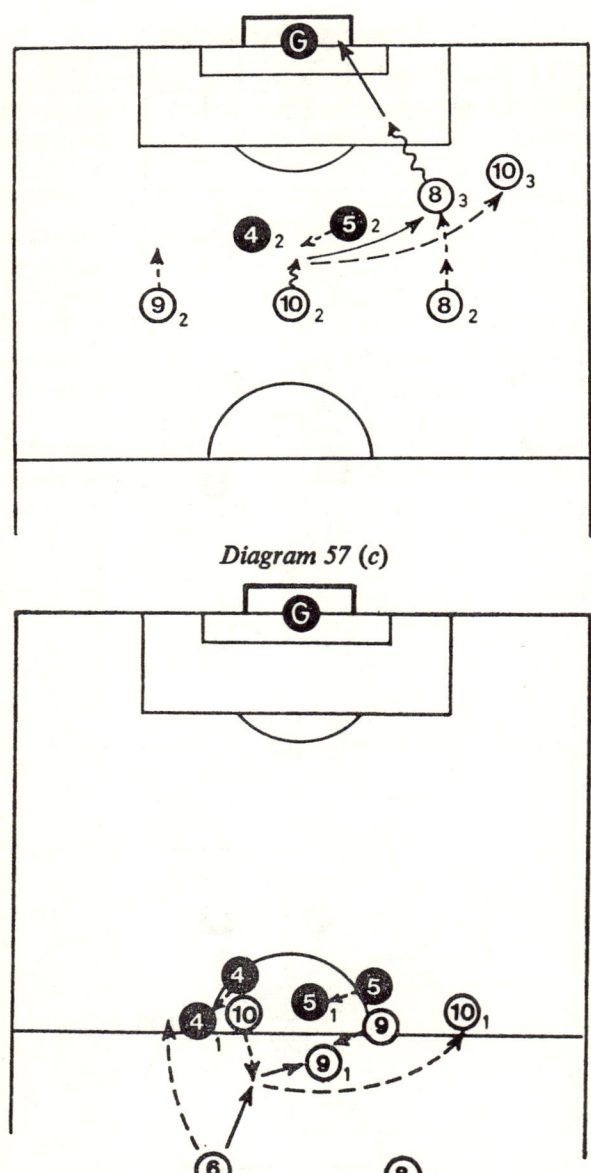

*Diagram 57 (c)*

*Diagram 58 (a)*

## Central combinations

a misplaced pass difficult to reach and control, then one of the defenders could again get into a position to block a shot at goal. If this happens then 10 should be nicely placed to receive an overlapping pass.

The game situations described in Diagrams 56 (a), 56 (b) and 56 (c) all began with a pass from 8 to 9. The same situation should now be set up based on a first pass from 6 to 10 as shown in Diagram 58 (a). The right centre-back lays off and 10 passes to 9 (and runs) and the moves develop exactly as they did when it was the right-midfield who initiated the attack (Diagrams 58 (b) and 58 (c) ). Diagrams 59 (a), 59 (b) and 59 (c) show how the coach should give the right centre-forward the opportunity to cope with a decision to withdraw taken by the centre-backs. In the moves described in Diagrams 57 (a), 57 (b) and 57 (c) it was the left centre-forward who had possession and

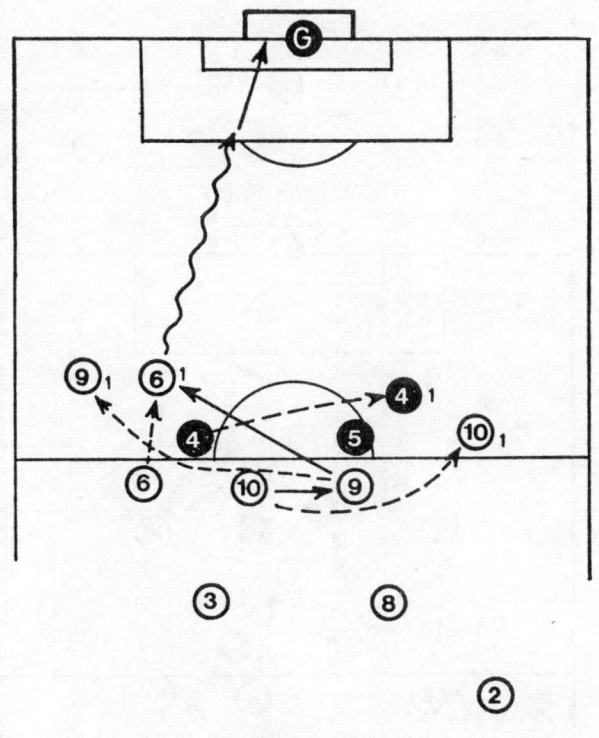

*Diagram 58 (b)*

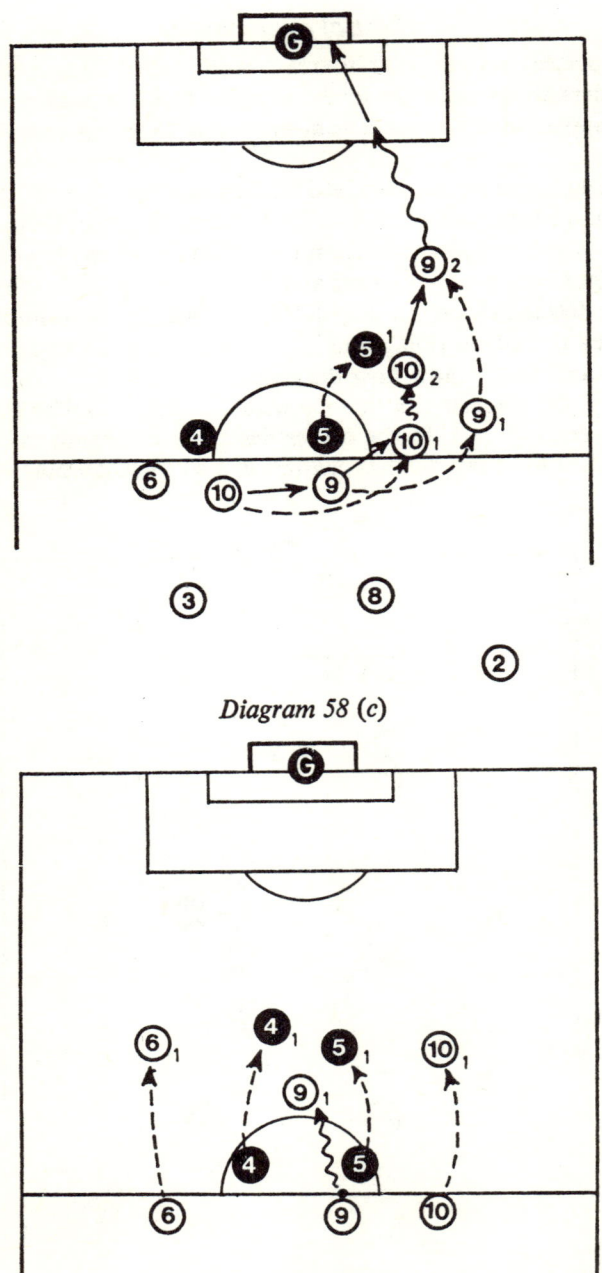

*Diagram 58 (c)*

*Diagram 59 (a)*

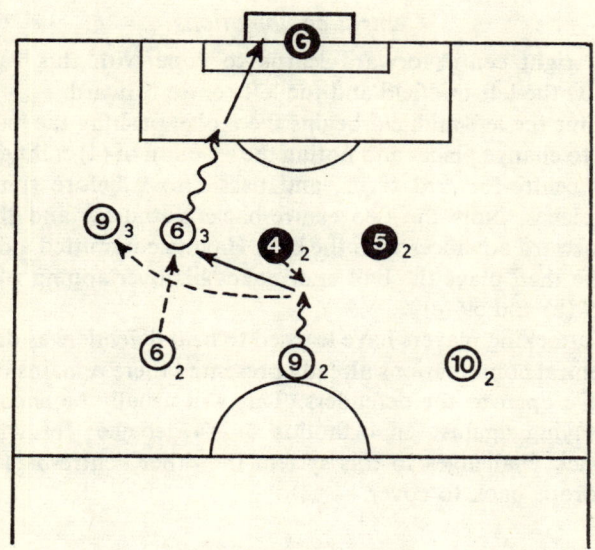

*Diagram 59 (b)*

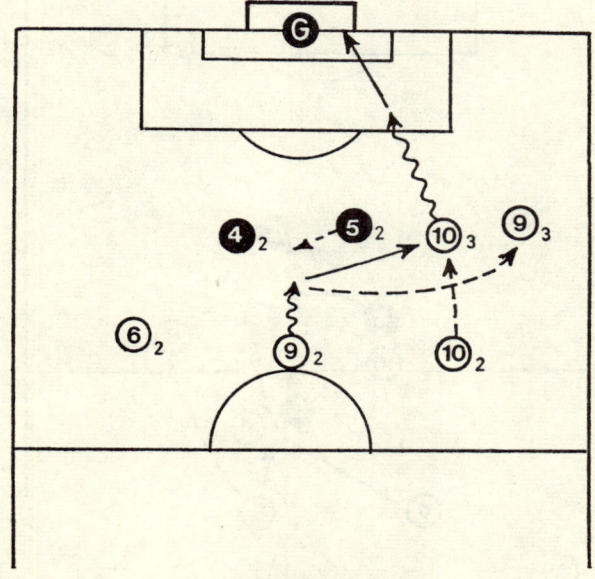

*Diagram 59 (c)*

## *Central combinations*

now the right centre-forward learns to cope with this variation, flanked by the left-midfield and the left centre-forward.

This time the left-midfield begins the move, pushing the ball to 10, running to change places and noting the reaction of (4) calling 'Turn'. The left centre-forward turns, and passes to 9 before running to change places. Now the two centre-backs withdraw and the right centre-forward advances with the ball. Having committed a defender to him he then plays the ball and makes his overlapping run (Diagrams 59 (b) and 59 (c) ).

If the attacking players have learned to beat defenders as described in the central combinations already presented there remains only one alternative open to the defenders. This will usually be encountered when playing against an orthodox 4–2–4 defence; for when one centre-back challenges in this system the other centre-back immediately drops back to cover.

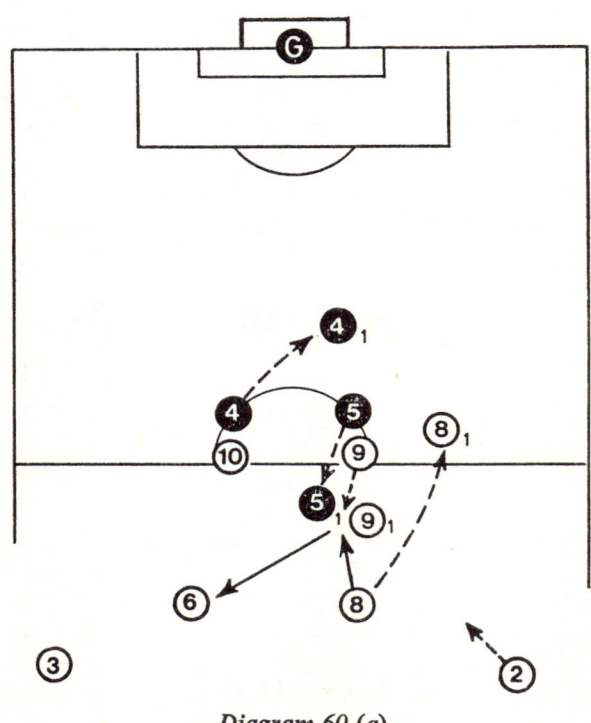

*Diagram 60 (a)*

## Central combinations

To counter this the coach should return once more to the basic starting positions for central combinations (Diagram 51). With the right-midfield making his pass to 9, the left centre-back comes to challenge. 'Man-on' calls the right-midfield as he runs to change places and meanwhile the right centre-back has left his opponent to cover space (Diagram 60 (a)).

With 8 running to right centre-forward, the attacking right-back advances to right-midfield (Diagram 60 (b)) as 9 plays the ball back,

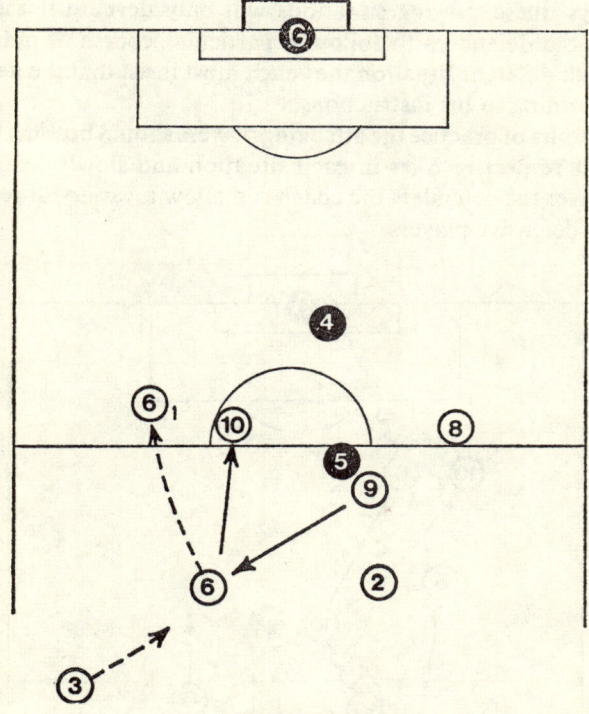

*Diagram 60 (b)*

first-time, to left-midfield. The defending right centre-back will still be moving away from his opponent 10, and 6 should now play the ball up to the left centre-forward, calling 'Turn' as he runs to change places. The left-back now comes out to play the role of left-midfield. It should be noted that both full-backs will follow up this attack, looking for the ball 'pulled' back for them to shoot.

## *Central combinations*

With the left centre-forward in possession and the right centre-back in a covering position (Diagram 60 (c) ) 10 should now dribble the ball forward at top speed. He should aim his run directly towards the right centre-back in a bid to commit him to challenge. Having committed the right centre-back to him, 10 should play the ball forward for the left-midfield and then follow the ball to overlap 6 in case a defender prevents him from reaching a shooting position.

Finally, the coach should set this move up again, starting with a pass from 6 to 10 as described in Diagrams 61 (a), 61 (b) and 61 (c). As always, these varying situations will only develop if the coach instructs the defenders to follow a particular course of action. To create each different situation the coach must insist that the defenders react according to his instructions.

After hours of practice the attacking players should become familiar with their respective roles in each situation and slowly relaxing his control over the defenders the coach can allow a variety of responses from the defensive players.

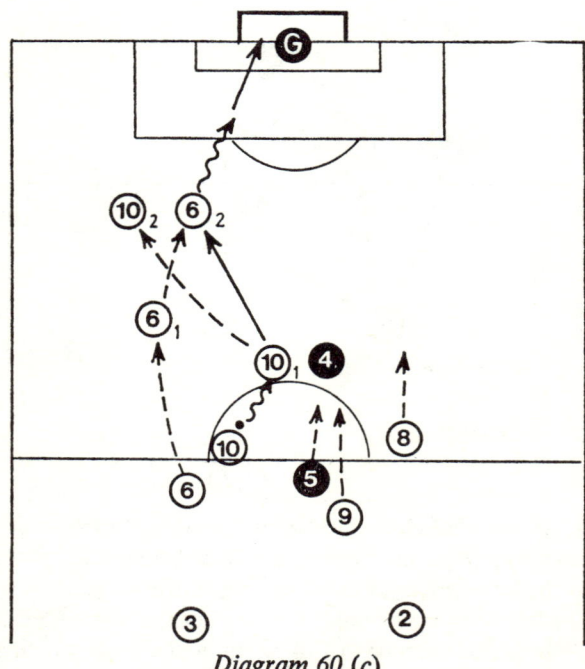

*Diagram 60 (c)*

## *Central combinations*

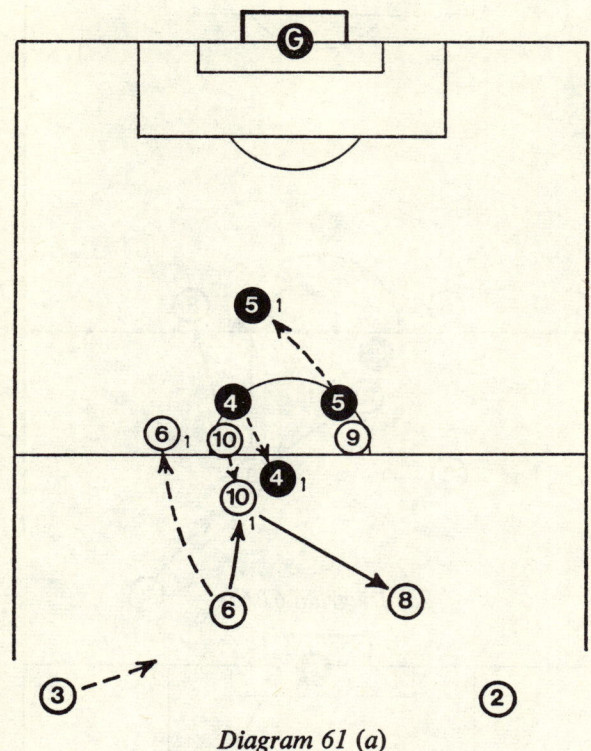

*Diagram 61 (a)*

Watching closely, the coach will know at once if the attacking players are not sufficiently familiar with their roles in a particular situation. With this realization the coach should stop the practice and create the required conditions by instructing the defenders to respond as he describes.

It should be continually stressed that every attack should be pressed to a shooting position and end with a shot at goal. It should also be emphasized that every time a player breaks through, the midfield players must follow up in support—some twenty yards behind the ball—and when the final assault develops on one of the flanks the ball can be pulled back for one of the midfield players to sprint forward and shoot. In this context the term 'midfield players' includes the full-back who replaces a midfield player.

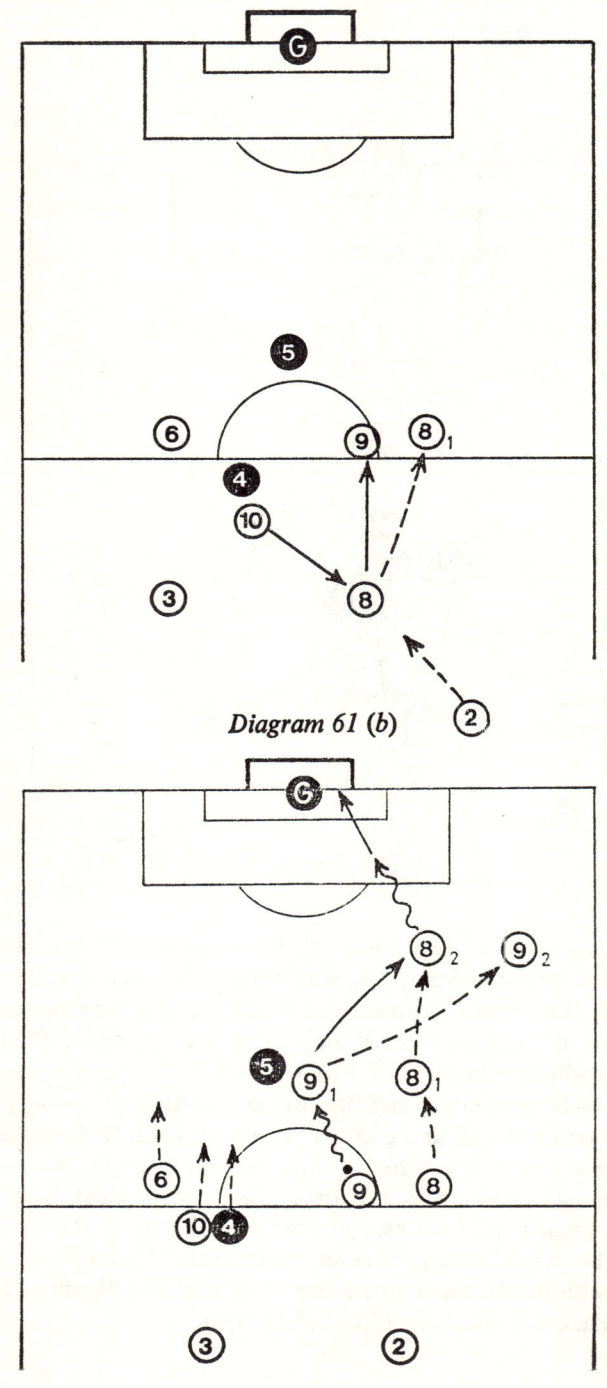

*Diagram 61 (b)*

# 9 — An analysis of the four major phases of the contemporary game and place-changing within this context. The demands made by modern football on the abilities of the players and the aims of coaching

Examination of the game as it is played today at professional level, reveals that while the play appears to flow quite evenly there are sudden changes of emphasis. These changes occur when possession of the ball switches from one team to the other. In certain circumstances—playing away from home in the European Cup for example—the objectives may be different, but in general terms both sides in a game will be prepared to attack when they have the ball. Having lost possession of the ball when their attack breaks down every team will attempt to reform its defence in the greatest possible strength.

Studying the reactions of both teams it will be seen that there are four quite distinct phases of the game and as the game flows from one phase to the next, different demands are made on each of the players.

**Phase I** (Defence)

With the opposition in possession of the ball, the objectives must be:
1. To challenge for the ball in the hope of regaining possession and to delay the development of the attack.
2. To closely mark the front players in the attacking team and cover the area in front of goal.

**Phase II** (Transition)

When the attack breaks down and possession of the ball is regained the defending team seeks to develop a quick counter-attack. The objectives are:

## *The four major phases of the contemporary game*
1. To transfer the ball quickly to a midfield player.
2. To re-position those players detailed to help in both defence and attack.


**Phase III** (Attack)

With the ball in midfield the attacking team seeks to effect a breakthrough before the opposition can reorganize its defences (see Phase I, page 167).


**Phase IV** (Development of the attack to a shooting position)

Having effected an initial break-through the aim must be:
1. To created a shooting space within the enemy defence.
2. To put an unmarked player into the shooting space and transfer the ball to him.

When the attack breaks down it makes no difference whether the move had reached Phase II, III or IV. The objective of the team which is now the defending side must be those outlined in Phase I.

Observation of the game at all levels reveals that a great deal of time is wasted between Phase I and Phase IV. It is clear that any delay in developing and pressing the attack to a shooting position must favour the defending side. Time is always the ally of defence.

Saving time must therefore be a major aim in attack yet in Phases I and II players can be observed running with the ball: teams can be seen exchanging square passes in midfield.

When an attack breaks down, the front players now have no immediate tasks to perform, and they are asked to obstruct and delay the defenders. If a defender (in possession) can be harassed he may:
1. Turn and pass back to his goalkeeper.
2. Attempt to run with the ball towards the touchline (away from his challenger).
3. Give a square pass to a colleague who is free.

All these possibilities will favour the team which has just lost possession. They need time to get their players back into defensive positions and the front player earns it for his colleagues by challenging for the ball.

Time is vital in counter-attacking. So vital that front players are asked to try and gain a few seconds by challenging, yet of their own volition many teams give their opponents time by exchanging square passes or by running with the ball in midfield. Time is also wasted by

## The four major phases of the contemporary game

wall-passes and by attempts to dribble past opponents (which are both dangerous and unnecessary).

If the team which is now switching from attack to defence thinks it worthwhile planning to win time, then surely it is in the interests of the attacking team to eliminate time-wasting from their build-up? It can be presumed that players who waste time in defence and in midfield do so for one of two reasons:

1. They are selfishly exhibiting their skill.
2. They do not know what else to do.

This is the first of many basic factors on which the arguments for *place-changing combinations* hinge. As a method of coaching it aims to eliminate time-wasting with its insistence on playing the ball forward—quickly.

Observation of *both* teams in the seconds following the breakdown of an attack, will be both interesting and informative. When the move breaks down the players who were attacking (and are now defending) will be sprinting back to take up their defensive positions. Draw an imaginary line across the pitch parallel to the goal-line, which passes through the centre of the ball at the moment when possession switches from one team to the other. Count at once the players of the defending team who are 'goal-side' of the imaginary line. Only players who are goal-side can play an effective part in preventing a goal being scored from a counter-attack, but see what happens when a defender wins possession and then the ball is passed back to the goalkeeper (Diagram 62). The attacking right-back had possession, overlapping on the right wing and finished his move with a high centre. The right centre-back (4) won his heading duel with 10 and nodded the ball down to the right-midfield (8). When the ball reached the right-midfield, the 'imaginary line' referred to earlier would place five attacking players *out of the game* in the defensive sense. These five are 2, 7, 9, 10, 11. If the right-midfield plays the ball back to his goalkeeper he immediately puts all five *back into the game*.

In a team coached in place-changing combinations the right-midfield would have been told to 'Turn', and now whatever move is made the five caught out of position are going to have a very difficult time getting back in the game. If the right-midfield *turns* and then without attempting to beat an opponent, without taking even one step with the ball, he immediately plays the ball forward, then his attacking colleagues outnumber the defenders by four to three. If

## *The four major phases of the contemporary game*

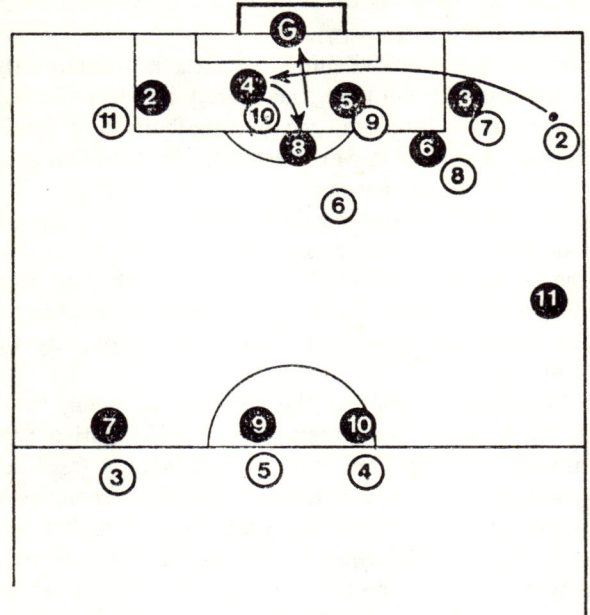

*Diagram 62*

the right-midfield plays the ball to 7, 9 or 10 and the recipient comes to meet the ball, if 8 is sprinting to change places, if 6, 2 and 3 are coming out to support the front man, then a combination is 'on'.

Alternatively the right-midfield could have passed to his temporarily unmarked colleague on the left wing. Unmarked the winger would be told to 'Turn' and having turned, the players left *behind the play* are increased by two—the attacking midfield players 6 and 8. Of course it must be understood that each of the players mentioned will be running at top speed in a bid to get back 'goal-side' but the team coached in *combinations* will certainly make it difficult for the opponents to recover in time.

In Phase II—the transition stage between defence and attack—the arguments for coaching in combinations are no less convincing. By tradition it has always been the skilful inside-forwards (now midfield players) who schemed the openings. Working behind the strikers, the midfield players sought to unbalance the defence with feints to pass

## The four major phases of the contemporary game

one way, checking and bringing the ball the other way. Dribbling past an opponent (or two) the old-time schemer hoped to free a 'front' colleague by pulling a defender out to challenge. Feinting and dribbling involves checking and changing direction—which take up valuable time—and inviting a tackle necessitates running with the ball. Opponents who were caught out of position are unhampered by the ball, do not need to waste time changing direction and will positively cover more ground than the schemer in any given period.

Observation will show that if a team does not develop its counter-attack within ten seconds of winning possession then they need not bother. If the attack is not pressed to a shooting position within twenty-five seconds—thirty seconds at the very outside—then a goal can only result if the defenders have made grave errors. In ten seconds it should be possible to have all ten players of the defending team back in defensive positions—no matter where they were when the move broke down.

With time so short, the midfield players must be discouraged from dribbling, standing with the ball, inter-passing with other midfield players. They must play the ball forward—quickly.

In organizing a counter-attack from midfield the players must already be aware that time is of vital importance. No doubt there are many players eager to transfer the ball quickly to a front player and they can be seen, looking, thinking and then deciding that the pass isn't 'on' because their front colleague is tightly-marked. Looking around from midfield in Diagram 63 the right-midfield now in possession must realize that time is against him.

Having gained possession following a misplaced pass or by interception or perhaps from a quick pass after a defender had won the ball in a tackle, the right-midfield must now make a decision. Behind his back the attacking left-winger (and maybe also the left centre-forward) is trying to cut him off from goal and offer a challenge. He must part with the ball quickly to avoid the risk of being caught in possession. The obvious 'easy' pass open to the right-midfield is the square ball to his colleague at left-midfield. Anticipating this, however, the right centre-forward is sprinting to intercept this pass—if it comes—but above all the square pass is a time-waster. If the pass is accurately given and successfully received the team in possession has achieved nothing. In the time thus wasted, both the opposing midfield players caught upfield have been running hard. Each is now a few yards closer to his defensive position.

*The four major phases of the contemporary game*

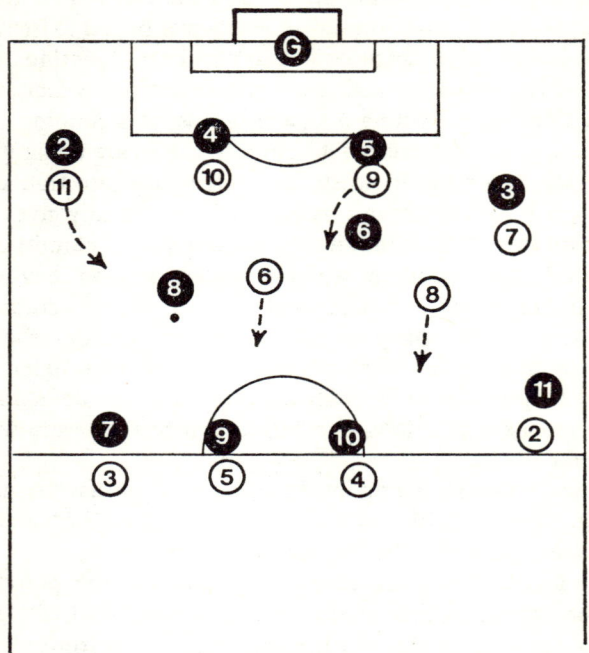

*Diagram 63*

In situations like this a great many midfield players will be anxious to play the ball forward quickly. But to transfer the ball to a tightly-marked colleague up front will only put the front man in serious trouble, unless the 'front' player is given immediate support. Without advice, without support, the 'front' player knows from experience that he is likely to receive an unpleasant kick on the heel, the ankle or the calf muscle. Perhaps something even more serious. Even more important, the 'front' man knows from experience that the knocks he receives in these situations will be for nothing. Finally, the 'front' player will discuss the general situation with his colleagues and insist 'never give me a short pass to feet when I have an opponent tight on my back'.

Coaching in combinations changes this situation in several important ways:

1. The players now realize that they must support the front player by running to good positions.

## The four major phases of the contemporary game

2. The front man, dropping back into space to meet the ball, is being given advice. If his opponent is coming 'man-on' then one touch will be enough to play the ball back. No longer does the front man have to screen the ball (with his legs) while trying to turn.
3. When defenders realize that they are being drawn forward quite deliberately and that another opponent, running off the ball, is racing 'in' on their blind side, then they will not willingly be drawn forward again. When this point is reached the 'front' men will be told to 'turn' and they will now do so without injury.
4. The midfield players learn through training in *combinations* that it is possible to go forward quickly and that a pass can be given to a tightly-marked colleague. No longer will they waste valuable time in midfield.

Perhaps this is a suitable point at which to discuss the often-used phrase 'good running off the ball'. It has been used so often that the expression is commonplace, but in no coaching book has it yet been defined.

Telling players to support the man with the ball by good running must leave them bewildered. Unless 'good running' can be more precisely defined then it has little value. The advantage gained in this respect from training in *combinations* is that in each situation 'good running' is defined precisely for each player. In Phase IV the advantages which accrue from coaching via combinations are no less important.

It has been continually stressed that in the final approach to goal all the players must move. From a flank approach, for example, the central strikers have been drilled to 'scissor', each of the centre-forwards heading for what is to him, the far post. If they are not followed on their scissor, then the central strikers get free, and if they are followed then the defenders marking the centre-forwards leave space behind them. Into that created space the midfield players are moving (together with one or more attacking full-backs), all looking for the reverse pass and the opportunity to shoot.

Whenever we have movement in attack, the defenders must concede space. They give this space to the moving man or they leave it behind when they follow their opponent. Either way there are definite advantages which accrue to the attacking team.

In coaching *combinations* the players are not merely asked to 'run

*The four major phases of the contemporary game*

off the ball'—which is so vague that it conveys nothing. They are drilled to move in well-defined directions and after a short time these movements off the ball become a part of the player's natural game.

*Above all, it must be clearly understood that the aim of coaching through combinations is not, and will never be, to obtain a stereotyped response.*

The objectives of coaching in combinations can be stated:

1. The individual players are linked together, moulded into one unit in which each player looks, thinks and moves as an individual within the unit.
2. The player with the ball at any given moment begins to look for a colleague running round his back. He begins quite naturally to look right and left for colleagues coming from behind.
3. Front players begin to move 'off the ball' armed with the knowledge that if they are followed by tight-marking opponents, then a colleague will exploit the space created.
4. Full-backs and midfield players will automatically be looking for exploitable space ahead of them. When it appears, they will move forward confidently and naturally.
5. Time-wasting square passes, back passes to the goalkeeper and running (or standing) with the ball will all be gradually eliminated.
6. The players will develop an understanding of the game in simple terms which will be shared by all. This will later give way to an awareness of their responsibilities to each other and from this awareness will come confidence in themselves and in their team-mates.

It has already been stated from time to time that the coach must give clear instructions to defenders when a new variation is introduced. This must be done to allow the attacking players to familiarize themselves with each possible reaction from the defender. Step by step, the coach releases the defenders from their prescribed response until the point is reached where the attacking players are completely familiar with all the combinations and variations.

The coach can now put on two-way drills involving twenty-six players (Diagram 64) and allow the attacking eight in each group complete freedom of action. This can also be granted to the defenders.

It must be stressed that the two groups—'square' players and 'circled' players—work independently of each other. No attempt to interfere must be made by a circled player when the square wave has

## The four major phases of the contemporary game

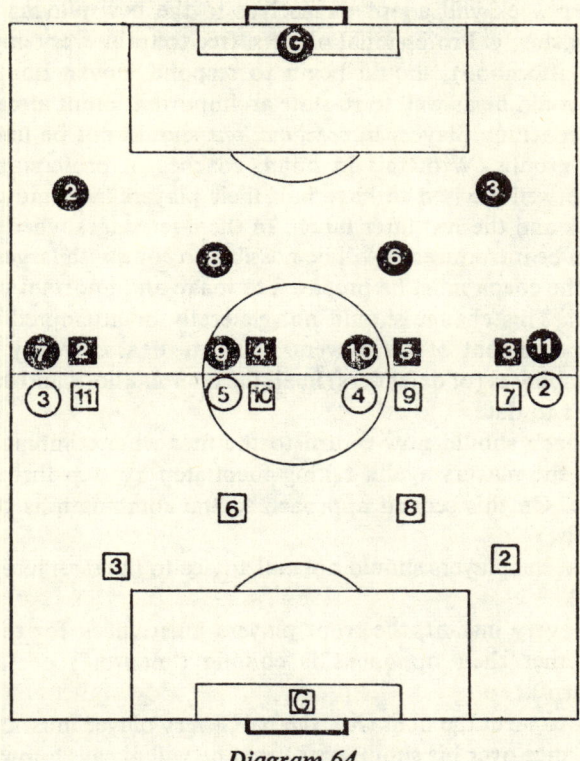

*Diagram 64*

possession. When the attack produces a shot at goal the move is ended and the defending goalkeeper re-starts the second wave, attacking the far goal. Here the goalkeeper can throw the ball out to a full-back or midfield player at his discretion. The circled players begin the session with a throw-out from their goalkeeper and for this first attack square players should be instructed to stand absolutely still. For subsequent waves of attack, the first group will trot back to starting positions while the second attack is developed, and so on.

Exactly how long it will take to reach this point will depend upon many factors. Among these factors will be:
1. The skill, understanding and enthusiasm of the coach.
2. The intelligence, ability and enthusiasm of the players.
3. The amount of time devoted to training each week.

It will be obvious that amateur players who train for only two

## *The four major phases of the contemporary game*

hours per week will adapt themselves to the new playing patterns relatively slowly. Professional players, free to train every day (morning and afternoon), should begin to respond almost immediately. Here it would be as well to re-state an important point already mentioned: coaching players in *combinations* should not be undertaken in large groups. With this in mind, coaches of professional clubs would be well advised to have half their players for training in the mornings and the rest after lunch. In the later stages when two-way drills can be introduced it will be possible to cope with larger groups.

Now the coach must be prepared to make an important change in emphasis. This change should not generally be attempted until the coach is confident of his players, ability to deal correctly with the varied responses (of defenders) in all the combinations and variations presented to date.

The coach should now return to the first wing combination and rehearse the players again, taking them step by step through each variation. On this second approach to the combinations the coach must insist:
1. That the players should not call advice to the man receiving the ball.
2. At every instant, the front players must check for themselves whether their opponent is coming ('man-on') or laying off ('turn').

Going to meet the man with the ball, every player must train himself to glance over his shoulders so that he will always know whether he is marked or not. In the last fraction of a second before playing the ball, the top-class player will now be able to adjust his move to the final response of his opponent. Having made this point it will be as well to explain why this course was not advocated from the outset.

In this volume a new method of coaching is being presented. Though many of the world's top coaches have worked on very similar lines no one has yet presented his ideas to the game at large. With this in mind it will be clear that this approach to coaching will be 'new' to 99 per cent of the millions with an interest in soccer. These millions will include coaches who work with boys of 9 or 10 years; men who train first-class amateurs and coaches of professional clubs. This book is aimed at everyone who has not yet been introduced to combinations and has not yet developed his own method of coaching the new game.

Players of professional standard in Britain and most of Western

## The four major phases of the contemporary game

Europe and National League players in Eastern Europe *should* be able to 'read' for themselves the situation which exists behind their backs. If they can, then at his discretion the coach can introduce the players to *combinations* without advice from the colleague who makes the pass.

For top-class amateurs, for regional league players, youths and schoolboys the coach would be well advised to include 'calling advice' as a basic part of the method. If the coach of a professional club finds that his players cannot read the situation for themselves then he must revert to the approach recommended in the earlier passages of this book and include advice. Similarly, the coach of a top-class amateur team may feel that his players are intelligent enough and sufficiently adaptable to justify a bid to introduce combination play without calling advice. If this should prove over-optimistic then he too should revert to the general pattern presented earlier.

At the highest level of the game it is absolutely essential that players be able to read the situation 'on their back'. A man who cannot do so, will for example, be told to 'turn' when his opponent lays off to cover space, but an astute defender will soon learn to turn this advice to his own advantage. Pretending to lay off, he will sprint forward to challenge immediately after the advice to 'turn' has been given. Conversely, the intelligent defender will feint to challenge for the ball and having heard the call 'man-on' the defender would immediately turn and sprint back to cover space. The player receiving the pass would play the ball back first time to a supporting colleague. In this case there would be no profit to the attacking team in terms of created space. There would only be a loss of time—wasted by playing the ball back when the recipient could (and should) have turned.

If the calling of advice is included in the general approach the change of emphasis should be introduced once the players are familiar with all the *combinations* and variations presented thus far. In general terms it can be anticipated that the method of coaching presented in this book will be completely new to the majority of players, and everyone—amateurs, professionals, youths and schoolboys—can be expected to improve at a rate which is proportionate to the length of time devoted to training each week.

For schoolboys under 12 years it will be advisable to begin coaching by way of the drills and exercises found in the next chapter. For boys over 12 years and for all other players new to place-changing

## *The four major phases of the contemporary game*

these exercises are intended to complement the periods devoted to coaching in combinations. It will be of interest to note that in the opinion of the author, boys who are introduced to *place-changing combinations* at 16 years and train for two, two-hour periods per week should be ready to accept the change of emphasis at the age of 18.

Coaching boys under 12 years should still be dominated by technical practice but there is no reason why the practices in the various techniques should not take the form of place-changing drills described in the next chapter.

At 12 years, boys can successfully be introduced to the *place-changing combinations* though time may still be spent on improving individual weaknesses in technique.

After the 16th birthday it should not be expected that the coach gives individual attention to players' technical weaknesses. The coach should now devote all his available time and energy to team play, concentrating on collectivity rather than individuality. The emphasis for the coach working with players of 16 years must now be on how to use their skills and not as previously on the acquisition of basic skill.

After this age, if technical weaknesses still exist in the play of an otherwise promising player, the coach may show the player 'how' to practice the required skill or skills and then leave the player to practice in his own time. Alternatively, the coach may decide to give private coaching in skills to one or more players—as a supplement and at another time.

The latter course will certainly be advisable if observation of match play indicates that while the players are moving well *off the ball*, attacks continually break down due to failures in technique.

# 10 — Drills and exercises aimed at developing the techniques required in place-changing and combination play

When senior players are first introduced to combinations the coach will observe that many of the players experience great difficulty. This will be particularly true for 'front' players but less obvious for full-backs.

Very largely this will be due to the fact that until now the 'front' players have been left almost entirely to their own resources. In fact they have developed their own highly personalized 'habitual' way of playing. Now required to think 'on the ball' and in certain situations to discipline their responses, the new game conflicts with the naturally acquired habits of these players.

Full-backs, who have never before been allowed to attack, will approach the new game with enthusiasm. They will experience little difficulty for while they have developed an habitual way of playing defensively, they have had no opportunity to develop any kind of habits for attacking play.

That players have habits there can be no doubt and this will not need further explanation for experienced coaches. It must be understood, however, that this conflict between the natural habits of the individual and the needs of the team will arise. Great patience and understanding must be demonstrated by the coach for it may be that some experienced players are so set in their ways that it will be very difficult to adapt themselves. If a player is *unwilling* to accept the discipline of the team game the coach must be very firm. But if a player is *unable* to do so, then the coach must temper his firmness with patience and sympathy.

In the final analysis it may become apparent that an outstanding individual may have to be dropped from the team. This will arise when it becomes obvious that the team plays better without the star than it does with him.

Realizing that naturally-acquired habits conflict with the develop-

## Drills and exercises

ment of a team game, a bid must be made to prevent players developing a personal style. For senior players of the moment this will be impossible, but much can be done to prevent future players having to overcome these problems.

Players begin to acquire habits at a very early age. They almost certainly develop one the first time they ever kick a ball, the habit of playing the ball with the right foot or the left foot. Perhaps this is not so much a habit as a preference, but whatever it is the chances are that the player will develop only one foot unless he is encouraged to perfect his technique with the left foot and the right foot.

Kicking a ball is not the same thing as playing, however, and habits begin to develop as soon as the young boy starts to play with his friends. Kicking a ball around in side-streets, the school playground or the back-field, plays a vital part in the development of ball skill and is indispensable in this respect but it is here that the habitual responses are developed. They are possibly fired by the widespread adulation displayed by the newspapers and the fans for the outstanding individual, and conditioned by this atmosphere youngsters grow up dreaming of individual success.

To become a star is certainly the aim of thousands of young players and while ambition should always be encouraged it must be understood that football is a team game.

The habits of the individual are not only a problem in an advanced team game which is the aim of the coach working via combinations. They have been acquired by every player, for all youngsters take part in impromptu games without supervision.

In street games the young player develops his ability but he certainly does not realize that he is simultaneously developing an individual and personal style of play. The most common fault among good ball players is easily observed even at professional level. In possession the player has his head down over the ball, both eyes riveted on the object at his feet. The star dribbler creates havoc when he beats an opponent or two, but never realizes it. He never sees the 'passing opportunities' earned by his skill because he never looks up and thus he does not see colleagues who would have open goals if only the ball could be given to them.

This tendency to ignore their colleagues is most pronounced in the best ball players. Later they have to be coached to acquire new habits —looking up from the ball, and looking around for their colleagues.

The less skiful also acquire habits. Many become very good at

## Drills and exercises

receiving the ball with the inside of one foot or the other and do not realize until much later that this particular 'habit' enables an opponent to anticipate which way they will move after the first touch of the ball. Others who cannot shoot with the left foot (for example) will always move to the right as they approach an opponent barring their way to goal. After a time this, too, becomes a habit—and predictable.

If all the kick-about games could be supervised by experienced coaches the players could be discouraged from developing habitual responses which will limit their ability later. Equally, the coach would have an opportunity of adding to the basic skills of the players in the years when ability with the ball is easily channelled.

We must recognize that youngsters will play for hours on end without supervision of any kind and the best that can be done is to ensure that in addition to free-play in street games every player receives at least two hours coaching per week. Ideally this should commence at ten years of age when his skills are already well developed but his habitual responses can still be overcome quite easily.

The practices and drills in this chapter form an ideal basis for the coaching of young players and from the age of 12 onwards they can be used to supplement the periods of coaching in combinations. Whatever the age at which players are introduced to combinations it will be found that time devoted to any of the exercises will bring a marked improvement in the play of the individual.

Summing up, it is clear that young players acquire a great many bad habits when they play for hours without supervision. With the right approach from the coach they can, at an early age, also develop 'good' habits which are consistent with the demands of modern football.

For older players these practices are no less important and will undoubtedly help the player to bridge the gap between his individualistic 'habitual' style of play and the needs of the team.

Before describing the various drills and practices a basic approach to coaching skills and habits can be established. Though this will be less true in the higher echelons of the game, the belief exists lower down that reading a coaching book and picking out a few training drills will improve the performances of the players. This is not necessarily so.

In any situation the coach would be well advised to follow a few

## Drills and exercises

simple rules. First he must decide on the pattern of play which is his long-term objective. Having decided on the kind of game he wants to develop he should picture his super team in his mind. Creating a mental picture will help and as the moves develop in his mind the coach should note on paper the skills demanded by his chosen style of play.

Following this pattern we can now analyse the place-changing game and devise basic drills which will help the players to become proficient at the type of game we are developing.

Above all the place-changing combinations will call for accurate passes given to the feet of a colleague. The man who gives the pass then runs to take the place of the player receiving the ball.

*Diagram 65*

Diagram 65 illustrates a very simple drill which will help develop both the skill (accurate-passing) and the habit (running to change places). Six players is perhaps ideal but if balls are in short supply eight or ten players can take part. Players A, B and C stand in Indian File and C has the ball at his feet. Facing C are three more players D, E and F, D being twenty to twenty-five yards from C. Younger players may be unable to pass a ball accurately over this distance and if difficulty is experienced the distance may be reduced to fifteen yards for boys of 10 to 14.

Player C begins the practice by pushing the ball to the feet of D and immediately runs to take up a position behind F at $C_1$, D controls the ball and then passes to B and immediately runs to take up position behind A at $D_1$, B passes to E, and so on.

It should be noted that good-class players can be expected to keep this drill going for several minutes with first-time passes. Less skilled players may be granted one touch to control the ball before passing and in special cases two touches. Progress should be carefully noted, however, and when performance improves the coach should switch from two touches to one and finally insist on first-time passing. Inaccurate passes may incur a penalty of ten press-ups or similar punishment.

## Drills and exercises

Four minutes of this will be enough at each training session but it should be understood that the coach can vary the tempo of the practice. If skill practice is the major objective the coach should encourage the players to control the ball quickly and make an accurate pass. This drill can also be used to improve speed if the coach insists on hard sprinting in the place-changing and kept up for longer periods than four minutes (under pressure from the coach) it is a more interesting way of developing stamina than the old-fashioned lapping.

This type of ball practice has been used in some countries for many years. Even the hardest physical effort is more interesting for the players if a ball is included.

Finally, it will be clear that within this framework the coach can introduce any desired ball practice. Passing with the inside of the foot or the outside, passing with the weaker foot, trapping in various forms, 'chipping', chesting and heading can all be insisted upon by the coach. In one basic drill the coach can improve skills, improve speed off the mark, develop general condition, and at the same time the players are becoming accustomed to moving after playing the ball.

After four minutes of this simplest of all place-changing drills the players can move on to another more complicated but still simple drill. Diagram 66 (a) shows how nine players can be accommodated, each file being at least twenty yards from the others. More players

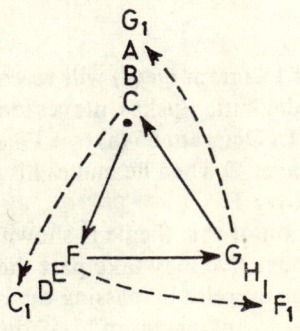

*Diagram 66 (a)*

## Drills and exercises

can be added if sufficient balls are not available. Once more it is player C who starts the drill by pushing the ball to F and running to $C_1$, F passes to G and runs to $F_1$, and so on.

Precisely the same drill is shown in Diagram 66 (b) except that the ball and the players are now moving round the triangle in the opposite direction. Three minutes in each direction will be sufficient at each training session unless particular stress is laid on the practice of the skill nominated by the coach, i.e. passing with the weaker foot. Here again the players can be given the opportunity to practise basic skill and improve general fitness and at the same time acquire the habit of moving after passing.

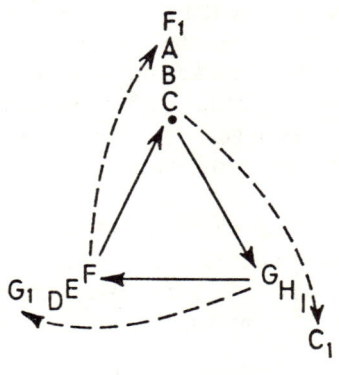

*Diagram 66 (b)*

Careful scrutiny of Diagram 66 (a) will reveal a close relationship with the Kocsis, Hidegkuti, Puskas moves described in Diagrams 1 (a), 1 (b) and 1 (c). In Diagram 66 (a) (see Diagram 1 (a) ) Kocsis is represented by the player G when he makes his pass to B (Hidegkuti) and Puskas is the player E.

Yet another variation of this theme is shown in Diagram 67. Any number of players above five may take part though nine are shown. The player B starts the exercise by passing the ball to A and running to the centre. A passes to any player of his choice and changes places with him (in this case D). From now on each player must pass to the man running into the centre and having given his pass he follows the ball into the middle. The player receiving the ball in the centre can

*Drills and exercises*

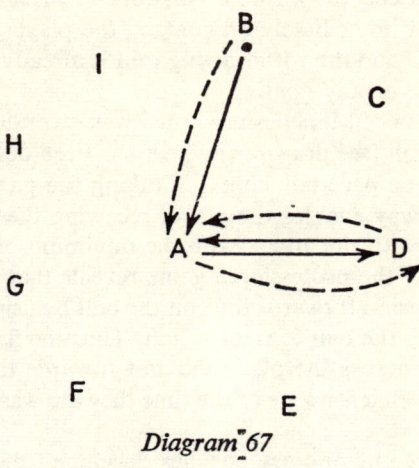

Diagram 67

pass to anyone he chooses and he, too, follows the ball to change places.

When the players have become accustomed to this drill a second ball can be introduced if at least nine players are taking part. It should be expected that at first the passing will break down soon after the introduction of the second ball but with perseverance, encouragement and discipline two balls will force the players to be even more aware of their colleagues. Developing the habit of looking around through the full 360 degrees of a full circle will be of great benefit in match play though not all players will be able to do this.

Returning to the mental picture of the team we seek to develop it will be noted that players will frequently be given a pass and told to 'turn'. A real ability to turn on the ball is rare indeed even in the professional game and practice in this skill will be imperative. In particular, the front players should be highly skilled at turning on the ball and to a lesser extent this ability will be demanded of the midfield players.

In match play at every level, precious seconds are thrown away because of total failure in this respect. Time after time, quick counter-attacks break down because too many opponents are allowed to get back in the game when a good 'turn' on the ball would have left them behind the play.

Dropping back to meet the ball played out by a defender, the front

## Drills and exercises

player should extend the inside of his foot to meet the ball. Withdrawing the foot immediately on contact, the player turns his body to follow the ball and the withdrawing foot is already taking the first step towards the enemy goal.

Bobby Charlton of Manchester United was exceptionally skilled at turning on the ball (see drawings) which has been described in other coaching books as pace-reducing (i.e. taking the pace off the ball). Turning in this way enables the player receiving the ball to control it and press on with the attack with the minimum of delay.

Observation of the professional game reveals that a high proportion of First Division forwards turn on the ball by using the inside of the foot to sweep the ball to right or left. Thus the first two or three steps taken are across the pitch and not towards the enemy goal. Other players, even less aware of the time they are wasting, 'turn' in a big semi-circle.

Many of the contemporary coaches developed their ideas in the more leisurely game of WM. Time in the WM game was of only relative importance and a corner-stone of coaching within that framework was the maxim 'play the way you are facing'. Now, however, the modern conception of team play demands that players shall be more mobile. Attacking with seven players and defending with eight makes it necessary that many players who have duties in defence and attack put in a great deal of hard-running. Attacks must be developed and pressed to a shooting position before the dual-purpose players can recover. *Play the way you are facing* often conflicts with the needs of the modern game.

Now the coach must insist that players 'turn' on the ball whenever possible—whenever the player receiving a forward pass has space at his back. The ability to turn on the ball is therefore a corner-stone of the new game but established players accustomed to 'play the way they are facing' will need a great deal of practise in the new skill.

The simplest form of turning practice is described in Diagram 68. Each of the three players A, B and C should be given two minutes

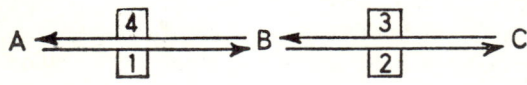

*Diagram 68*

## Turning on the ball

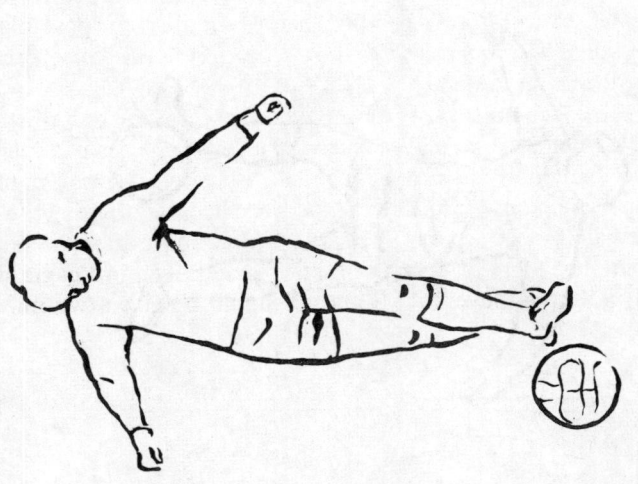

Fig. 1. Stretch the left foot out to meet the ball

Fig. 2. Receive the ball with the inside of the left foot

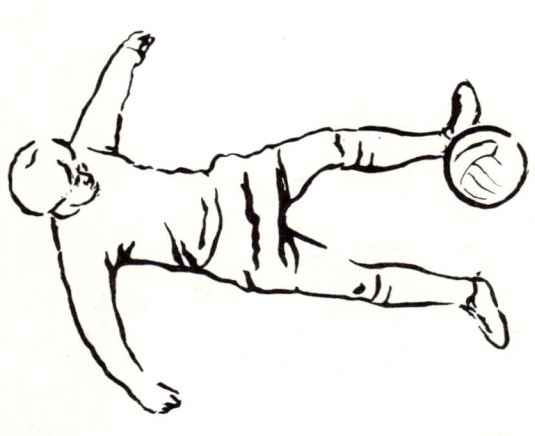

Fig. 3. Withdraw the left foot immediately on contact    Fig. 4. Left foot takes first step towards enemy goal

Fig. 5. Ball runs on while body weight is shifted

Fig. 6. Right foot comes round to push the ball on

Fig. 7. The turn completed with minimum delay

## Drills and exercises

sustained practice in receiving passes and 'turning' in the manner described earlier. A and C should initially be approximately thirty yards apart and the practice begins with a pass from A to B. A should aim his pass at the right foot of B who uses the inside of his right foot to take the pace off the ball and turning his body (to the right) through 180 degrees now has the ball under control facing C. B pushes the ball to C who controls the ball and plays it back to B, this time aiming his pass at the left foot of B who turns to the left as he takes the pace off the ball with his left foot.

After two minutes B should change places with A and later C should have two minutes practice at turning. It should be noted that two minutes practice is insufficient and that four minutes or perhaps six would be better. The players, however, will tend to become bored when asked to push passes to their colleague in the centre for long periods and changing the roles after two minutes will help prevent them reaching this state. Two periods of two minutes for each player will take twelve minutes and this will be the maximum the coach should insist on for each training session.

Once the players have become reasonably skilled at the new form of *turning on the ball* the more elaborate practice described in Diagram 69 brings further advantages. Here the players are given

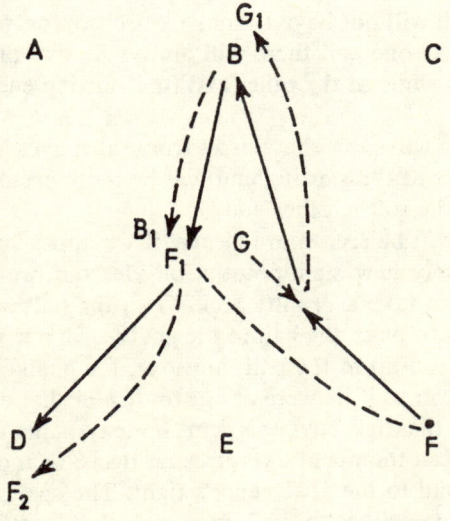

*Diagram 69*

## Drills and exercises

another opportunity to improve their turning ability and in addition they are asked to change places with the man to whom they pass the ball.

It must be noted that in Diagram 69 there should be at least ten yards between A and B, B and C and that A, B and C should be around forty yards from D, E and F. The practice begins with a pass from F to G who is positioned between the two lines of players. Player G runs to meet the pass from F, turns on the ball and then having *turned* G now passes to A, B or C. Meanwhile F sprints into the middle after passing to G and when G has passed the ball to the player of his choice he also runs to change places with the man to whom he passed.

In Diagram 69, F passes to G and runs; G turns, passes to B and runs; B passes to F and runs into the middle while F turns at $F_1$, passes to D and runs, and so on.

If the players are training outside in very cold conditions or if the coach desires to use this practice as a form of fitness training, then two players (C and F for example) may be eliminated. In this way the players will be called upon for greater activity but another factor will be eliminated along with the two extra players.

When only five players take part in the exercise described in Diagram 69 it will be clear that for 50 per cent of the time the man turning on the ball will not have to make a decision on which player he will pass to. At one end there will always be two players ready to receive a pass while at the other end (the starting end) there will be only one.

Observation will show that passes from the player in the middle to the lone player at the starting end will be more accurate than those from the middle to the other end.

The effect will be seen more clearly if we approach this question from an entirely new standpoint. Consider the problems facing a player about to take a penalty kick. With the ball on the spot, the player decides to place the ball to the goalkeeper's left-hand side. As he begins his run-up to the ball, however, the goalkeeper moves his left hand or arm as if he were about to dive in that direction. If the player taking the kick buys this feint he may panic and change his mind. At the last moment he reverses his decision and now attempts to place the ball to the goalkeeper's right. The chances are that the ball will now go neither to the left or right but straight at the goalkeeper.

## Drills and exercises

In fluid situations a player with the ball is just as likely to change his mind about whom he will pass to when faced with a choice between two or more colleagues. When the new decision is made very late the player making the pass will frequently pass into the space between the two players just as the penalty-taker who changes his mind shoots straight at the goalkeeper. The problem here is one of body position and balance. With regular practice a player develops the ability to adjust his body position and balance in these situations and for this reason the choice inherent in having three players at each end should not be discarded without good reason.

It has already been suggested that professionals or players of National League standard should be introduced to *combinations* without the benefit of advice from colleagues. Other players of lesser ability will benefit from advice but in either case they will need a practice aimed at developing the ability to *read* the situation *on their back* or developing the habit of calling advice every time they give a pass.

In Diagram 70 we have an exercise which can be for either purpose.

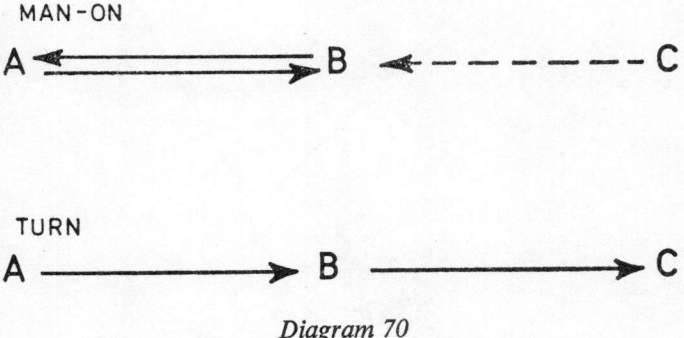

*Diagram 70*

For professionals who will be asked to make their own decisions when receiving a pass the emphasis in the exercise outlined in Diagram 70 is placed firmly on the player B. Three players A, B and C stand twelve to fifteen yards apart. A begins the exercise by passing the ball to the feet of B and as A makes his pass C has two options:
1. He can remain where he is.
2. He can sprint forward to challenge B and attempt to intercept the pass.

## Drills and exercises

The coach should insist that B moves to meet the ball as soon as the pass is made by A and in addition to watching the ball he must look over his shoulder to note the reaction of C. If C has remained where he was then B *turns* on the ball and having turned and now facing C, B passes to the feet of C.

C now returns the ball to B, and here it is A who has the options open to C a moment ago. If A comes forward to challenge then B should note this (by glancing over his shoulder) and moving to meet the ball he pushes it first-time back to C. Players A and B now reposition themselves and C begins the exercise again with another pass to B, and so on. The coach should pay particular attention to the way in which the third player reacts when the other two players are giving and receiving a pass. If the response is not varied the exercise has little value and the coach should continually stress the importance of varied responses on the part of the third player.

For players of lesser ability the emphasis in the exercise described

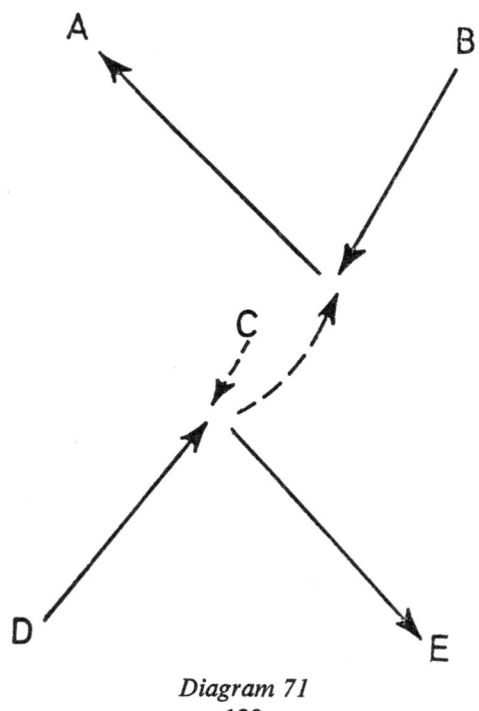

*Diagram 71*

## Drills and exercises

in Diagram 70 will be more evenly distributed. Again the players A, B and C should be twelve to fifteen yards apart. A begins the exercise with a pass to B, and meanwhile C has the same options to come forward and challenge B or to remain where he is. In addition the player giving the pass must note the reaction of C and call appropriate advice to his partner B.

As A pushed the ball to B, he must note the reaction of C. If C sprints forward to challenge then A must call 'Man-on' and B will respond by moving to meet the ball and playing it back, first-time, to A. If C elects to lay off, then A will call 'Turn' and B will turn in the modern manner before playing the ball to C.

The exercise begins again with C pushing the ball to the feet of B; now it will be up to A to decide whether to sprint forward and challenge (man-on) or lay off (turn). In each case C must now call appropriate advice and B must respond to the advice as described.

In the exercises already described in this chapter the players will find ample opportunity to practice the skills demanded by the modern game. Accurate passing is required by all these exercises while some are aimed at passing with place-changing and others relate skill practice to the responses of opponents. Still more seek to develop the ability to turn on the ball quickly and efficiently.

It is not suggested, however, that the coach should draw up his training programme to include them all. The practice(s) from which the players will derive the greatest benefit will be indicated by the players in match play. If the coach observes his players closely in competitive games it will soon become apparent that attacking moves break down because of a failure in terms of skill.

Above all, however, there is one skill at which there can never be enough practice—shooting at goal. In all the *combinations* it was continually stressed that every move should be pressed to a shot at goal. Though it may be fair comment to suggest that until recently too little thought was given to approach-play and the creation of a shooting position, it would be foolish to neglect the finishing touch now.

It should be clear that dead-ball shooting is of little value though it seems certain that players enjoy it. If match-like situations for shooting can be created this will be of infinite value and still enjoyable, but it would be as well to consider first why many good shots do not bring goals. Observation suggests that goalkeepers have an easier time then they might expect for two major reasons:

## Drills and exercises

1. The shot is delayed while the ball is teed up.
2. The shot is not hit with sufficient power.

In all training sessions, therefore, the coach should insist that every shot be hit early (i.e. first-time) and that they should be hit with maximum power. Hit it early—and hit it hard must be the maxim for shooting. There is another important point which must be borne in mind here. Players very often fail to score from favourable positions because they try to make sure. Placing their shots beyond the reach of the goalkeeper is all very well but an agile 'keeper will frequently save well-placed shots which lack power. Alternatively, the bid to place a shot beyond the goalkeeper's reach may be too successful and in this event the ball may rebound from the woodwork or pass harmlessly past the wrong side of the post.

Even amongst the most accomplished players it will be found that power and precision are incompatible. With this in mind and remembering that we shall demand maximum power behind every shot it will be sound advice to recommend that shots should be aimed at the goalkeeper's knees. 'Hit your shots early, hit them with everything you have—and try to kill the goalkeeper' should be demanded by the coach in charge of a shooting practice.

Bearing in mind that full-backs and midfield players will often be presented with shooting opportunities this is probably the best place to start. Very largely these players will be invited to shoot when passes are laid back for them to run on to and shoot from the edge of the penalty area, or just outside it. This is the type of shooting practice from which these players will benefit most.

In Diagram 72 a shooting practice is outlined for midfield players and full-backs. One of the centre-forwards should be positioned around twelve to fifteen yards from goal with the midfield players (8 and 6) and the full-backs (2 and 3) positioned a further twenty yards away. Reserve team players in these positions are also included (i.e. 2R and 3R, etc.) and four balls are distributed as indicated by large black dots. In the right-hand file the first and third players have a ball while in the left-hand file it will be the second and fourth players who have a ball.

The first player in the right-hand file begins the practice, pushing the ball to 9. The centre-forward drops back to meet the ball and plays it away first-time to 8 who sprints forward and shoots. Having made his pass to his shooting colleague the centre-forward should be asked to sprint towards goal seeking a shooting chance himself. This

## Drills and exercises

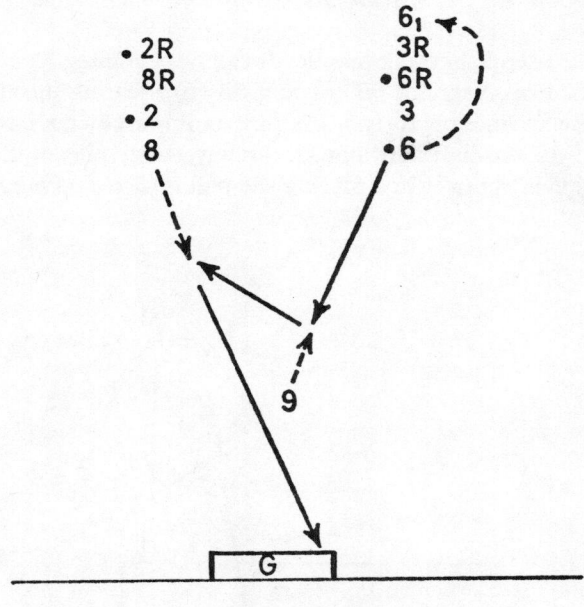

*Diagram 72*

may be presented when the goalkeeper stops but fails to hold the first shot or when the ball rebounds from the crossbar or a post.

In each case the player who made the first pass to 9 goes to the back of his file (6 moves to $6_1$) while the shooting player retrieves his ball, retains it and takes his place at the back of his file.

The coach should supervise this practice constantly and indicate when the second pair can begin. He will also demand accurate passing and insist that the centre-forward follows up each shot energetically and then re-positions himself quickly. Because the centre-forward will be far more active than all the other players the coach should have another centre-forward standing by. When the centre-forward begins to tire—indicated by increasingly inaccurate passes—the second centre-forward should be substituted to enable the first player to recover.

The practice continues with passes from 2 to 9 and first-time into space for 3 to shoot; then from 6R to 9 and on for 8R to shoot, and so on. It will be noted that because the shooting player retrieves his

## Drills and exercises

ball after the shot it will be his partner who shoots second time around.

Another useful shooting practice for players coming from behind is described in Diagrams 73 (a) and 73 (b). Bearing in mind that having the inclination to shoot is just as important as having the ability to hit the ball hard and accurately, every player should be drilled to call 'shoot' when playing the ball into a *shooting space*.

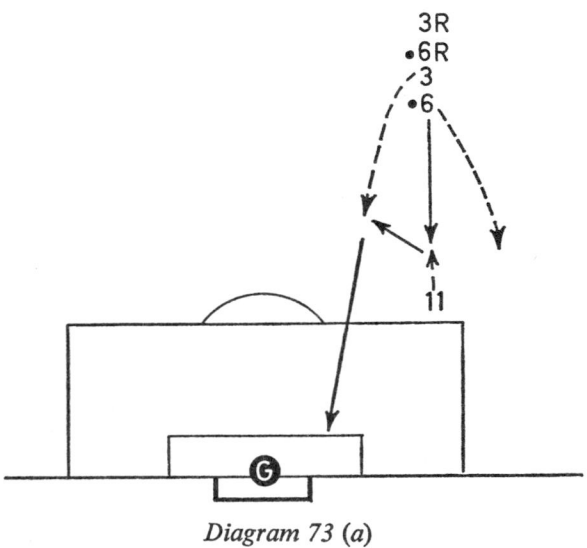

*Diagram 73 (a)*

The practice described in Diagram 73 (a) is for the left-flank players. Again the coach can have the reserve wingers standing by to substitute for the first-choice player from time to time. Those involved are the left-midfield and left-back from the first team and their understudies.

Each of the left-midfield players has a ball shown on the diagram by a large black dot. The left-midfield plays the ball up to the left-winger, positioned just outside the penalty area, and then runs to change places. The winger drops back to meet the ball as soon as the pass has been laid and plays the ball back first time into space. Meanwhile as soon as the left-midfield has made his pass and gone, the left-back comes forward looking for the ball being laid in front of him and shoots first-time. After each shot it should be the re-

## Drills and exercises

sponsibility of the shooting player to retrieve the ball, though spare balls may be left behind the goal. Here the spare left-winger may be employed retrieving the ball when wild shots miss the target. On the second run by the starting pair the roles should be reversed. The left-back should play the ball up to the winger and make the overlapping run while this time it is the left-midfield who comes from behind to shoot and then retrieve the ball.

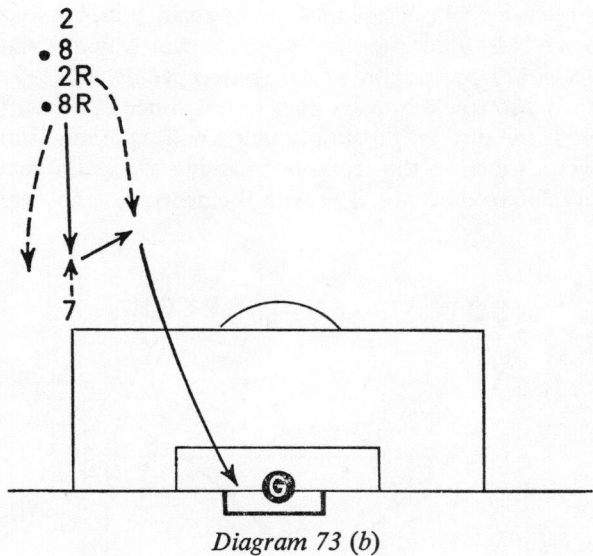

*Diagram 73 (b)*

In Diagram 73 (b) the same practice is described for the right-flank players.

It will be noted that amongst the established defensive players there is a tendency to get *underneath* the ball when shooting, and it should be emphasized that having the weight of the body *over the ball* is vital. Coaching manuals concentrating on the technique of playing football have already dealt with this topic, however, and the point will not be further explained. For the future it may be advisable to convert young forwards to play in defensive positions, but this point will be dealt with more fully in a later chapter.

Defensive players accustomed to playing a purely destructive role may well find it impossible to play a full part in the *place-changing* game. This will be particularly true for full-backs but if running at

## Drills and exercises

speed with the ball under close control cannot be expected there is no reason why such players cannot come from behind to shoot.

Another point on shooting which should be stressed is that a cross-shot is invariably preferable to one aimed at the near post. Goalkeepers always deal more confidently with a shot at the near post for there is rarely an opponent close at hand to impede him. With a cross-shot, however, the goalkeeper is often hesitant. This hesitation stems from the knowledge that opponents are lurking somewhere on his 'blind' side and will be rushing in, hoping to get a touch to the ball. Secondly, the near-post shot which is slightly off target will either go straight to the goalkeeper or wide of the near post. This is also true of the inaccurate shot aimed at the far post but here there is the distinct possibility that a colleague might in fact be able to get a touch to the cross-shot passing across the face of the goal. This chance does not exist with the near-post shot which goes wide.

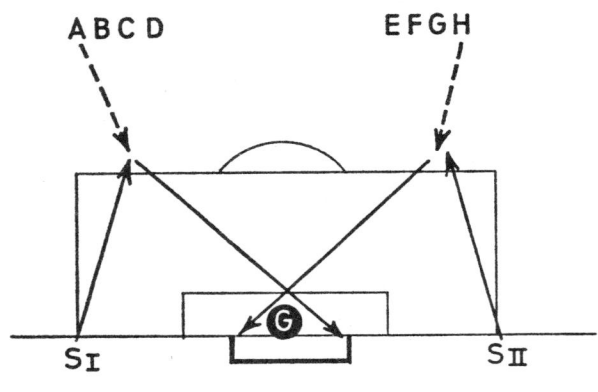

*Diagram 74*

A very simple shooting practice for defensive players may be rewarding in terms of enabling the player to adjust his body balance correctly. Such a simple practice is outlined in Diagram 74. Here the emphasis will be on the pure technique of shooting, the correct distribution of bodyweight and balance. At first the ball should be pulled back along the ground but when the players begin to show improvement in the techniques of shooting the service should be varied with chipped or lobbed passes. The two players serving

## Drills and exercises

shooting passes should be changed after a few minutes and with each change the position of the server should be modified to provide variation in the angles of the shooting pass. Server S<sub>I</sub> serves exclusively to the right-flank players A, B, C and D while server S<sub>II</sub> serves only to the left-flank players E, F, G and H.

The server plays the ball back and the shooting player immediately runs to meet the ball, shoots and retrieves his ball, leaving it beside the server before returning to his starting position. At first the order of shooting may be laid down by the coach (A, B, C, D in that order) but later it can be left to the discretion of the server to call a name.

In addition to variations in the passing angles obtained by changing the position of the server the type of service can be varied when the players begin to show improvement. Lobbed or chipped services will force the shooting players to produce a variety of volleys and half-volleys in order to get their shots in first-time and finally the coach should stress the importance of forcing the shooting players to shoot with their poorer foot. Which foot the shooting player uses is determined by the precise angle of the shooting pass. This should be explained to the players giving the service who should be encouraged to deliver more difficult serves as their colleagues become more proficient.

Shooting practices for front players have already been dealt with extensively in other publications. In terms of practising the techniques of shooting they are all of value but once the ability to shoot has been acquired, other factors must be considered. In the modern game it will be very rare that a front player is left unmarked in the shooting area for a free shot and practice with a dead ball will be of no value at all except for very small boys.

Front players standing motionless within the shooting area will always be tightly marked and quickly challenged and all shooting practices for front men must be designed with these factors in mind. The essentials are simply stated:

1. The player receiving a shooting pass should be on the move as he meets the ball.
2. The ball must be hit early (first-time).

It will be of value to impose a first-time shot condition in all training games—goals do not count unless they are scored with first-time shots. This will help develop the inclination to shoot *early* but further practice in first-time shooting will also be required.

In the highest class it will not be enough that a would-be scorer is

## Drills and exercises

on the move. If it is accepted that front players will usually be marked tightly within the shooting area then it follows that if they move they will be followed. If the front player moves slowly he will be overtaken by his opponent who will be in a position to block even a first-time shot. If the front player makes his move too early he will arrive too soon in the shooting position and being forced to wait until the ball arrives he gives his opponent time to catch and cover him.

The front player has the initiative for the defender marking him must always wait for his opponent to move but the initiative will be lost if the front player moves too slowly or too soon. A player can always get 'free' by moving suddenly but this freedom is only temporary and against well-drilled defenders will be limited to one yard (in terms of space) or half a second (in terms of time). This will be enough time and space *if* the player and the ball arrive in the shooting position simultaneously. Half a second early and the free player will be covered when the ball arrives—half a second late and the player is too late. The shooting chance will have come and gone.

The secret is to 'go' into space at the last possible fraction of a second and to arrive LATE—not too late, but certainly late. Going *late* and hitting the ball *early* are the twin secrets of players who are frequently amongst the goalscorers. Such players are born with the ability to time their approach to the shooting position. It cannot be taught or acquired but it can be sharpened by experience, and the coach should aim to supplement match experience with training.

Diagrams 75 (a) and 75 (b) describe a shooting practice designed specifically to bring out the desired features in the play of the centre-forwards. In Diagram 75 (a) the practice begins with a pass from the right-midfield to the right centre-forward. Being unopposed the right centre-forward turns in the approved manner and immediately passes to his colleague on the right wing and then sprints towards the far post. The winger takes one touch to control the ball and crosses it into space ahead of his colleague (9) who shoots first-time.

The right-midfield then serves a second ball to the right centre-forward from the reserve team (9R). He *turns*, plays the ball out to the reserve right-winger and sprints to meet the cross and shoot. In each case the shooting player retrieves his ball, returning it to the right-midfield before re-positioning for the next move.

It will be clear that the right centre-forward must time his approach to the shooting position in relation to the service from the winger. In

*Drills and exercises*

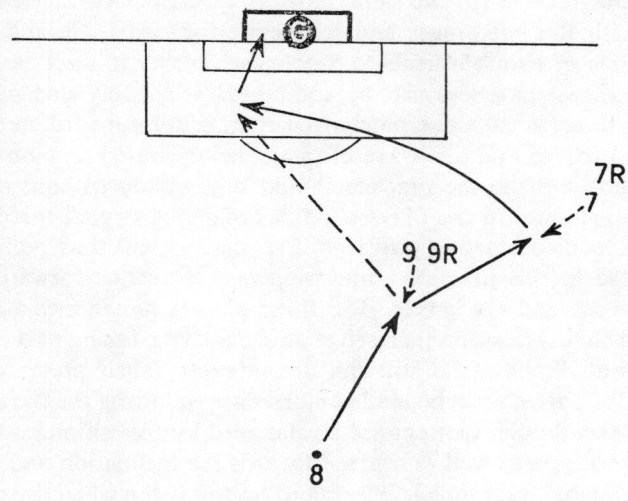

*Diagram 75 (a)*

match play this approach can be varied very slightly by changes of direction and by slowing down to be followed by sudden acceleration. The practice will lose all its value, however, if the winger does not play his part promptly and accurately and the coach should pay particular attention to the winger.

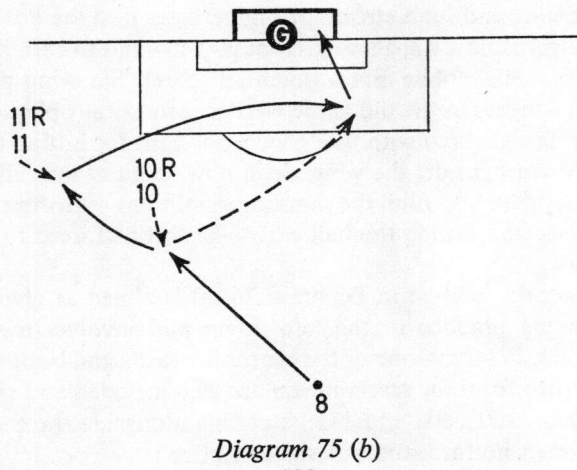

*Diagram 75 (b)*

*Drills and exercises*

In Diagram 75 (b) the same move is described for the left wing pair with the left-winger and left centre-forward (11R and 10R). After one or two rehearsals to enable each player to understand his role the two practices can be combined. With only one midfield player to serve balls alternately to a right centre-forward and a left centre-forward and one wave of attack being started as soon as the first shot is made the practice should flow evenly without putting undue pressure on the players. After each shot at goal the players return to their starting positions. Ten players will thus be accommodated in this practice—four wingers, four centre-forwards, the goalkeeper and the server. The front players not immediately involved should position themselves as if they were taking part in each wave but should stand still and not interfere. Their presence is of value for passes must be made and received allowing for their being there even though they cannot be classified as opposition.

For wingers as well as centre-forwards the inclination and ability to hit the ball first time is important. So too is the winger's sense of timing in approaching the shooting position and to sharpen the ability, inclination and shooting skill of the wingers the practice outlined in Diagrams 76 (a) and 76 (b) is specifically designed. It will be noted that in both practices the chances are that the wingers will be continually forced to shoot with their 'wrong' foot. This is not necessarily a bad thing for while the players may face initial problems of technique they can be overcome. Indeed they must, for the days are long gone when a winger's contribution to the team effort was to wait on the sideline and hit a stream of high crosses into the goalmouth.

The winger is now a striker—a front player—and to earn his place he must be both mobile and a potential scorer. Shooting positions offered to wingers in the old game were invariably at oblique angles and could be delivered with the 'good' foot used for hitting the high crosses. Moving inside, the winger can now shoot at the full face of the goal but if he is to fulfil the shooting conditions set forth earlier—going in late and hitting the ball early—he will be forced to use the wrong foot.

The practice outlined in Diagram 76 (a) is aimed at giving first-time shooting practice to the left-winger and involves a midfield player acting as server, one of the centre-forwards and both wingers. The front trio from the reserve team are also included and shown in the diagram as 7R, 9R and 11R, standing alongside the three first team players who form the first wave of attack.

## Drills and exercises

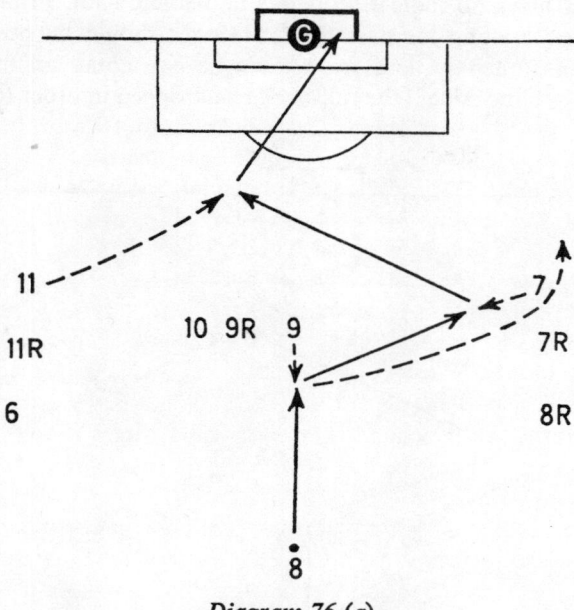

*Diagram 76 (a)*

With only two attacking waves there will be a certain amount of time lost in waiting for the players to re-position after they have taken part in an attack. Inclusion of the third team players if there is a third XI will make the practice run smoothly. If this is not possible then the first team left centre-forward (10) and the two midfield players may be included as a third wave.

The practice begins with a 'turn' pass from the server to the right centre-forward who turns and with his second touch of the ball sends it on its way towards the right-winger. As soon as the right centre-forward has made his pass he must spring round behind the right-winger (place-changing). The right-winger does not stand waiting for the ball to come to him, but sprints to meet the pass as soon as it is laid. He may be allowed a touch to control the ball and turn, but preferably the right-winger's pass should be made early and at all events with the second touch.

As soon as the ball has been played forward into the shooting space, the left-winger must sprint inside to meet the ball and without any hesitation shoot first-time. Care should be taken to see that the

## Drills and exercises

left-winger gives no indication of his impending shot. Prior to the right-winger making his pass the left-winger should be positioned close to his touchline and from there he can come on from his opponent's 'blind' side if the full-back has dropped in order to cover.

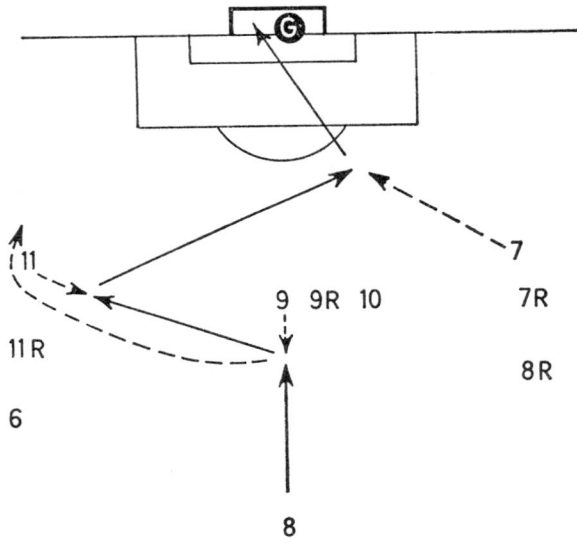

*Diagram 76 (b)*

Diagram 76 (b) describes the same shooting practice for the right-winger. It should be emphasized in both practices that when the shooting winger has hit the ball towards goal, the other winger and the centre-forward should close in on goal at top speed. Following-up, they will be on hand to score should the goalkeeper fail to hold the ball or if it should rebound from the framework.

The matter of following-up a shot at goal is entirely a question of habit. Though the advisability of following-up will be obvious it is something which even top-class players do not do naturally but it can be acquired if it is insisted upon by the coach in all appropriate training situations.

Another very simple and comparatively free shooting practice is described in Diagram 77, for four players and a goalkeeper. The goal here should be made by using corner flags unless goal-posts are avail-

*Drills and exercises*

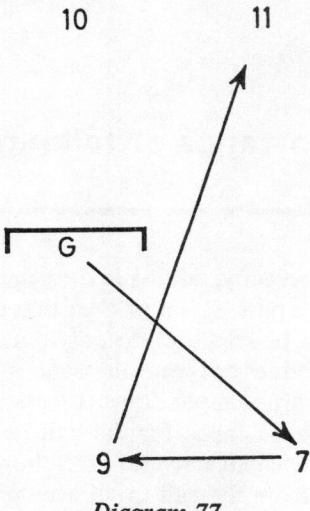

*Diagram 77*

able without nets and with at least forty yards of grass free of obstruction on either side of the goal. Two of the four players for practice are positioned on each side of the goal, and they should not be allowed to stand closer than twenty-five to thirty yards from goal. The practice begins with a throw-out by the goalkeeper to one of the four players. As he receives the ball the player (7 in the diagram) has two options. He can pass to his colleague 9 with head or foot or he can shoot at goal himself. Whichever choice he makes he must either pass or shoot himself first-time.

In the diagram 7 has passed first-time to his colleague 9 who shoots first-time. The ball passes wide of the goal in the direction of 11. The last named now has the option of a first-time pass to his colleague 10 or a first-time shot at goal.

The goalkeeper turns to face each pair in turn and if he saves a shot and holds the ball, the goalkeeper once more throws the ball out to the player of his choice. The coach should pay particular attention to the goalkeeper as well as the four shooting players. Under pressure from the coach, the goalkeeper should be urged to make an attempt to reach every shot and should not be allowed to rest even momentarily.

# 11 — The importance of talking in the game

Until comparatively recently, talking in the game was almost entirely limited to calling for a pass. It is now clear that this is a foolish thing to do and it may now be seen that the only time a player should call for a pass is when he does not want the ball.

To call for a pass now simply draws attention to oneself and if a player was free when he called for the ball he is very likely to be tightly marked when the ball arrives. In fact, however, the opposition may have benefited from the call to an even greater extent and an astute opponent is likely to intercept what may have been a good pass. Calling *for* the ball is now quite definitely out of date though in certain circumstances 'decoy-calling' like decoy-running (the two invariably go togther) may be of real value.

If calling for the ball is now to be avoided the advantages of talking within the team can hardly be exaggerated. Tremendous benefits accrue to teams which *talk well* and in a game between two teams of similar ability it may be that talking represents the difference between winning and losing.

Before going any further it will be as well to establish the fact that talking is not prohibited and will not be penalized by good referees. Unfortunately, many players are adversely affected by ill-informed schoolteachers who prohibit talking in the game—in the interests of discipline. Thus there are many young players who grow up with the conviction that talking and calling contravene the laws of the game. This belief is perpetuated at junior level by poor referees who penalize players that call advice to colleagues and do not indicate who the advice is intended for by mentioning the name of the player. Teachers and referees who are in these categories do the game and the players a great dis-service for talking is in reality an integral part of the game. It should be made clear that there are only two situations in which talking or calling contravene the laws of the game:

1. Using foul or abusive language.

## The importance of talking

2. Seeking to gain an unfair advantage by calling to mislead an opponent.

The use of foul or abusive language needs no further explanation but a word about calling to mislead an opponent will not be out of place. If a player calls 'my ball' as he attempts to head or otherwise control the ball he may or may not be guilty of an offence. This depends on the proximity of opponents and their chances of winning the ball had the advice not been given.

The majority of players who call 'my ball' are not deliberately misleading an opponent but seeking to advise a colleague. Players who intentionally mislead opponents usually do so very quietly with a soft 'leave it' or 'keeper's ball' almost whispered as they move to play the ball. Keeping their voices down such players are unlikely to be heard by referees or schoolteachers who are more than a few yards away.

Giving advice to a colleague is of definite advantage and for this reason talking was included in the combinations to get everyone into the habit of giving advice. Players making passes were instructed to give advice regarding the situation on the back of the player receiving the ball, but it does not necessarily follow that only players who make passes should give advice. Experience will make it clear to the coach that some players are unable to read situations quickly and accurately while others may be exceptionally good at this aspect of the game. Giving advice along with the ball when a player makes a pass he enables his colleague receiving the ball to concentrate entirely on the ball. But this will be true only as long as the advice given is 'good' advice. Calling 'turn' in *man-on* situations will clearly be of advantage to the opposition and if the coach becomes convinced that one or more players cannot be relied upon to give sound advice, they should be discouraged from giving any at all. It will be found that once the more intelligent players have been encouraged to give advice they will begin to do so in every situation and not only when they themselves give passes. The best players will begin quite quickly to read the situation constantly and with encouragement from the coach these players will fill the gap left when the coach begins to discourage one or more players who are unable to give sound advice promptly.

In general situations already dealt with in earlier chapters there are three basic calls which should be used by all players when they give a pass to a colleague:

1. Man-on.

## *The importance of talking*

2. Turn.
3. Go with it.

The meaning of 'man-on' is quite clear. In full, the advice is man on your back, and means quite simply that it would be dangerous to turn, play it away first-time. As long as the man receiving the pass sprints to meet the ball and acts on the advice, even the most tightly-marking opponent should be rendered impotent. The meaning of 'turn' is just as clear. It means quite simply—you have time and space in which to control the ball and turn before you can be challenged by an opponent. 'Go with it' seems to be more complicated but is nevertheless essentially simple. This advice should be given to a player who has no opponent on his back and relative to the speed at which the ball is travelling, would be wasting time and space if he stopped the ball by 'turning' on it. When a player receives a pass and *turns* he is bringing the ball under his control and turning towards the enemy goal. He is also taking the 'weight' from the ball—the speed at which it was travelling. In some situations the player could have let the ball pass him by without touching it, turned and sprinted after the ball and still gained possession before he could be challenged. In a situation like this, the player receiving the ball would waste time and space by 'turning' in the approved manner. Diagram 78 illustrates one of the 'go with it' situations.

Heading up to the situation which exists in this diagram the left winger dropped back to receive a pass from his colleague at left-back. His opponent (2) came forward to challenge and being told *man-on* the winger played the ball to the left-midfield. While the left-winger was dropping back the right centre-forward moved across behind the defenders as shown in the diagram. Having got out on to the left wing without being followed and ensuring that he is on-side by looking back along the line of defenders the right centre-forward is now free. The left-midfield spots his colleague unmarked on the wing and plays the ball to him. If the left-midfield reads this situation correctly he will not push a pass to the right centre-forward now at $9_1$ but will hit the ball past his colleague and play the ball in such a way that the ball turns in flight—IN towards goal.

Clearly such a pass is not a man-on pass but neither is it a turn pass. To turn—taking the speed off the ball and then pushing the ball forward as he builds up speed—would waste very precious time. With the ball on its way from 6 to 9 the enemy would certainly react. The right-back would be sprinting at top speed to get back *goal-side*

## The importance of talking

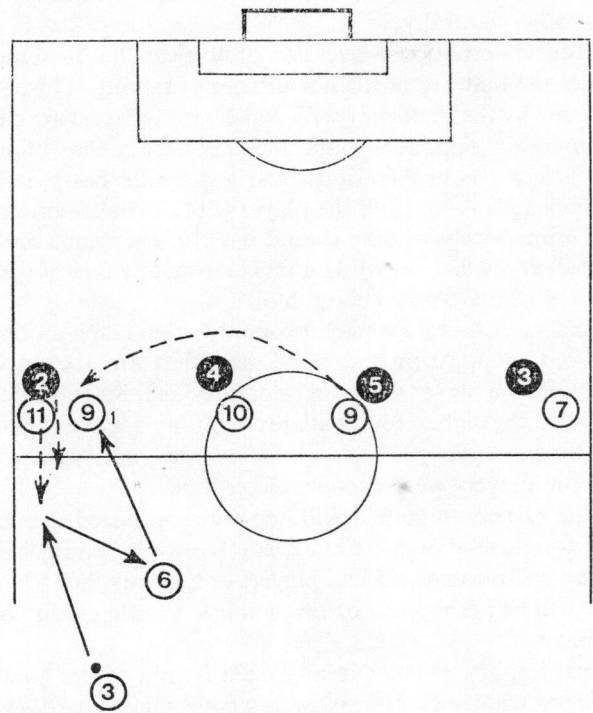

*Diagram 78*

of the ball and simultaneously the left centre-back would be sprinting across-field to cut his opponent off. Every fraction of a second will be vital here and if the pass from 6 to 9 is heavy enough the right centre-forward would be best advised not to play the ball but let it pass, turn and follow it. He would not stop the ball or turn with it—he would let the ball travel *and go with it* at top speed.

There are many other situations in which the level of team play will improve if the players off the ball give sound advice to their colleagues. The player who was born a natural leader will do so without prompting but other players less gifted can also make an important contribution in this respect if they are encouraged to do so. It was for this specific purpose that the giving of advice was made an integral part of the *place-changing combinations*. In turn, each of the

## *The importance of talking*

players was called upon to talk, and after some time many players will do so quite naturally.

Even at full international level it is quite clear that in some teams the players are unaware of the advantages of talking. This is clearly demonstrated by the frequency with which good players are caught in possession by an opponent who challenges from the 'blind' side. When an attack has broken down and a defender has switched the ball to a colleague in midfield the player with the ball is often unable to decide immediately who he should pass to. He stands motionless with the ball at his feet—inviting a tackle from any one of the enemy front players who are now behind him.

Front players who tackle back promptly often catch an opponent by surprise. Coming from the 'blind' side they are able to win the ball and make the player who lost it look foolish. Such incidents can be observed at the highest level but are commonplace even at National League standard. They could all be avoided and many blushes spared if the players were encouraged to talk.

In a team of good talkers it will be very rare indeed that a player is caught in possession by a challenge from his 'blind' side. The enemy may try to catch midfield players in this way, but in the good side there will be perhaps six or seven voices warning their colleague of the danger.

The most important voice in any team is that of the goalkeeper, for a 'keeper who does not advise his colleagues regarding his intentions will surely involve everyone in a great deal of trouble. In addition to watching the ball and anticipating how the opposition will develop their attack, the top-class goalkeeper should also be alert to the danger of an opponent sneaking into the shooting area unopposed. Like a radar scanner, the goalkeeper should be constantly surveying his penalty area. From his position on the goal-line, the 'keeper has everyone in front of him and in this sense he is unique. No other player is so well placed to command the defence and spotting an unmarked infiltrator he should decide which of his colleagues is best placed to cover the unexpected threat and issue instructions. The goalkeeper's *talking* responsibilities do not end here, however. Indeed, this is only the beginning. Whenever the goalkeeper decides to intervene he should make his intentions clear to all his colleagues. If he decides that he cannot reach a high cross in time it is the 'keeper's responsibility to make this known *and* nominate the defender who will deal with it. Very often two or more defenders can

## The importance of talking

be seen attempting to head the ball away following a corner-kick. Sometimes two defenders will so impede each other that neither is able to time his jump correctly, with the result that they both miss the ball. If the goalkeeper reads the situation and calls sound advice —'John's ball' is quite enough—then many potentially dangerous situations can be avoided.

When the goalkeeper decides to intercept a pass or a high cross he should always inform his colleagues. ''Keeper's ball' is a suitable call in this situation and one which cannot be misunderstood by friend, foe or referee.

Hearing their colleague's advice, defenders who were intending to attempt to clear the ball themselves should now do two things:
1. They should ensure that they do not inadvertently obstruct the goalkeeper.
2. They should drop back to cover the goal in case the 'keeper should fail to reach the ball or be unable to hold it.

Even when moving to reach a shot at goal it will be a great advantage if the 'keeper calls for the ball to be left for him. Obviously there will be many occasions when the absence of time precludes this but the word ' 'Keeper's' given in good time when the goalkeeper has a longer-type shot covered, can prevent many deflections off defenders and not a few own goals.

Scoring against one's own team is always a disconcerting experience. A great many of the own goals that are registered stem directly from the lack of advice given by the goalkeeper. Even in the simplest situations, misunderstandings can occur between the goalkeeper and his defensive colleagues, sometimes when there is not an enemy player within twenty yards of the ball.

Passing the ball back to the goalkeeper can be potentially dangerous and when a defender passes back 'blind'—that is without first verifying the position of the goalkeeper—the danger is multiplied. Quite often at amateur level a defender can be seen passing back 'blind' but this also occurs amongst professional teams. Sometimes a defender passes back to his goalkeeper in a situation where he had time and could have turned away to move the ball upfield—only to discover that his *silent* colleague was standing behind him or was on his way to pick up a harmless centre. All these situations can be avoided if the goalkeeper is alert, aware and advising his colleagues promptly of his every move.

**Whenever** danger threatens his goal the 'keeper must continually

## *The importance of talking*

make a series of decisions and if he makes these decisions known loudly, clearly and promptly he will avoid a great many embarrassing situations and prevent any number of critical moments from arising.

Another situation which often causes trouble is one in which a defender is covering the ball as it travels towards his goal with the goalkeeper coming out. The goalkeeper must make it quite clear if he wants the ball left strictly alone ('keeper's) or whether his colleague should play it back to him.

Many players are unable to concentrate on their own duties and still have time to spare for issuing advice and instructions to colleagues. Goalkeepers may come under this category and it would be unwise to press such a player too far. For a goalkeeper, however, '*Keeper's ball*' is the minimum requirement and it should be heard loud and clear every time the goalkeeper intends to go for the ball.

For outfield players the giving of sound advice in good time is no less important and there are many ways in which players off the ball can be of real assistance to their colleagues. In particular, advice is of real value when two players of the same side are going for the ball simultaneously. In these situations one often hears the cry 'one of you' but although well-intentioned this is not the answer. Given this advice it may well be that both players will assume they are the 'one' to go for the ball, impeding and perhaps injuring each other. Alternatively they can both decide to leave the ball to their colleague.

In these situations the only answer is for a player or players off the ball to decide which of the two players is best placed to play the ball. Making this decision, the player off the ball should call 'John's ball'. This decision should be based upon several factors:

1. Is one player facing the enemy goal?
2. Is one player going forward to meet the ball while the other is moving backwards?
3. Is one player in a position to shoot first-time.

A player who is facing the enemy goal, moving forward to meet the ball and in a position to shoot first-time should always get the decision.

Whenever two players of the same team are moving to play the ball simultaneously, it is invariably true that one is better placed to use the ball than his colleague. Having decided which player is in the best position the two players should be informed promptly with a simple call, 'John's ball'.

With these simple calls: man-on, turn, go with it, 'keeper's and

## *The importance of talking*

John's ball or Jim's ball, we can ensure that every player gets good advice as he moves to receive or play the ball. There are other situations, however, where advice can be even more important. In a team with advanced talking standards, silence, or the absence of a man-on call, will keep the player in possession aware that he has time. In lesser teams it will be of value to encourage players off the ball to tell their colleague *on the ball* that he has time. The word 'time' is quite suitable and self-explanatory, and can be repeated several times over a few seconds in suitable circumstances. This saves the man on the ball from wasting valuable time glancing over his shoulder to ensure that he is not being challenged from behind. In possession the player can now concentrate on what lies ahead of him and decide his next move.

Calling 'time' and 'man-on' is elementary, however, and the more intelligent players will be ready to go on immediately to more advanced talking. The really top-class player will be able to sum up the attacking possibilities and advise his colleague in possession where the attack should be pressed. Keeping his voice down a good player off the ball can be of considerable help to a colleague in possession and this is especially true when the opportunity exists to create a shooting position by changing the direction of attack from one flank to the other.

Whenever a player receives the ball and turns to face the enemy goal he will always have a 'blind' side. If he uses the inside of the right foot to turn on the ball he will be facing his left flank colleagues as he turns but to note the positions of colleagues on his right he will have to make a conscious effort and look right. The reverse will also apply for a player who takes the ball on the inside of his left foot to turn. In this case he will be 'blind' to those players on his left.

Should there be the chance of a good opening on the blind side of the player receiving the ball, an intelligent colleague positioned close by will help a great deal by advising 'look left' or look right' as the case may be. This advice should be loud enough to be heard by the player receiving the ball but no louder, and having given his advice the donor will help even more if he sprints away in the opposite direction.

## 12 — Combinations for attack only

There are many circumstances in which a coach will want to play cautiously and in these conditions he may well order his full-backs and midfield players not to commit themselves to attack. Against overwhelming superior opponents or when the team has been reduced to 10 men through injury it may be decided that the front players must not count on support from behind. Even in the most favourable circumstances there will be occasions when the backs and midfield players cannot re-position themselves in time, for example when heavy pressure is relieved by a thirty or forty yard pass to a front player.

Depending upon the shape of his team and the number of front players, the coach should devise a series of combinations for three or four front men. These *combinations* should also be based on *place-changing* which is rapidly becoming a prerequisite of modern attacking play.

Place-changing in attack is nothing more complicated than the old art of position switching but if place-changing is to be continuous it will bring in its wake new problems of condition and technique. To be constantly changing positions will make greater physical demands on the front players though modern methods of preparation can overcome this and there is no reason why the front players should not be as fit as the midfield players who have always been expected to stay in the game for ninety minutes.

The new technical problems are more difficult to overcome for if the front players are constantly changing positions then it follows that they will be asked to fulfil the roles of other front players. Wingers for example will be called upon to shoot (first-time) with their wrong foot and all the front players in turn will be expected to *pull* the ball 'back' from either wing while moving at speed.

The advantages far outweigh the disadvantages, however, for against an attack which includes place-changing as one of its major weapons the opponents face ever greater difficulties. In a defence

## Combinations for attack only

based on loose man-to-man marking combined with zonal responsibilities in covering, the defenders will find they are constantly being forced to decide whether to mark their man or cover their zone. With the defender's individual opponent frequently leaving the defender's zone this leads automatically to one of two possibilities:
1. Front players will often get free.
2. Defensive zones will frequently be left uncovered.

Both these eventualities are to the advantage of the attacking team. If the defence is based on very tight man-for-man marking and the front players are constantly changing positions then it follows that the defenders will be repeatedly called upon to perform their skills in unnatural surroundings. Passing back to the goalkeeper or clearing the ball upfield may be a simple matter for a full-back in his natural and best zone but it may be fraught with danger on the 'wrong' flank. Similarly there are many defenders skilled at timing their tackles when using their best foot who may be helpless on their poorer side and totally unable to slide-tackle when on the wrong side of the field. Underlying all the defender's problems is the theoretical fact that each defender still has two jobs:
1. He has to mark (tightly or loosely) an individual opponent.
2. He has to cover a zone in the defence.

When the front player remains permanently in a position which can be related to the number on his back then the task of the defender remains simple for he can fulfil both roles without difficulty. When the front player *moves*, however, the defender must make a decision. He must decide whether to mark his man or cover his space for he can no longer do both. Before leaving the theory of man-for-man marking in defence consider the duties and responsibilities of the full-backs. The left-back for example has to cover the left flank of the defence and mark the opposing right-winger. In orthodox play this player will be the opponent wearing the number 7 shirt, but in fact the right-winger is the opponent who is positioned on the extreme right flank of the attack. Marking number 7 the left-back is correctly positioned, but consider what happens when an attacking colleague runs round behind the right-winger in Diagram 79. The 'winger' dropped back to receive a pass and deciding to lay off, the full-back allowed his opponent to *turn*. As 7 turns on the ball his colleague at right centre-forward moves across the winger's back as illustrated and immediately the left-back is thrown out of position. Number 9 is now the effective right-winger.

*Combinations for attack only*

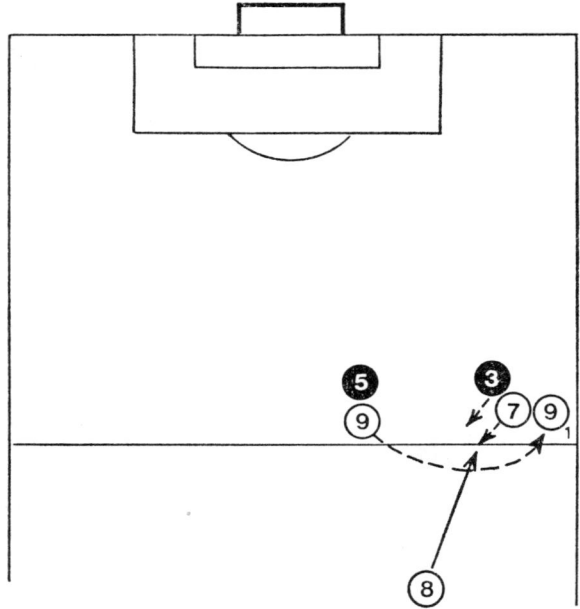

*Diagram 79*

If the defender who normally marked number 9 has followed his man to the wing then the right centre-forward has created space within the defence which can be exploited by a colleague. If the defender has not followed the right centre-forward then he gets free on the right wing and being positioned to the right of number 7 he becomes the effective right-winger. The left-back is now covering the wrong man.

Movement off the ball has always been desirable but it can never be achieved by merely asking the players to move. Neither will it help very much if schemes are devised in which all the front players are called upon to change their positions in certain circumstances or at a signal from one of their colleagues for this will lead to players running haphazardly and frequently taking up positions in which they will be ineffective. All changes of position should be related to the position of the ball and the moving player should always run into space *within* the defence and never beyond the line of defenders

*Combinations for attack only*

where he not only isolates himself from support but also runs the risk of being played offside. Front players should run *across the field* in their attempts to get free and *show themselves* unmarked to their colleague in possession.

If the moving player does not get free it will be because his individual opponent has elected to follow him and in that eventuality the defending side concedes two important advantages. Moving off the ball, the front player has left space behind him which can be exploited by a colleague and he has also drawn his opponent into a position where the defender's qualities will not be seen to the best advantage.

## PLACE-CHANGING OFF THE BALL

Keeping the full-backs away from the centre of the field is one of the primary aims of modern wingers and for this reason it will be unwise to encourage wingers to change places off the ball. In a 4–2–4 formation, however, the two centre-forwards are in an excellent position to change places frequently and should be encouraged to do so for they can change position within the defence without increasing the number of defenders covering the central approach to goal.

With the ball in right-midfield the right centre-forward is the closest front player to the man in possession and therefore a likely recipient of a pass. If he *shows himself* to his midfield colleague by dropping back a yard or two the left centre-forward can change places to advantage as illustrated in Diagram 80 (a). If the defending centre-backs both elect to mark their opponents tight then valuable space is created within the enemy defence—space which could be exploited by the right centre-forward who realizes he has drawn his opponent close to him and can turn and sprint for goal. This turn should be the signal for the right-midfield to drop the ball into the space ahead of 9, as the right centre-forward makes his break.

Alternatively, the defenders may elect to stay in position and cover their zones and in this case the left centre-forward (10) is very likely to get free at $10_1$. He could receive a 'go with it' pass from midfield and break through for a shot at goal.

It should be clear that the defenders will not be unprepared for positional switching off the ball and will almost certainly have established an understanding on general policy. Either the defenders

*Combinations for attack only*

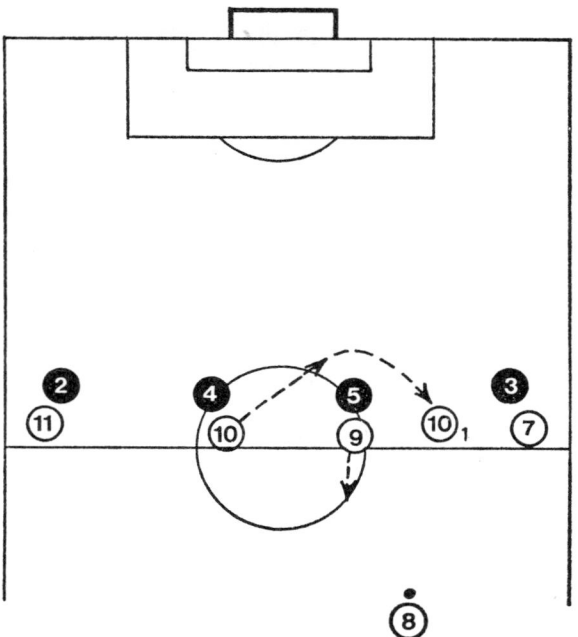

*Diagram 80 (a)*

will all mark their individual opponents *or* they will all cover their respective zones.

Finally, it is very likely that the right centre-back (in Diagram 80 (a)) might assume that his opponent will run himself offside. If the left centre-forward makes his run early (as 8 is receiving the ball or better still is moving to receive the ball) then he should have time to change direction and take up position at $10_1$, and turning to look back across the field towards the left wing, ensure that he is not offside.

In Diagram 80 (b) this situation is re-created in a three against two form with the right-midfield in possession playing with two colleagues at centre-forward. Opposition is provided by two centre-backs.

The coach should instruct the right centre-forward to drop back slightly and insist initially that the centre-backs stand fast. As 9 drops back, the left centre-forward makes his run and when he has

*Combinations for attack only*

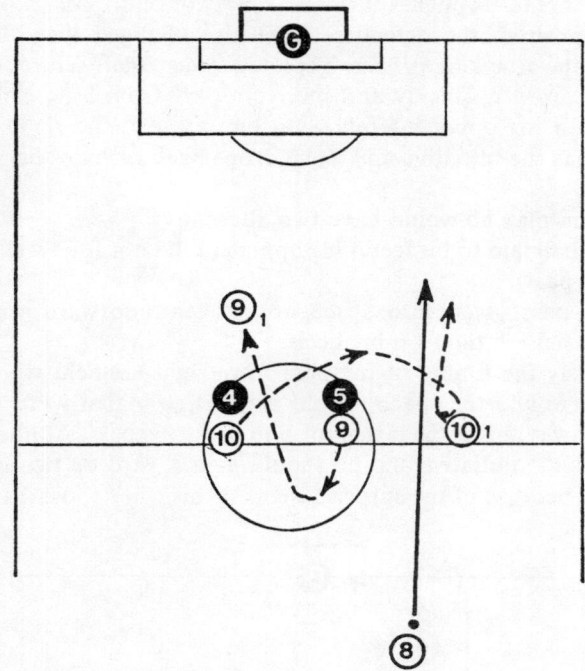

*Diagram 80 (b)*

turned to face the left wing at $10_1$, the right-midfield hits a 'go with it' pass to 10. The right centre-forward (9) should now complete the change of position by veering left as he sprints to goal in support of his colleague in possession. Each move should be rounded off with a shot at goal.

With practice the players should soon begin to break through regularly when the defenders elect to cover their zones. Now the coach should change the defensive emphasis from zone to strict man-for-man marking. Creating the same situation in Diagram 80 (c) the coach should now instruct the defenders to mark their opponents tightly. When the left centre-forward makes his place-changing run the right centre-back follows him closely The right centre-forward again drops back to meet the right-midfield but this time his opponent will follow him closely.

Studying the diagram it may appear that the defence has now pre-

*Combinations for attack only*

vented a break-through for while the two centre-forwards have changed position the defenders have also changed over. In fact, however, the attacking pair have created space at left centre-forward and if 9 can turn quickly and receive a pass from 8 he can break away. With his opponent following him closely, the right centre-forward has the initiative and as he drops back he hides his real intention.

In match play he would have two alternatives:
1. The ball laid to his feet if his opponent did not follow closely (a turn pass).
2. The pass given into space at left centre-forward when his opponent is tight on his heels.

Obviously the timing of the pass from right-midfield will be important here and the coach should make it clear that when 9 turns to sprint away this is the signal for 8 to make his pass. Although it is 9 who has the initiative and he should gain a yard or two over his opponent because of the surprise element this will be lost if the pass

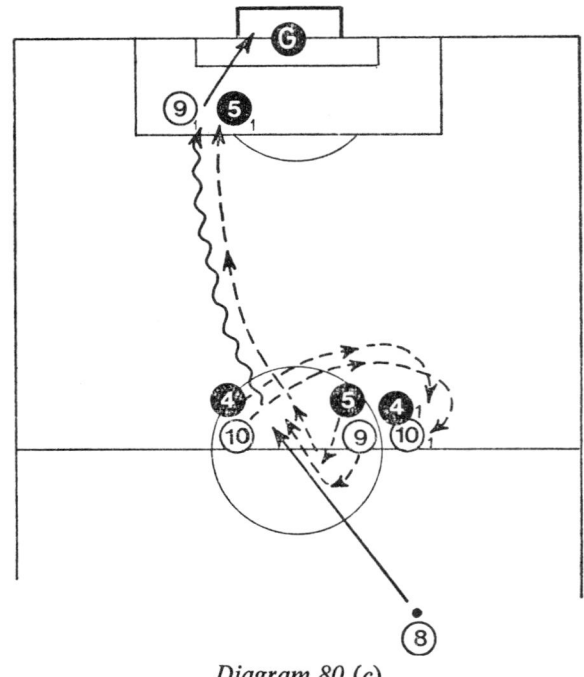

*Diagram 80 (c)*

## Combinations for attack only

from right-midfield is delayed. In this case there will be a considerable danger of 9 running offside, but this will not arise if he drops back to meet a pass at feet and the ball is given into space in the moment that 9 turns to go.

This is perhaps the ideal moment to introduce a factor of vital importance which exists every time any kind of pass is made. In poorly-coached teams at all levels moves break down repeatedly because passes are not given in relation to the next move. Even in the most simple situations the pass should be given to a colleague in such a way that he can easily 'screen' the ball from his opponent. All too often passes are hit towards a team mate without thought and what might have been a good pass is turned into a 50–50 'fight' ball because it cannot be screened.

In Diagram 80 (c) the right centre-forward has made his break with his opponent on his right. As 5 turns to follow his man he will

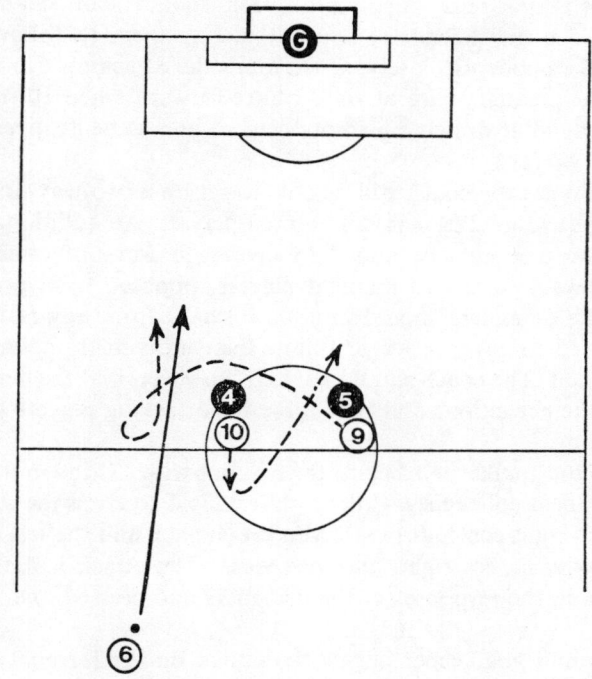

*Diagram 80 (d)*

## Combinations for attack only

surely follow goal-side and here the ball from 8 should be delivered to the left-hand side of his colleague 9. Given promptly and with the pass given just the right 'weight' the ball will arrive exactly as 9 wants it—with his body screening the ball from his opponent.

Now the coach should turn his attention to the similar situation described in Diagram 80 (d) and here he should introduce the two centre-forwards and two centre-backs from the reserve team. With the addition of a left-midfield we now have another three-against-two situation and the only difference here is that the break-through will now be engineered from left-midfield. In this case it will be the right centre-forward who moves *off the ball* in a bid to make space or get free.

At first the coach should once more instruct the defenders to cover their zones and 9 should now make his place-changing run from right to left and turn to look back across the defence and ensure he is on-side. The left-midfield then plays the ball through for 9 to turn and *go with the pass*. Again the coach should soon change the emphasis for the defenders, now instructing them to follow their individual opponents closely. Once more the attacking trio should exploit the created space at right centre-forward when 10 turns to sprint away after drawing his opponent to him as he dropped back (Diagram 80 (e) ).

At this point the coach will be able to set up a two-way drill with two goals (two goalkeepers) and all ten players. An additional midfield player can also be added to give each wave of attack two centre-forwards and two midfield players, opposed by two centre-backs. The defenders should now be released from any restriction and allowed to cover space or follow their individual opponents as they think fit. The coach should see to it, however, that the defenders do vary their reactions and thus force the attacking players to read the situation.

One of the goalkeepers begins the practice with a throw-out to one of his midfield colleagues. If the right-midfield received the throw it will be the right centre-forward who drops back and the left centre-forward who moves right, and vice versa. The attack is developed according to the responses of the defenders and pressed to a shot at goal.

The second goalkeeper begins the attack on the far goal with a throw out and meanwhile the players involved in the first attack have time to re-position. The moves are then repeated with attacks flowing

## Combinations for attack only

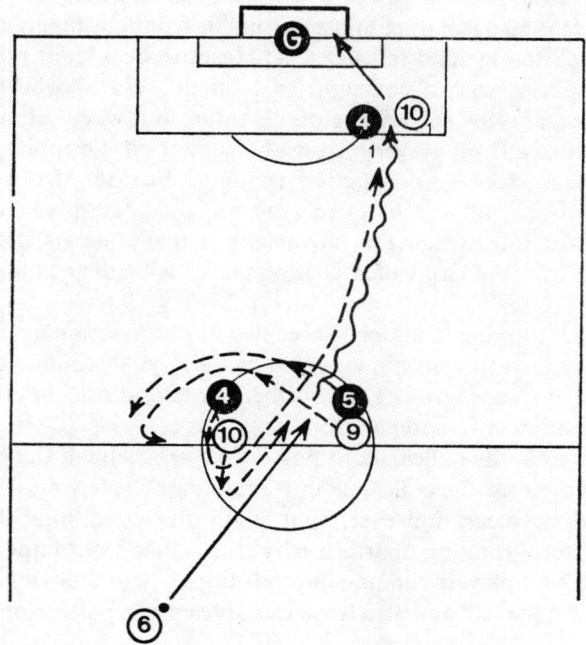

*Diagram 80 (e)*

first to one goal and then to the other and as always in two-way practices, a tally of goals scored can be kept.

## PLACE-CHANGING IN ATTACK AFTER PASSING

Front players who remain in fixed positions make life easy for their opponents and it can truthfully be stated that if the front men run in any direction it is better than remaining static. To insist that front players should constantly change position would be of benefit but this would inevitably lead to players taking up positions in which they would isolate themselves from their colleagues and the ball. It would also lead very rapidly to a state of near exhaustion if the front players were to carry out this instruction with real enthusiasm.

In general terms it can be stated that by running away from the ball towards the enemy goal the front player isolates himself from support and also risks being played offside. Running to meet the ball

## Combinations for attack only

is hardly an improvement for while the offside danger is eliminated the runner is also isolating himself from his front colleagues and if he drops back too far and too often he ceases to be a front player and changes places with a colleague in midfield. When colleagues are *coming from behind* this can be of advantage but when a longer type pass is hit to a front player he must be supported. Dropping back in these circumstances is negative running. For the front players *positive running* off the ball can now be fairly described as lateral-running for only when the movement is made across the line of defenders can the front men change places with their colleagues in attack.

If lateral running in attack is accepted as *positive running* it will not entirely remove the mystique which has always surrounded this expression. We can, however, go further for lateral runs in attack can be divided into two categories:

1. Towards the colleague in possession or receiving the ball.
2. Away from the colleague in possession or receiving the ball.

It will be clear, however, that given the conditions described above, lateral running in attack may still be haphazard and can still result in front players running into positions where they isolate themselves from the ball and also leave the colleague in possession without support.

It is with these thoughts in mind that the combinations presented here were drawn up. There are many more possibilities for the experienced coach but these combinations bring out the two forms of lateral running—towards the player in possession and away from the player in possession. Underlying them all is a point which should be continually presented to the players: if a colleague runs away from the ball and towards you then he is changing places with you, and you must now move to change places with him.

Awareness of the opposition has always been a priceless asset in the make-up of front players but awareness of his colleagues is equally important. It will be clear that when a centre-forward moves laterally and away from the winger in possession, he will either get free on the far wing *or* create space in the centre. If the far winger now moves inside then the probabilities are that the far winger will be able to exploit the space in the centre *or* the centre-forward now positioned on the far wing will be able to take full advantage of his freedom.

Introducing the front players to lateral running combined with

## Combinations for attack only

*place-changing* the coach will do well to keep things as simple as possible. The best point at which to start will be place-changing in pairs as illustrated in Diagram 81. Two players should be selected who are normally adjacent to each other in the orthodox attacking formation, for example the two centre-forwards. Positioned ten to fifteen yards apart with the player 9 in possession the practice begins

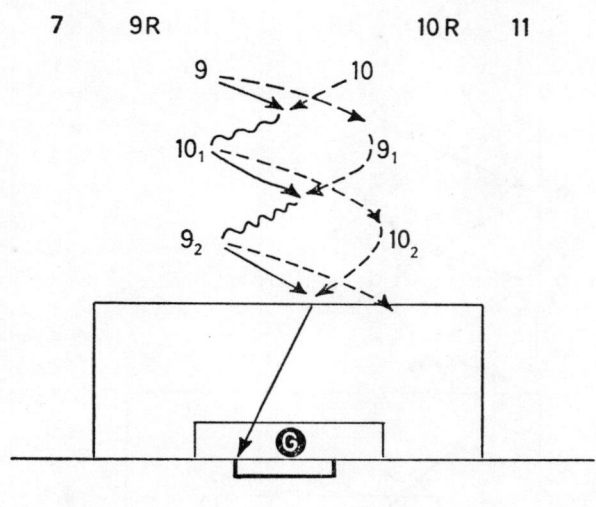

*Diagram 81*

with a diagonal pass for 10 to run on to. As soon as 9 has made his pass he runs across the back of his colleague to change places; 10 runs to meet the ball, controls it and dribbles forward three or four paces and then turns to play a reverse pass diagonally forward to his colleague; 10 then runs round the back of his colleague to return to his orthodox position. The moves are repeated combining reverse-passing with place-changing and when the ball reaches the edge of the penalty area the player running on to the ball must shoot first-time.

Waiting behind the first two players 9 and 10 the coach might well have two or three more pairs who can attack in turn. This will give the players time to retrieve their ball and return to their starting positions without wasting time. The second pair may be the first choice right-winger and the right centre-forward from the reserve team followed by the reserve left centre-forward and the left-winger

## *Combinations for attack only*

from the first team. It will also be a wise move to change the pairs quite frequently.

A second place-changing exercise is described in Diagram 82. Again this is for two front players and once more it will be wise to choose players from adjacent positions in the orthodox team shape and change the pairs frequently. In this exercise the ball is pushed

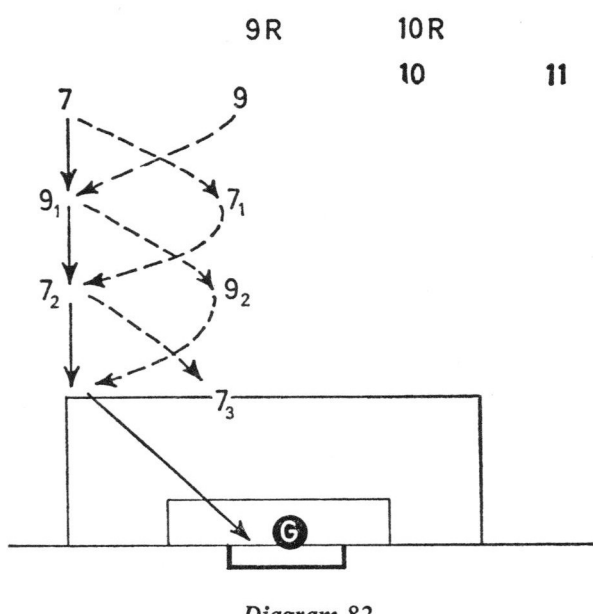

*Diagram 82*

directly forward towards goal and the second player sprints diagonally forward to overtake the ball, turn on it and push the ball directly forward once more. After making his pass each player sprints away immediately on a place-changing run and having made the change he turns to face his colleague. The players should be cautioned to watch the ball and their colleague at all times and no move should be made towards the ball until the forward pass has been made. In each case the player off the ball should ensure that he is always half a yard behind the ball until the pass is made, and in this way the danger of running offside will be obviated.

Two more pairs can be included waiting their turn to attack and

## Combinations for attack only

once more the player receiving a pass on the edge of the penalty area finishes the exercise by turning on the ball and shooting with his second touch. His partner follows up looking for a rebound and finally retrieves the ball before making his way to his starting position, as the second pair begin their move.

The basic themes behind the practices in Diagrams 81 and 82 can now be extended and adapted for three players. In Diagram 83 an

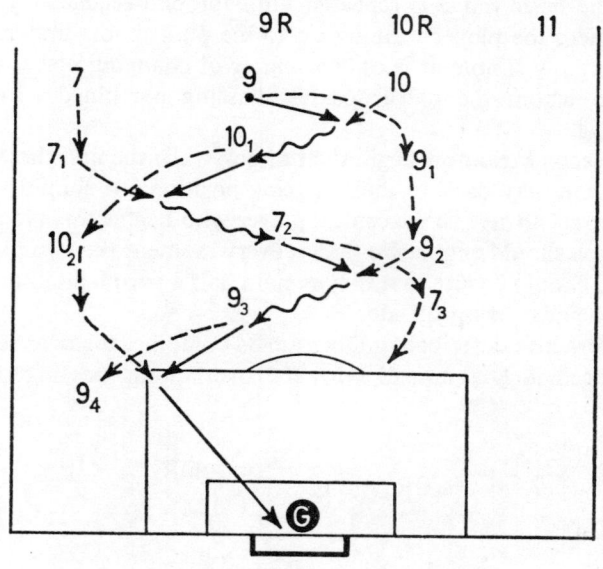

*Diagram 83*

exercise is described for three front men. For a 4–3–3 team it will be a simple matter of using the three front players from the first team with their respective understudies forming a second wave. For teams playing with four players up (as illustrated) it will be best to select players whose orthodox positions are adjacent, in this case right-winger and the two centre-forwards. In the second wave the coach for a 4–2–4 team would be well advised to include the two centre-forwards from the reserve team with the left-winger from the first XI. The two reserve wingers can be standing by, perhaps to field the ball when shots fly wide of the goal, and with frequent changes of the players the coach can keep them all active. The right centre-forward

## *Combinations for attack only*

begins the practice with a pass to his colleague 10, given diagonally forward. As the left centre-forward runs to meet the ball the man who gave the pass sprints to change places by passing round the back of the player he passed to. The left centre-forward controls the ball and carries it into a central position between his colleagues and then releases a pass, given diagonally forward for the right-winger. The left centre-forward then sprints round the back of his colleague on the right wing as the winger moves inside with the ball under close control. The basic move is repeated until the ball reaches the penalty area where the player running on to the pass shoots first-time.

Essentially simple, it is only a matter of changing places with the man to whom the player passes. Passing combined with place-changing.

The second trio now begin their attack while the first three players make their way back to their starting positions. It should be noted that it must always be the central player who begins this practice and the coach should emphasize that at every moment the two players off the ball should ensure that they remain half a yard behind the ball to guard against being offside.

The practice described in Diagram 84 combines the reverse passing introduced in Diagram 81 with the overlapping passing theme of

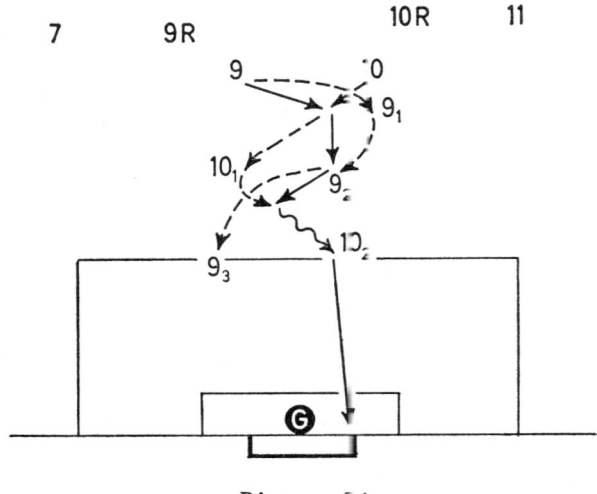

*Diagram 84*

## Combinations for attack only

Diagram 82. In pairs, adjacent players attack in waves and should be positioned seven or eight yards apart—approximately fifteen yards from the penalty area. After the third pass, the player receiving the ball picks it up in his stride and shoots with his second touch.

The players should become familiar with their respective roles in all these combinations relatively quickly. As soon as the players reach the point where they move off after playing the ball without any hesitation they should be introduced to opposition.

One defender will be quite sufficient at first and in the early stages the coach should instruct the defender to remain relatively passive. It will be enough if the defender offers a challenge to the player in possession and when the first pass has been made he should be free to intervene if he can—but only by interception. Tackling should be discouraged until the players become more accustomed to opposition.

Even in the three-man combinations it will be enough to introduce one defender at first and restrict him to a limited role of challenge and interception.

As soon as possible, however, the coach should aim to lift all restrictions from the defender but care should be taken that this is not done too early. This will be evident if an unrestricted defender is too successful and in such circumstances the coach should reintroduce the restrictions on the defender for a further period.

When the restrictions on the opposition are finally lifted the attacking players should be encouraged to improvise on the basic themes when in possession. It should be quite clear that the aim here is not to restrict the initiative of the talented player but to ensure that his front colleagues are constantly re-positioning in close support.

In particular the exercise described in Diagram 83 is full of possibilities for improvisation. If the defender positions himself in such a way as to bar the prescribed pass from 10 to 7 for example, then he must leave ample room for either an overlapping pass or a reverse pass to 9. Even when the coach adds a second defender to provide greater opposition it will be seen that all the advantages are in the hands of the attacking trio. If they move without hesitation after parting with the ball; if they call good advice; if the player in possession commits one of the defenders to him before passing; if the players off the ball time their approach to meet a pass at the latest possible moment—then the defenders will be powerless.

The key to it all can be seen clearly in Diagram 85 in which the

## Combinations for attack only

*Diagram 85*

central figure is player C approaching the ball passed from his colleague B. In this situation player C is unopposed temporarily and before the defender 2 can recover to offer a challenge there should be time for B to have moved across the back of his colleague C.

Assuming that one defender is covering player A, this will leave the second defender to face two men. The lone defender cannot possibly cover all the alternatives open to player C for however he approaches the man receiving the ball he must leave at least two simple alternatives open to C.

Three basic alternatives are shown in the diagram:
1. A direct pass from C to B.
2. A forward pass for B to run on to.
3. A change of direction away from B and into space.

Positioning himself to cut off the direct pass to B, the defender lays himself open to the forward pass on to which player B would run from the 'blind' side of the defender. Finally, if the defender elects to play safe and position between the two possible passing angles from C to B then he gives player C both time and space to move away.

If player C should turn away from his colleague B, then the defender must come across to challenge for if he does not then C would turn towards goal and finally shoot himself.

Whenever the defender commits himself to the pursuit of player C then the passing angles to B are immediately open again.

Given *running off the ball* as described in Diagram 83, these three basic possibilities are 'on' every time a player received the ball. Automatically the attacking trio have two against one wherever the ball goes. The essence of the practice is that the player receiving the ball should recognize the possibilities and take the correct decision in relation to the reactions of the defender. This of course is in addition to the prime purpose of familiarizing the front players with the advantages of place-changing after passing, and developing in them the habit of *moving* after playing the ball.

The theme underlying all the combinations so far presented in this

*Combinations for attack only*

section has been place-changing with the man in possession or the man receiving the ball. This tends inevitably to confine the game to short or relatively short-passing but perhaps the most effective combinations are based on longer-type passes.

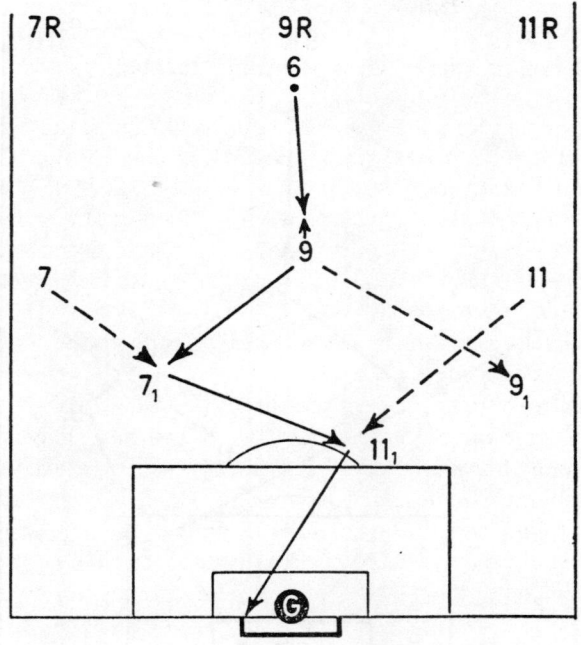

*Diagram 86 (a)*

Diagram 86 (a) illustrates a move already much in evidence amongst the most advanced teams. Because of the longer distances involved it demands greater accuracy in distribution but it is still essentially simple. To save time the coach would again be advised to employ two or preferably three groups of players so that following each attacking wave, the players have time to regain their starting positions.

In the first wave the attack begins with a turn ball served to the right centre-forward who drops back to receive the pass, turns and plays the ball towards his colleague on the right wing. In the moment that the pass is made, all three players must move off at speed. The

*Combinations for attack only*

winger sprints to meet the ball, while the right centre-forward and left-winger change places. Playing the ball first-time, the right-winger puts the ball on for his colleague on the far wing as he speeds into the centre to shoot first-time. In Diagram 86 (b) a variation of this

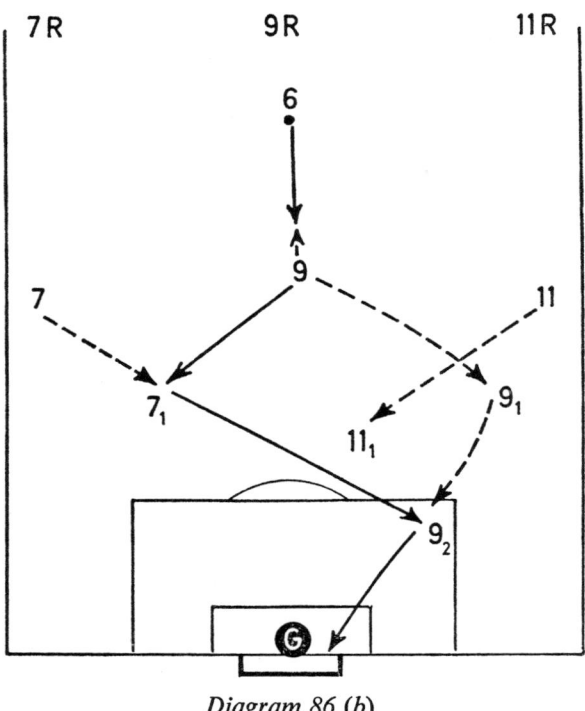

*Diagram 86 (b)*

basic move uses the left-winger as a decoy and gives the right centre-forward a shooting chance as he veers in from the left wing.

Initially the coach would be well advised to instruct the right-winger to aim his passes for each of his front colleagues in turn. He should also emphasize to each of the players (9 and 11) running off the ball that whether they receive the pass or not each run must be realistic and wholehearted.

Once the players have become familiar with their respective roles, opposition can be introduced. One defender (D) will be quite suffi-

*Combinations for attack only*

cient for inexperienced players and he should be positioned as illustrated in Diagram 86 (c). The coach should instruct the defender to vary his responses and particularly in the early stages should not make feints. With the ball on its way from 9 to 7 the defender must make his decision and move promptly and decisively to cover the

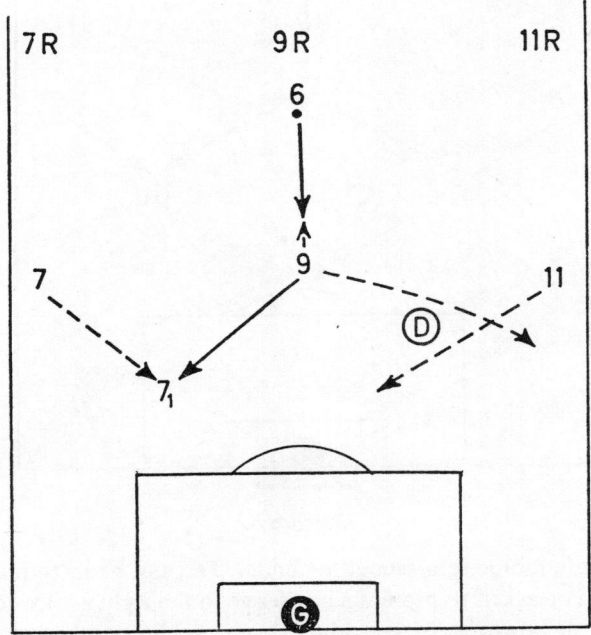

*Diagram 86 (c)*

man of his choice. If the defender elects to cover the left-winger then the ball should go from 7 to 9 while if the defender moves to pick up 9 the shooting chance will go to the left-winger.

Diagram 87 describes an exactly similar move except that the ball goes first to the left wing and back to the moving players on the right. Diagrams will not be needed to illustrate the alternative passes from the left-winger but both the right-winger and the right centre-forward should be sufficiently rehearsed before opposition is introduced as in Diagram 86 (c) but this time positioned between the right-winger and the right centre-forward.

At the discretion of the coach, who will alone be able to judge the

*Combinations for attack only*

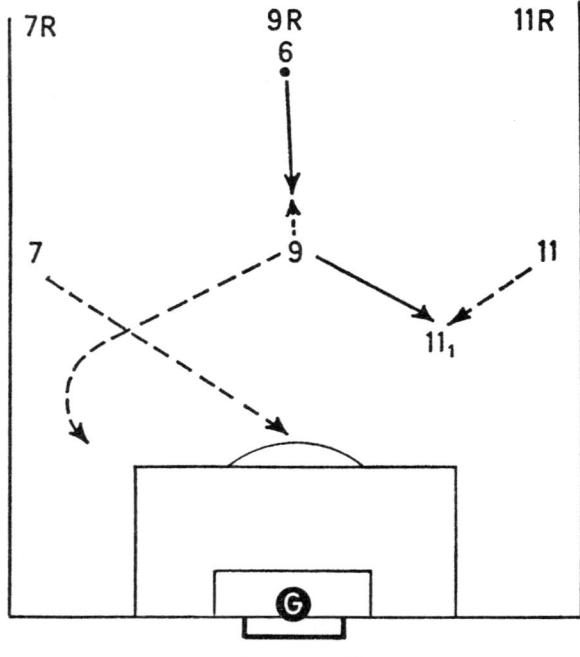

*Diagram 87*

appropriate moment, a second defender, D2, can be introduced and he should be asked to present a challenge to the right centre-forward. He should, however, be restrained from tackling and merely show himself at first (see Diagram 88).

The right centre-forward now receives a 'turn' pass and however the opponent positions himself he must allow 9 to pass to one wing or the other. Having passed to the winger, the right centre-forward immediately sprints away to change places with the other winger.

In this three-against-two practice the coach should withdraw the original defender to a position which would closely resemble that of the *libero* or free-back. From his starting position in the centre the free-back must move across to challenge the winger who received the pass from the right centre-forward.

At first the coach should instruct defender D2 to pick up the winger running into the shooting position *or* follow the right centre-forward. Step by step the practice becomes more realistic and more

## Combinations for attack only

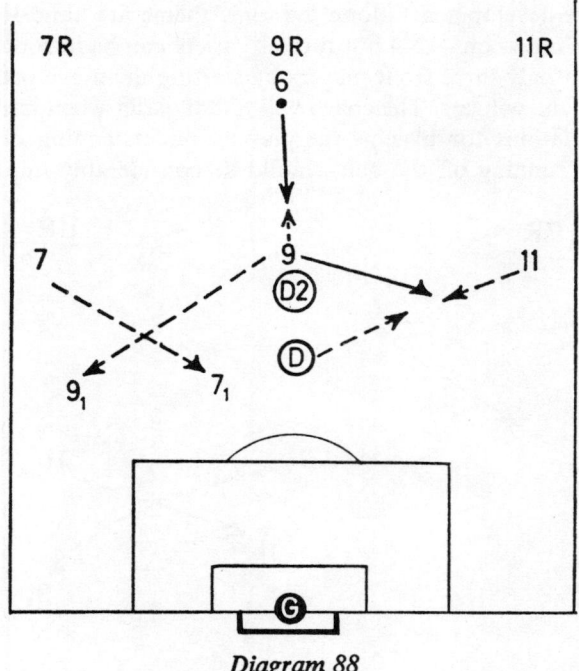

*Diagram 88*

free. Even greater freedom can be introduced later. After giving his pass to the wing, the right centre-forward can choose between:
1. Changing places with the winger he passed to.
2. Changing places with the other winger.

The right centre-forward may also make feints at this stage, in moving first towards one winger and then turning to sprint in the other direction. When defender D2 is free to react as he wishes the same freedom can be granted to defender D. It should be made clear, however, that the winger sprinting inside to pick up the pass from 9 should go in alone and shoot himself if the defenders pursue the other two players. Finally, the coach can add the last touch of realism by releasing defender D2 from his restrained challenging role when 9 drops back to pick up the turn pass from the midfield server (6). Now defender D2 can go forward to challenge for the pass from 6 to 9 and if he does so then 9 should play the ball back to 6 and make his run. From 6 the ball is put up to the free winger and

## Combinations for attack only

the attack develops according to the reactions of the defenders.

Further developments along the same theme are almost limitless in a team based on 4-2-4 but further variety can be introduced to a team with only three front players by starting the move with a pass to one of the wingers. The coach will find it easier when introducing these variations for by now the players' understanding of the expression 'running off the ball' should be considerably improved.

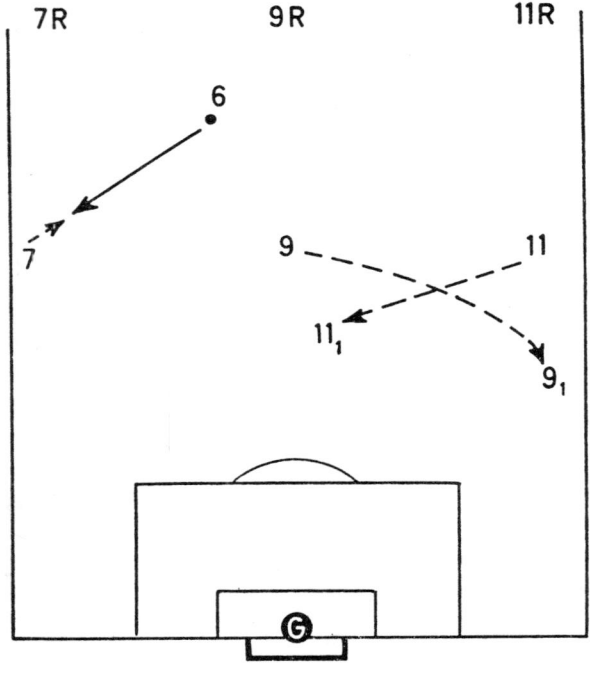

*Diagram 89 (a)*

In Diagram 89 (a) it is the right-winger who received a turn pass from midfield and as he *turns* his two colleagues off the ball make their *place-changing* runs. Turning on the ball, the right-winger hits an early pass first to the number 9 and then to the far winger running in, and in each case the recipient shoots at goal.

After a few rehearsals the coach can once more introduce an opponent who should at first be instructed to follow either 9 or the 'free' winger and to make his choice both early and definite for each

## Combinations for attack only

rehearsal. Soon the right-winger will be hitting his passes to the colleague best placed to get in a shot at goal and as further progress is made the coach can introduce a second defender to challenge the right-winger (Diagram 89 (b) ).

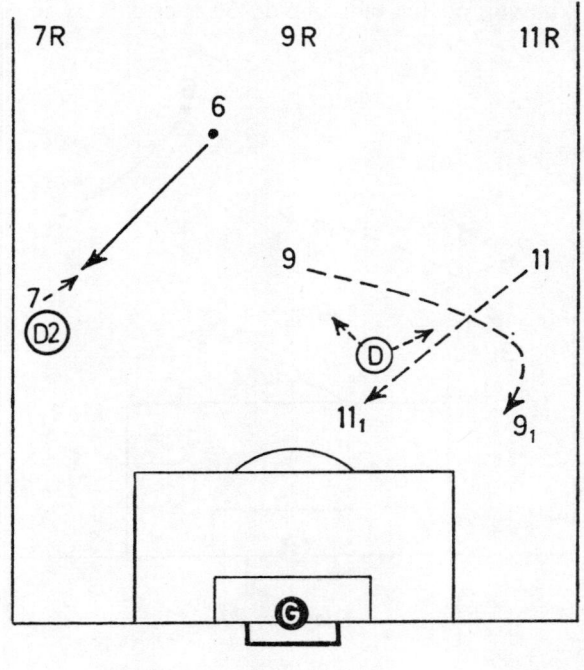

*Diagram 89 (b)*

Exactly the same practice can be developed commencing with a *turn* pass from midfield to the left-winger. This time it will be the right centre-forward (interchangeable throughout these practices with a left centre-forward if applicable) and step by step the practices become more and more realistic as defenders are introduced and the restrictions on their reactions are removed (Diagram 90).

To avoid wasting time two or preferably three waves of attack can take part in turn and when defenders are introduced they too can be replaced. After each wave of attack has come to an end with a shot

## *Combinations for attack only*

at goal all the participants, including the defenders, should immediately leave the playing area and make their way back to their starting positions along the sidelines.

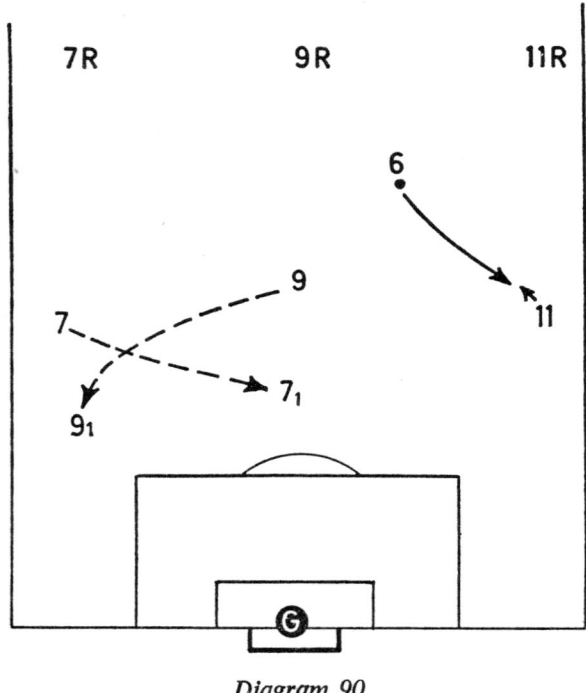

*Diagram 90*

# 13 — Place-changing in relation to the super-defence and the free-back

More and more people are thinking about football than ever before, but the more they think the worse the game becomes. This was the opinion of the former Hungarian centre-forward Nandor Hidegkuti in 1961. At that time Hidegkuti was the coach of Fiorentina and he was experiencing at first hand the problems posed by the deep defence and the free-back.

Since then the catenaccio-type defence has been exported across the world and in the 1967–68 season almost the whole of Continental Europe dedicated itself to the free-back. Not everyone gave in easily, but those who resisted the negative appeal of catenaccio soon learned the error of their ways. Between 1962 and 1966 everyone came to realize that to attack was to court disaster. Dominating a game for eighty-five minutes but losing 1–0 was a common experience in that period, particularly against the most successful Italian clubs. Finally, it was accepted that the way to score goals was to defend in strength and launch quick counter-attacks, for to attack in strength merely exposed one's own goal.

No other tactical development has ever been accepted so readily, and world opinion now seems to have hardened into the view that there is no other way to play. The Uruguayans, who played to the old attacking centre-half system as late as 1954 and reached the World Cup semi-final in that year, have gone over wholeheartedly to catenaccio. In less than twelve years they flirted briefly with WM and 4–2–4 and finally settled for the *libero* in time for the 1966 World Cup. Where once the Uruguayans attacked with eight men, they now defend with eight. Now, however, it is time the game moved on to something more positive but before doing so it would be advisable to take a long and coldly analytical look at catenaccio.

We can state without fear of contradiction that the key man in the catenaccio-type defence is the *libero* or free-back. Until his introduction, the responsibility for covering in defence was shared by the

## *Place-changing* versus *catenaccio*

defenders collectively, and inevitably the weaknesses in the old defensive system were easily exposed. Each defender had three primary duties:

1. To mark a particular opponent.
2. To cover his own defensive zone.
3. To give support when required to his colleagues.

In the catenaccio defence, the full-backs and centre-backs are relieved of their covering responsibilities. Withdrawing a player from midfield to play 'free' behind the defensive wall, we charge him to cover each of his colleagues in turn. The full-backs and centre-backs are now able to concentrate on their individual opponents, while the *libero* covers space. Against tighter marking and quicker tackling the front players are considerably less effective than they once were and wingers, for example, have been so discredited that they are on the point of becoming extinct. Though centre-forwards remain the primary goalscorers, it is rare that any central front player gets more than one goal in a game and against Italian defences the norm is closer to one goal in three games.

If we consider the theory of catenaccio more closely, we shall see that there are inherent weaknesses in the apparently impregnable defence. Disregarding the goalkeeper, we can say that there are three lines of defence in the modern system:

1st line—the midfield players.
2nd line—the close-marking full-backs and centre-back(s).
3rd line—the *libero*.

For the midfield players, the major role in defence is to challenge any opponent who attempts to carry the ball up to the second line of close-marking defenders. Should an opponent succeed in breaking through the midfield barrier, then either one of the backs must leave his immediate opponent or the *libero* has to come forward to challenge. The midfield defenders will prefer, therefore, to make an opponent pass, rather than risk an unsuccessful tackle.

Because their role is to challenge rather than to cover or close-mark the midfield defenders tend to concentrate in the area around the ball. Opponents who advance *off the ball*, are able to get within striking distance of the second line of defenders for the attention of the midfield players is centred on the area around the ball.

If we now study the situation which exists in Diagram 91 we shall see a defensive line-up similar to that presented by FC Internazionale in the period 1965–67. With the enemy right-midfield in possession,

## *Place-changing* versus *catenaccio*

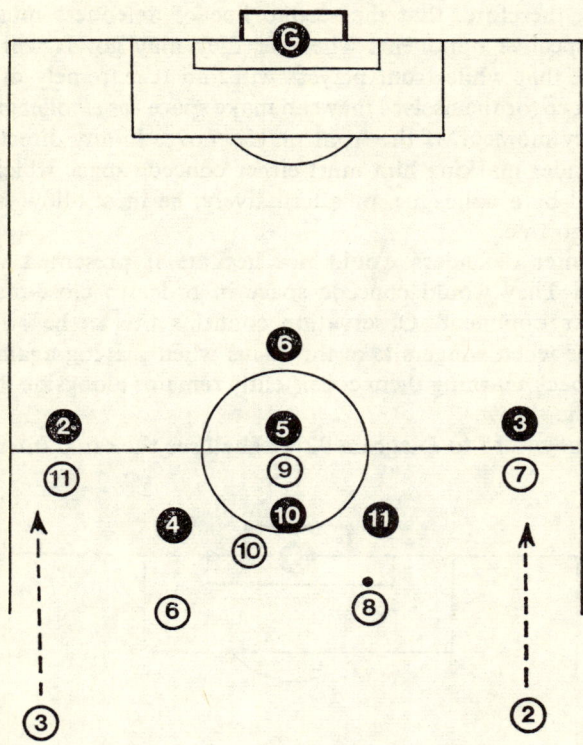

*Diagram 91*

the Inter midfield trio Bedin (4), Suarez (10) and Corso (11) are charged with preventing a break-in from midfield. Neither Suarez nor Corso was a particularly strong tackler, so generally they preferred challenge and interception. Because none of this trio was infallible they inevitably positioned in close support of each other. This being so it was inevitable that Inter conceded space on the flanks in midfield. At any moment, the opposition's full-backs could have advanced to a position very close to their front colleagues on the wings.

The second line of defenders are charged with close-marking a particular opponent in an attempt to prevent him getting even one touch of the ball. Whenever a front player receives a pass his opponent must be close enough to offer an immediate challenge. It is

## *Place-changing* versus *catenaccio*

obvious, therefore, that the second line of defenders must follow their respective opponents wherever they may go. It will now be apparent that while front players will find it extremely difficult to make space for themselves they can make space for a colleague at any and every moment. If the front player moves in any direction then the defender marking him must either concede space which can be exploited by a colleague, or alternatively, he must allow his opponent to go free.

The Inter defenders would not hesitate if presented with this problem. They would concede space in order to close-mark their particular opponent. Observation confirms this to be so, for on occasions when wingers take throw-ins when playing against Inter, the full-back marking them consistently remains alongside the player taking the throw.

If we now turn to Diagram 92 we shall see the same Inter defence

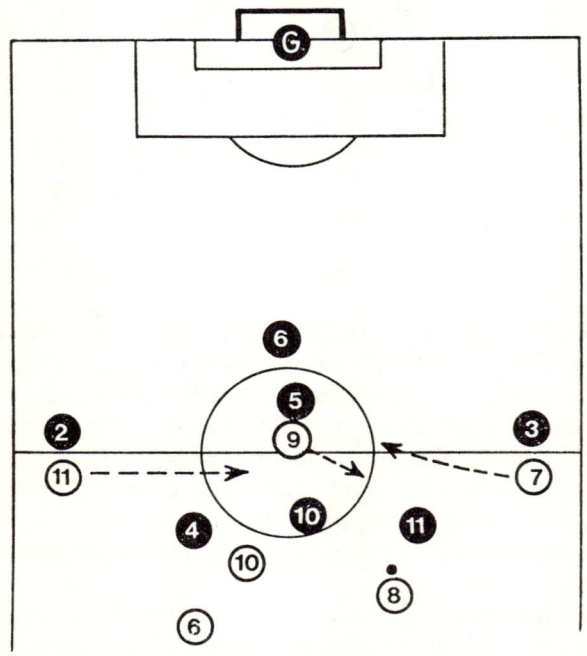

*Diagram 92*

## Place-changing versus *catenaccio*

taken as the standard catenaccio guide. Given the same situation as that taken from Diagram 91, imagine what would happen if the three front players 7, 9 and 11 were to move across the pitch, ostensibly looking for a pass from 8. The Inter defenders 2, 3 and 5 would assuredly have accompanied their respective opponents in order to be close enough to offer a first-time challenge should they receive a pass.

Now consider the position of the *libero*. When first introduced he was little more than an extra cover for the old centre-half who was quite frequently beaten by the top-class centre-forwards of the day. Once the system became more fully organized, the *libero*'s duties evolved to the point where he was asked to cover each of his defensive colleagues in turn, whenever they were drawn into a duel for the ball. Later still, when it became apparent that unmarked opponents could, and would, come from behind, it fell to the *libero* to watch for such a player and cover him. Observation of the former Inter *libero*, Armando Picchi, revealed that for some time before he was transferred to Varese, he could be seen constantly turning his head, looking from one side of the defence to the other. When an unmarked opponent did attempt to slip past the first and second lines in the Inter rearguard there was Picchi to challenge the interloper.

The *libero* can now be seen to have two primary roles:
1. To cover space behind the second line of defenders.
2. To pick up any unmarked opponent who comes from behind.

If we return for a moment to Diagram 92, we shall see that the right-winger (7), left-winger (11) and centre-forward (9) are all *showing themselves* for a pass. Which of the attacking trio would be in the most threatening position if he should receive a pass and slip past his close-marking opponent? Where should the *libero* position himself? With three opponents converging on the centre circle the *libero* would probably be best advised to take up a central position covering all three of his defensive colleagues, and he would probably move just a shade to his left.

The *libero* is now fulfilling the first of his primary duties in covering the space behind his colleagues who form the second line of defence. He is not, however, fulfilling his second task, which is to pick up any unmarked opponent who comes from behind.

If we combine Diagrams 91 and 92, and reproduce them as Diagram 93 we shall see the crux of the *libero*'s dilemma.

With the wingers (7 and 11) creating space on the flanks, and the

*Place-changing* versus *catenaccio*

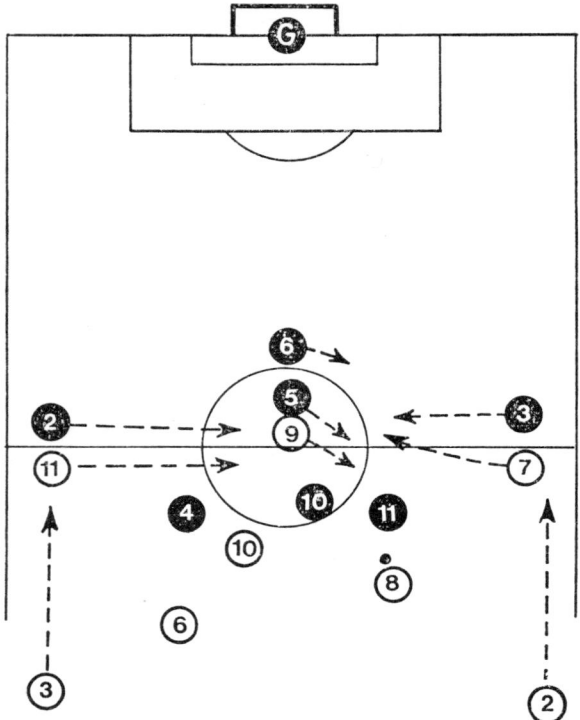

*Diagram 93*

enemy full-backs moving up fast as the space is created for them, the *libero* now has three duties to perform:

1. He must cover the central space behind his colleagues.
2. He must pick up the enemy right-back 2.
3. He must pick up the enemy left-back 3.

Clearly the *libero* is placed in an impossible situation. The best hope here for the defending side, will be that one of the midfield players will be able to dispossess the right-midfield. If all else fails the *libero* will want to retreat, but what if the player in possession should hit a cross-field pass to the left wing, dropping the ball nicely ahead of the left-back as he sprints into space?

This is the move made in Diagram 94 (a) and to counter this attack the *libero* would obviously move across to challenge the enemy left-

## Place-changing versus *catenaccio*

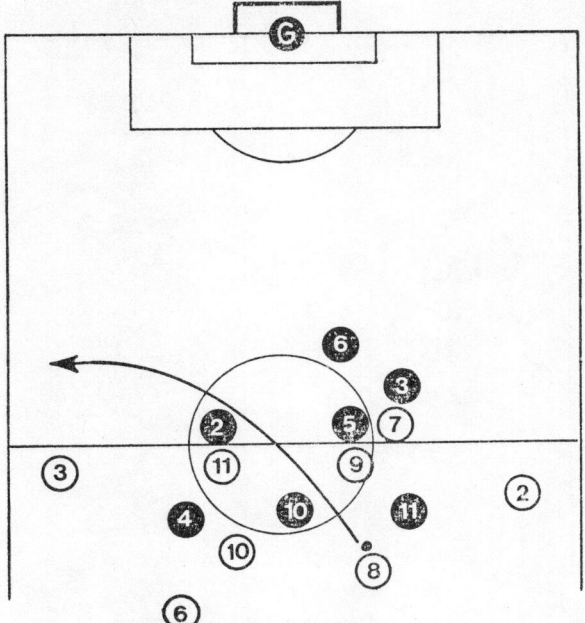

*Diagram 94 (a)*

back, before he moved in on goal. While the left-back advanced with the ball and the *libero* attempted to intercept him the attacking trio 7, 9 and 11 would all be speeding away to goal looking for the conventional centre and if each of the close-marking defenders does his job properly the situation may yet be saved. Meanwhile the attacking team's midfield players would advance in supporting positions while the midfield defenders would attempt to get back to their penalty area.

For the attacking team, this situation is full of possibilities. For example (Diagram 94 (b) ), the right-winger (7) could have run to meet his colleague on the ball. Clearly his close-marking opponent (3) would be not more than a yard behind but he might be able to take a pass from his left-back colleague and play it on, into space. From there the left-back could go in towards goal and (a) shoot himself or (b) play the ball across goal to either 9 or 11 ... each going 'late' into space. The left-back might even have ignored his right-winger (7) and hit a first-time cross-field pass to his colleague at right-back!

*Place-changing* versus *catenaccio*

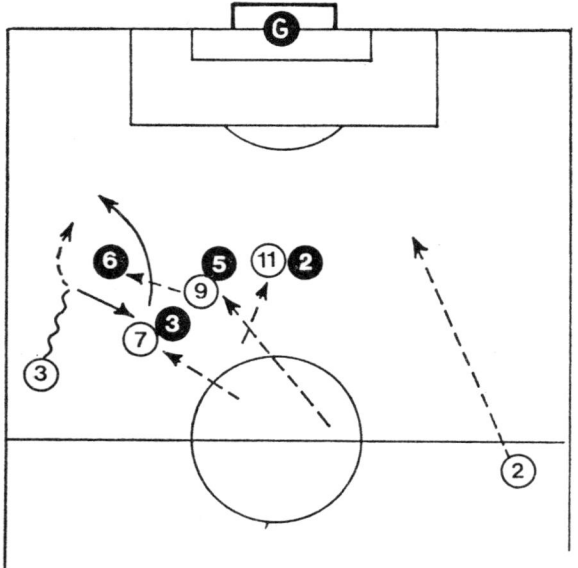

*Diagram 94 (b)*

If we return to Diagram 93 for a moment, we shall see an even better move for if the player in possession had played the ball out to his colleague at right-back, the *libero* would surely have been forced to commit himself to the unmarked man coming from behind in possession. Had the right-midfield followed the ball to change places with his colleage 2 (overlapping him) then the *libero* would have been immediately faced with a very unpleasant two against one. This is the situation in Diagram 95 (a) but as the *libero* begins to move across and challenge the right-back, the best move would be a cross-field pass from 2 to 3 (Diagram 95 (b) ), and with any luck at all, the left-back would be in for a shot at goal.

It must now be stated quite clearly that it is not expected that any team will ever be able to produce combined movements precisely as they have been developed here on paper.

However, it can be stated quite definitely that this is the type of football which will come from skilled and intelligent players after they have been coached in place-changing combinations aimed

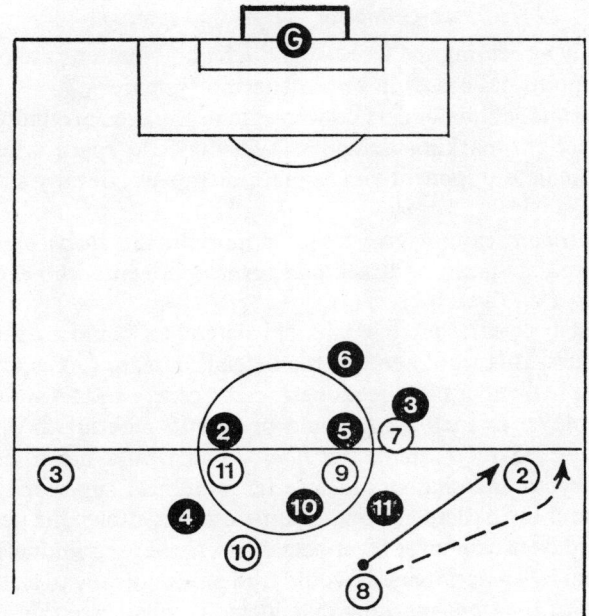

*Diagram 95 (a)*

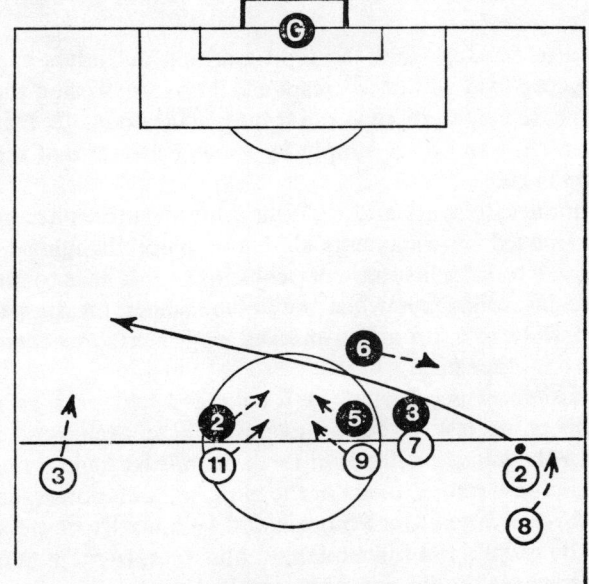

*Diagram 95 (b)*

## *Place-changing* versus *catenaccio*

specifically at beating the free-back. Such combinations are aimed at fundamental weaknesses in the catenaccio system:
1. The midfield defenders concentrate in the area around the ball.
2. The tight-marking defenders will concede space when their immediate opponent runs square or moves laterally across the pitch.
3. The *libero* cannot give close support in the space behind the immediate point of attack *and* cover opponents who *come from behind* on the flanks.

It must be clear that the midfield defenders could in theory be given zones. This would enable the defending team to keep an extra man loose in front of the three zones—right, centre and left-midfield—and the player in each zone would be free to pick up an opponent who attempted to outflank the *libero*. This would mean, however, that the defending side would lose its numerical superiority in the area around the ball and in one-against-one situations, the defending midfield players can never be unbeatable. Whenever a midfield player was beaten by an opponent, it would lead automatically to a challenge from one of the tight-marking defenders. To challenge the player in possession would now mean letting one of the front men go free, and for this reason the midfield players cannot be restricted to zones.

It will also be clear that the tight-marking defenders cannot be asked to accept the additional responsibility for covering their particular zone. If they were, then the front players could get free whenever they wished to do so, simply by leaving the zone of their particular opponent.

If the midfield players and tight-marking defenders are going to be sorely pressed by opponents skilled at place-changing then the *libero* is going to have his share of problems too. If he is to give close support to his colleagues when they come under pressure then he cannot possibly pick up an un-marked opponent who *comes from behind* on the other flank.

Combinations which include a long cross-field pass as a basic feature will be no less successful against a catenaccio-type defence than they will against a defence of three or four backs in a line.

We should now return to one of the basic combinations specifically designed for the wings. Once more it will help clarify matters in the minds of the players if a full explanation is given to them before the practice begins. It should not, however, be lengthy. Explain, briefly,

## *Place-changing* versus *catenaccio*

what is involved and then set-up the situation described in Diagram 96 (a).

With the left-back in possession, the aim is that stated earlier: to go forward quickly, before the opposition can re-group their defences. The fact that the enemy now includes a free-back (6) makes no

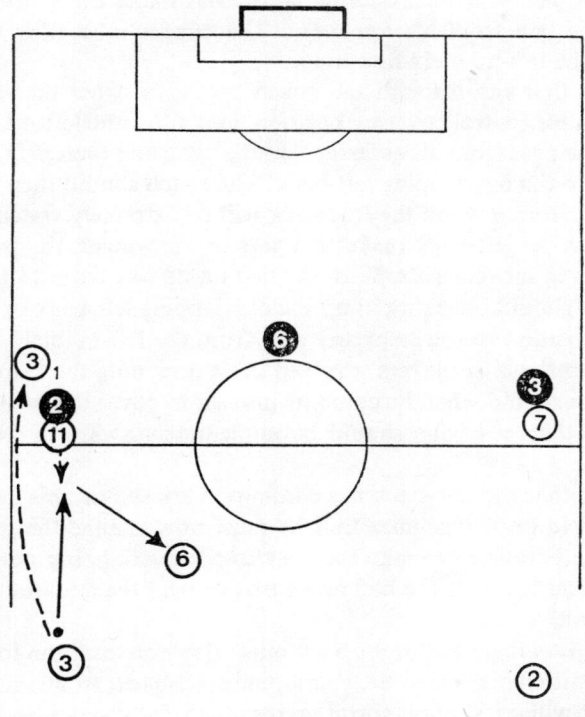

*Diagram 96 (a)*

difference in this respect. To play the ball to his colleague at left-midfield would represent no real advantage and the left-back should be instructed to play the ball quickly to the feet of his colleague on the left wing and having made his pass he must immediately run to change places with the winger.

With a free-back as an integral part of the enemy defence, the right-back who provides opposition in this practice would always come forward to challenge. It is the free-back's responsibility to cover

## *Place-changing* versus *catenaccio*

space and the right-back must concentrate on his individual opponent. At first, however, the coach would probably be best advised to restrain the right-back if he should be too successful in his duels with the left-winger.

The pass from left-back to outside-left will always be a man-on pass in this practice, and the winger must be urged to drop back towards the ball with real determination and make every attempt to screen the ball from his opponent. The winger must play the ball back to the left-midfield first-time.

In this first run-through the coach should instruct the *libero* to remain in his central covering position, and allow the left-midfield to receive the pass from his colleague on the wing and then play the ball forward to the overlapping left-back. The coach should then make it clear that from now on the free-back will be extremely watchful and as soon as the left-back makes his pass to the winger, the free-back will begin to move across. With the ball on its way from 11 to 6, the free-back should have picked up the overlapping left-back or at least be in a position to intercept any pass from the left-midfield.

All the attacking players involved must now note the response of the free-back and when he commits himself to cover the overlapping left-back then everyone should be immediately aware of what will follow.

Noting that the free-back has committed himself on this flank, the left-midfield must recognize that he must now change the direction of attack. Feinting to make the pass to the overlapping player, the left-midfield controls the ball and turns to read the situation on the other flank.

The right-winger and right-back must also note that the free-back has committed himself to the overlapping left-back. In this situation, the right-winger should sprint across-field into space, where he threatens to receive a pass from the left-midfield and simultaneously, the right-back sprints forward to become the effective right-winger.

The defending left-back now has a choice:
1. He can follow his personal opponent.
2. He can remain in position and cover the space on the left flank.

The defending left-back should now be instructed by the coach to follow his personal opponent into space and with the right-back sprinting forward, the left-midfield will hit a cross-field pass to him as in Diagram 96 (b).

It should be noted that in this situation where an opponent is

## *Place-changing* versus *catenaccio*

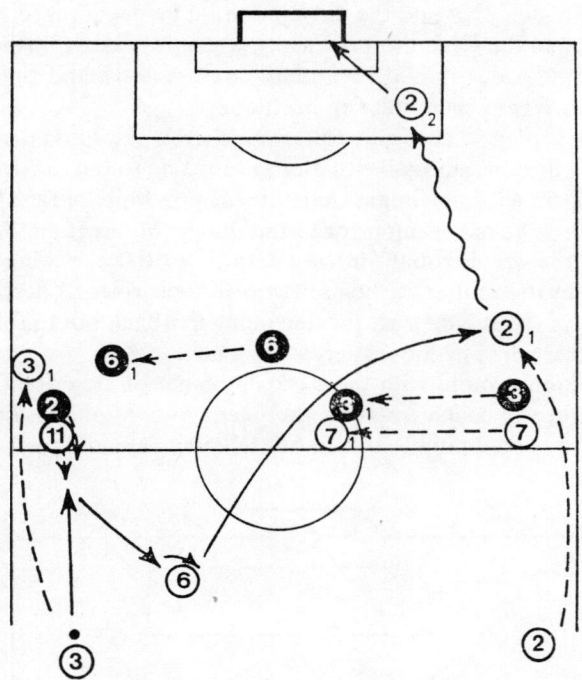

*Diagram 96 (b)*

positioned between the player making a pass and the player receiving the ball, the pass should be given plenty of height. Ground passes certainly look prettier, but they are also more easily intercepted.

Over and over again the coach should drill the players in this same move. The coach could also have a discreet word with the free-back and ask him to remain in the centre for the ninth or tenth rehearsal. When the free-back does not commit himself to the overlapping left-back, then the left-midfield should note this and aim his pass to the overlapping player.

Later the coach can re-create this situation, but for the moment he should content himself with the major objective which is to change the direction of attack when the free-back commits himself.

It should also be noted that every attack should be pressed to a shot at goal. Even if something goes wrong with the pass from 6 to 2 it should not be impossible to improvise. Things will inevitably go

## *Place-changing* versus *catenaccio*

wrong in match play and the players should be encouraged to adapt themselves to the circumstances. Only when possession of the ball is won by a defender should the attack be broken off and the players allowed to regain their starting positions.

In match play it does not follow that even the most disciplined defences will respond to all situations according to their instructions. An intelligent left-back might well note the proximity of the attacking right-back as he moves up prior to the change of direction. With this in mind, the coach should intervene once all the attacking players have begun to familiarize themselves with their roles as described in Diagram 96 (b) and instruct the defending left-back not to follow the right-winger when he moves across the pitch.

Starting once more with the basic combination described in Diagram 96 (a) the coach instructs the *libero* to continue 'selling himself' to the overlapping left-back but tells the defending left-back to

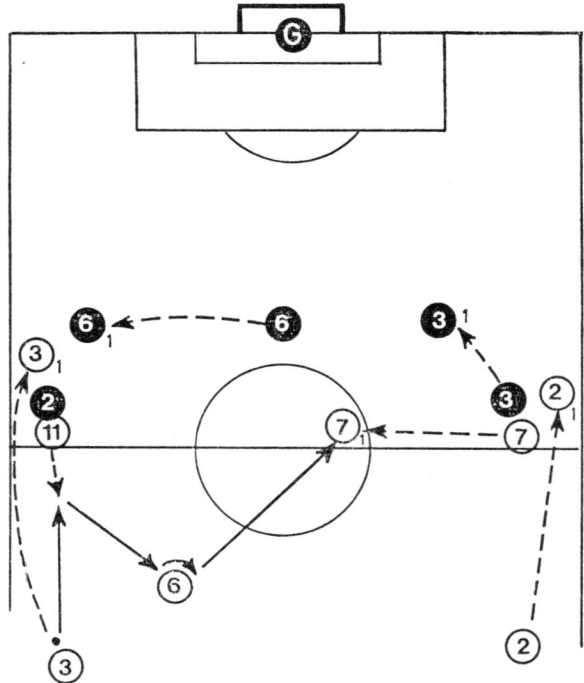

*Diagram 96 (c)*

## *Place-changing* versus *catenaccio*

withdraw to a position from which he can watch both the right-winger and the attacking right-back.

In Diagram 96 (c), the left-back and left-winger have executed their man-on pass and changed places. The free-back has committed himself to the overlapping left-back, but acting on the instructions of the coach, the defending left-back has withdrawn. This time the left-midfield turns on the ball to change the direction of attack, but noting the response of the left-back he now plays a turn-ball up to his colleague 7, who has run inside. The right-winger turns, and veering slightly to the right he moves towards goal with the ball under control. The coach should now instruct the defending left-back to stand off. Facing two opponents in match play, only the most foolhardy defender would rush into a tackle and this would open the way for a simple pass from 7 to 2, who is now overlapping his winger once more.

For the sake of simplicity the next phase of this attack is continued in Diagram 96 (d).

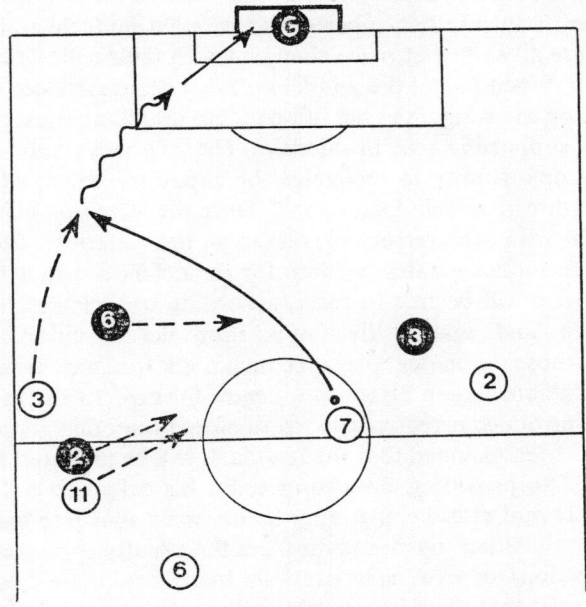

*Diagram 96 (d)*

## *Place-changing* versus *catenaccio*

With the ball on its way from 6 to 7, the free-back will be sprinting to re-position himself to face this new threat. At the same time, the left-winger will make his run infield, looking for a pass from his colleague 7, and the defending left-back should be instructed to follow his opponent. The way is now clear for a cross-field pass from 7 to 3 as described in Diagram 96 (d). From there, the attacking left-back may well be able to reach the penalty area and shoot himself but at all events he should be able to commit the free-back to him once more, and at least offer a shooting position to a colleague.

Precisely the same practices should also be set up including the right-midfield and this time the move should begin with a man-on pass from the right-back up to his colleague on the right wing. It will now be the overlapping right-back to whom the free-back is committed in the first phase, and the right-midfield who will initiate the change of direction.

Before leaving this particular combination, the coach would be well advised to reorganize the overlapping combination which begins the practices outlined in Diagrams 96 (a), (b), (c) and (d). It will not always be the right- or left-midfield who receives the ball back from the winger. It must be remembered that the right-midfield and centre-midfield are all skilled at place-changing with their colleague on the right wing. When one of the midfield players changes places with his colleague on the wing, then the full-back on that flank must advance to play a supporting role in midfield. The full-backs must also be given the opportunity to recognize the situations which call for a change of direction as in Diagram 97. Once the attacking players are all familiar with their respective roles in all the variations, the coach can then introduce greater freedom for the defenders. In each case, the defenders will be free to react, according to their instincts and intelligence, and against 'live' opposition the conditions closely resemble those of match play. To make the practice even more realistic, the coach can also add a centre-forward to the attacking side and introduce a centre-back to reinforce the opposition. Until now it has been assumed that the free-back will be prepared to commit himself to providing close support for his defensive colleagues, but in Italy and elsewhere, it may be observed that free-backs are frequently unwilling to operate far from the penalty spot. Acting on the instructions of extremely cautious managers, these free-backs have accepted that there is not necessarily a direct relationship with the play in midfield and the serious matter of scoring goals. There is

## *Place-changing* versus *catenaccio*

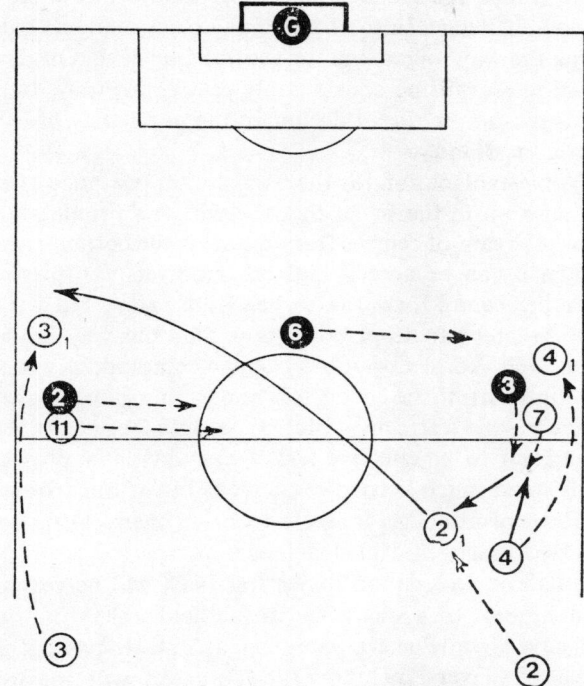

*Diagram 97*

a strong school of thought which insists that the place for a free-back is on the penalty spot and observation confirms that it is not uncommon for free-backs to decline the opportunity to intervene in midfield. Only when failure to intervene would immediately lead to a shot at goal is the free-back allowed to commit himself. Otherwise, the free-back must keep himself firmly entrenched behind the defence where he will be able to challenge anyone who attempts to break-through the line of defenders and reach a shooting position.

It must also be understood that against a team which plays to a 4–2–4 pattern, the catenaccio-type defence would be particularly strong in the central regions. Here one will normally find two centre-backs (each marking one of the centre-forwards) and the free-back or *libero*. In these conditions it becomes increasingly difficult to make progress in the central area for in addition to the three centre-

## *Place-changing* versus *catenaccio*

backs there is also the midfield screen or players whose job it is to offer the first challenge. In total there may be as many as five defenders barring the way to goal via the central approach. On the flanks, however, progress will be considerably easier, not easy, but easier, and for this reason the recent decline in the popularity of wingers is difficult to understand.

One possible explanation for the partial disappearance of wingers, may be bound up in the belief that the winger's primary role is to send across a stream of centres from out near the corner flags. If this were so then it can be agreed that other players can provide high crosses for the centre-forwards to head into goal, but the winger has a much greater part to play in attack than this very limited role.

Since the 1966 World Cup it has become commonplace to see fullbacks moving deep into the enemy half and having gained possession it is the custom to send a stream of high passes into the penalty area. This may well appear to be effective and it can obviously provide spectators with some much-needed excitement but it must be accepted that this form of attack is unlikely to bring many goals against a well-organized and well-drilled defence.

It must also be understood that a free-back will be very unlikely to commit himself to a challenge in midfield unless his defensive colleagues have already been circumnavigated. Inter-passing amongst enemy midfield players, including the full-backs, will not disconcert an experienced free-back in any way for he has learned that the commonest form of attack is to inter-pass in the comparatively open midfield regions until a position is reached from which a high cross can be placed into the penalty area. Knowing that this will be the final pass, the *libero* will certainly be wise to remain behind the line of defenders. What will disconcert the free-back is an attempt by any opponent to *come from behind* for one of the prime reasons for the existence of the free-back is that he should provide an extra man in defence. An opponent who breaks past the line of defenders immediately disturbs this balance in favour of the defence, and if the extra player is committed on one of the flanks then either he draws the free-back to him, or he is left free to exploit a temporary numerical advantage on the wing.

This being so, it follows that *place-changing combinations* will still be of great value against catenaccio, even without the change of direction. If the final pass is still to be a high cross delivered into the penalty area, it must be clear that even this primitive form of attack

## Place-changing versus *catenaccio*

will have a better chance of success if the free-back has first been drawn away from the centre.

If the free-back will commit himself when an extra opponent comes from behind on the wing, then the combinations described in Diagrams 91 to 97 will be of real value. If the free-back will not leave his customary beat behind the centre-backs then the more simple wing combinations will enable progress to be made on the flanks without intervention from the *libero*.

If the *libero* should be tempted to intervene in midfield he will soon be persuaded to remain in position behind his colleagues, if a well-executed change of direction leaves him standing. Once convinced that he is gaining nothing by challenging he will prefer to withdraw towards the penalty area.

Whatever the circumstances, and whatever tactics are adopted by the opposition generally, progress will always be easier along the flanks than it is through the centre. Coming from behind along the wings will enable progress to be made, and in all flank attacks against a catenaccio-type defence the position most sought after should be that described in Diagram 98. Whether it is the right-winger, right-back, right-midfield or indeed the left-winger is not of real importance. The aim must be to put someone 'IN' in possession, in the area around 7 in the diagram. The closer to goal that the 'winger' can get, the better, for as he approaches the near post the danger of a direct shot from him becomes greater. In the face of this threat the free-back will finally be forced to commit himself and the goalkeeper will also be drawn across his goal to cover the shot to the near post. From any range within reason, and from any angle, the most advantageous move will be to 'pull' the ball back from the wing for a colleague to shoot from the edge of the penalty area.

Looking for the pull can be rewarding for almost the entire team but it should be clear that this does not generally apply to tightly-marked front players. Anyone else, coming from behind, can seek a shooting position on the edge of the penalty area. Two obvious nominations here will be the attacking right-back and the right-midfield, though all three midfield players and both full-backs should be encouraged to look for the pull. Shooting first-time, following a pass pulled back from close to the bye-line, affords particular advantages. To begin with, the goalkeeper must now re-position himself quickly after going to cover the shot to the near post and he may fail to orientate himself in time. In addition the player receives a con-

*Place-changing* versus *catenaccio*

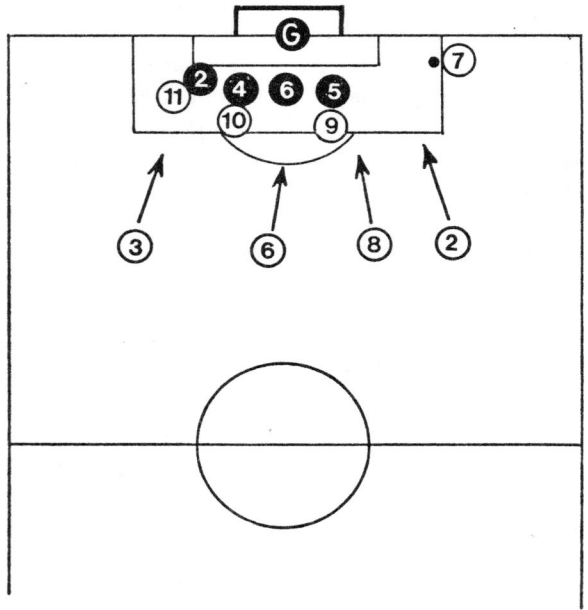

*Diagram 98*

siderable advantage from the fact that the area between the goalkeeper and the shooting position is relatively crowded. Each player inside the penalty area helps to 'unsight' the goalkeeper and this is just as true for the cleverly-flighted chip or lob, as it is for the full-blooded drive.

Pulling the ball back from the bye-line will clearly be an advantage but while midfield players and full-backs who manage to get themselves 'in' on the flanks will develop this habit quite quickly, it must be expected that natural wingers will not find it so easy. As already explained, this is due to the naturally acquired habits of players accustomed to playing 'for themselves'.

Full-backs, and to a lesser extent the creative midfield players, will not face this conflict between habit and the demands of the modern game, for they will rarely have been encouraged to put themselves into this type of position. Instructed to 'pull' their passes back away from goal, they will do so readily.

Wingers, however, are quite accustomed to approaching goal

## *Place-changing* versus *catenaccio*

from an oblique angle and observation shows that a very high proportion of wingers exploit this situation by shooting towards the near post. Those with a more advanced sense of team play can easily be picked out for they will invariably attempt to give a scoring chance to one of their colleagues in the goal-mouth.

Pulling the ball back away from goal will be clearly advantageous and seen to be so, from a seat in the stand or on the trainer's bench. To the winger on the spot, however, it will appear to be a retrograde step and one which will not naturally enter the winger's mind.

If natural wingers experience unusual difficulty, if for example it is noted that in match play a winger rarely, or never, pulls the ball back, then the coach should withdraw any options that may have been granted earlier. In training, the coach should insist that the winger 'must' always pull the ball back and gradually remove this condition only when this particular player is seen to be *pulling* the ball back in match play.

# 14 — The ideal team shape

The shape of a team is determined by joining up all the playing positions with a single unbroken line. For example it was the shape of the old 3-2-5 team which gave the WM system its name. Not all team formations have such an easily remembered shape, however, and it is for this reason that the various playing formations are now referred to by numbers rather than shapes.

To discern the shape of any team it is necessary to forget about the ball. Indeed it can truthfully be said that to 'see' anything in a fluid game like football, basketball or rugby, it is vitally important to tear one's eyes away from the star player with the ball. Only one player can have the ball at any given moment and following the ball, the vast majority of spectators cannot possibly see the game. Ball-watchers will never notice the vitally important parts being played by the remaining twenty-one players who do not have the ball. They will never notice how the great players change their minds about where to drop their pass when an opponent moves to cover the danger; they will never see an equally good player making a decoy-run to create space, and they will never recognize team shape.

The shape of any team is relatively unimportant except in the realm of tactics but this is a field which has nothing to do with players. Tactics are the sole concern of the manager, coach or trainer, whose job it is to choose the eleven players for any one match.

Having decided on the players, many contemporary coaches then decide on the tactics and the team shape. Indeed, it is said to be a grave error to try and make the players suit the tactical requirements.

While it is true that reference must be made to the abilities and intelligence of the available players and it is conceded that the tactical requirements of the team must be considered, there remain several fundamental factors which must be taken into account at all times.

First we can all agree that we must have a goalkeeper. In fact, the laws of the game demand that one player must be the goalkeeper,

## The ideal team shape

but from this point on, the possible permutations are enormous. The choice regarding team shape is now so wide, varying from 4-2-4 to 4-4-2 and 1-4-3-2 that very few personalities within the game will ever reach agreement on an ideal formation. To ignore several fundamental features as many do, is to make a serious error however.

## FUNDAMENTAL CONSIDERATIONS IN DEFENCE

In defence the first point to consider is that each of the enemy front players must be marked by a defender, but the term man-for-man marking is in fact relative. Loose man-for-man cover can be just as effective as the tightest marking, which seeks to deny an opponent even one touch of the ball. To what extent the defenders can devote themselves to their individual opponents depends entirely on the covering system adopted.

If the responsibility for covering in defence is shared equally, then the marking on individual opponents must be relatively loose. Only with the introduction of a free-back can defenders be left to fight private battles with their individual opponents. It should be borne in mind, however, that even the most reliable *libero* is not infallible.

The major covering problem in defence is the delegation of responsibility in the central zone and the most economical solution will be to nominate two centre-backs. This is the basis of the defensive aspects of 4-2-4 and 4-3-3. The key here is the degree of understanding developed by the centre-backs, for when one of the centre-backs is drawn into a duel for the ball (on the ground or in the air) then it is vitally important that his partner drops back to cover space.

Against an opponent who fields two centre-forwards this degree of understanding will be severely tested if each of the centre-forwards is intelligent and moves around in a bid to create space, i.e. the centre-forward tries to draw his opponent away from the central zone.

Observation of the defence under pressure will reveal whether the degree of cover reaches an acceptable level, but if it does not then the only answer will be to delegate one player to cover space. In a 4-2-4 or 4-3-3 defence playing against a team with only one centre-forward this will not be a problem. One of the centre-backs can be given the job of watching over the centre-forward while his partner covers space.

Neither will this be a problem for a team with four in the back

## The ideal team shape

line if the opposition fields two centre-forwards but only one winger as in 4–3–3 or 1–3–3–3 and many other combinations. Here the coach will have a completely free choice and he can re-deploy the full-back who has no winger to oppose him. If the covering of the centre-backs is considered to be adequate then the extra back can be used:

1. To reinforce the midfield players.
2. To act as a defensive screen in front of the defence.

If the covering of the centre-backs is considered to be inadequate then the extra back may be used (a) to provide cover by positioning himself 'free' behind the defensive line, or (b) to mark one of the enemy centre-forwards. In this last instance, cover could then be provided by one of the centre-backs.

There is one real alternative to all the established defensive systems, borrowed from the Swiss 'bolt'. In possession of the ball, the attacking team will be wasting a player if he is left free behind his defensive colleagues. Once possession is gained then the free-back could relieve one of the centre-backs who would thus be able to play at least a supporting role in midfield. When the attacking team lost possession then the centre-back would sprint back to pick up his personal opponent and relieve the free-back.

This would demand all-round ability from the centre-back and also make greater demands on his stamina, but it should not prove impossible in a team with a high individual work-rate.

Overall, however, it is clear that two centre-backs should be able to develop an understanding which will enable them to do an adequate job and except under very special circumstances the introduction of a free-back should not be necessary.

## FUNDAMENTAL CONSIDERATIONS IN MIDFIELD

The link between defence and attack has always been vital and never more so than in the modern game. The major consideration here must be the adequacy of the midfield pair (in 4–2–4) as far as their defensive responsibilities are concerned, and the desirability of having as many players as possible with the opportunity to *come from behind*. Although the full-backs can now take an integral part in developing and pressing attacks, it will be the midfield players who will have to accept the greater part of the physical burden involved.

## The ideal team shape

Screening their defensive colleagues when possession of the ball is lost; sprinting out in support of their attacking colleagues when the defenders regain possession and exploiting space within the enemy defence will make too great a demand on two midfield players.

It must also be considered that when one midfield player goes forward in a place-changing combination, this will leave only one support player in midfield. With three midfield players the physical burdens are shared over a broader base and when one midfield player sprints forward in a bid to exploit space he leaves at least two colleagues behind as alternatives should a front player receive a man-on pass.

Finally, and this is perhaps the most important consideration, a player with a very strong shot will probably find more opportunities to exploit his talent *coming from behind* than he would if he were to be permanently positioned up front. As a front player, the potential scorer will attract the personal attention of a defender, but coming from midfield he will be much less easy to mark. Except in very special circumstances the advantages of fielding three midfield players far outweigh the arguments in favour of 4–2–4.

## FUNDAMENTAL CONSIDERATIONS IN ATTACK

With three midfield players stated to be a priority and four players at the back an absolute necessity, this leaves only three players to remain permanently positioned up front. This seems to indicate that advocates of 4–3–3 and 1–3–3–3 have already presented the ideal formation.

However, the vast majority of teams which play with three men up do not include two wingers and this feature can be considered no less important than four at the back and three in midfield.

One of the biggest advantages which accrue to teams which include wingers is the fact that by his mere presence the winger pulls at least one defender out to the flank. With two wingers the advantage gained is more than doubled, for now there must be at least two defenders positioned very wide apart and therefore less able to play a full role in covering. This is only the beginning, however, for in addition the winger is able to create space on the flank. The opportunity to create space is granted to all tightly-marked front players, but to appreciate the special advantages of wingers, consider the position of teams which base their 4–3–3 system on three centre-forwards. To a lesser

## The ideal team shape

extent, this same disadvantage will apply to 4–3–3 teams which include one winger.

With three centre-forwards positioned up front, the defenders marking them are kept in close contact with each other and are nicely placed to give cover to each other as and when the need arises.

In addition, space is now at a premium in the central zone, while space constantly exists on the wings. Any attempt to exploit the spaces on the flanks takes the front players away from goal and by moving out to the wings they will invariably be escorted by their tight-marking opponent. Thus they will be instrumental in closing the space on the wing if they wander very far, yet handicapped by lack of space if they remain in the central region.

By spreading the three front players across the field, we immediately force the enemy to spread his defensive resources. No longer are the defenders close enough to support each other should the need arise.

With wingers positioned on the flanks the attacking team is able to create space on the wings at any moment of its choice. Space can still be created in the centre too and space there will now be of even greater importance because the other defenders are less able to cover.

In the moment of breaking out from defence to attack, the team with two wingers has a tremendous advantage over a team with only one. Winning possession of the ball, the initiative changes hands and in the moment of gaining possession speed is vital. The ball must be pushed forward quickly if the enemy midfield players are to be denied the opportunity to get back and reinforce their defensive colleagues in time.

Forced to play the ball forward quickly, the team without wingers has no option but to launch all their attacks on the central zone, which is always the most heavily defended. With two wingers up front, the task of the defenders is more than doubled for until the pass is made to a front player, they cannot know from which point the attack will come. The defenders must keep their defences well spread out across the entire width of the pitch.

In the light of all the above considerations it would appear that 4–3–3 is the ideal framework for the modern game and the inclusion of two wingers is essential. Given the overall shape of 4–3–3 with two wingers the key-note should be flexibility. With 4–2–4 the players remained positioned in accordance with the team shape, but in the new game which is evolving the emphasis is on running off the ball

## The ideal team shape

and constant effort. With greater flexibility, the team will have a constantly changing shape, first contracting and then suddenly expanding in all directions at once. There remains one more important feature which must be emphasized. More and more the modern game is demanding all-round ability from each player and it will be of no particular advantage to insist that defensive players take part in attack if they lack the ability to exploit the opportunities earned by the hard running of their colleagues.

It is becoming increasingly clear that with the exception of the two centre-backs and the goalkeeper, the needs of the game will demand a higher degree of skill from everyone.

Full-backs must now be able to demonstrate the talents demanded from wingers in the WM game, while the midfield players will need to become even more complete players.

Finally we shall reach the point where individual standards will be so high that at the professional level the specialists will disappear. Instead of backs, midfield players and front men, we shall have only multi-purpose players able to fulfil any role in the team game.

## 15 — The theory of modern coaching, which must be related to the demands of the game and the importance of the correct psychological approach

Surveying the present state of football, it can be seen that defences are generally in command and this domination will continue until the game as a whole adjusts itself to modern conditions. The prime factor in these new conditions is tighter marking, for this leads inevitably to quicker tackling and a reduction in what we may call the 'reaction-time' available to players receiving the ball.

Forty years ago, it was possible for a player to wait for the ball to come to him, when a colleague made a pass. Receiving the ball, the player of 1920 would control the ball, look up, and decide what to do next. Then, on the basis of what he had seen, the player would either pass, shoot, or move forward with the ball. Observation of the contemporary game indicates that many players still adopt this basic approach which can be summed up thus: control, look, pass.

This approach may still be of value in midfield, if the primary objective is to retain possession, for in this area the defenders do concede time and space. Even in midfield, however, there is one major disadvantage acting against players who adopt this leisurely approach to the game: time is in favour of the defenders. Every second during which a direct assault on goal is delayed enables the defenders to regroup and to receive reinforcements from midfield.

If the 'control, look, pass' sequence wastes too much time in midfield, it is fatal closer to goal, and it is now quite clear that the players must know what they are going to do before they receive the ball. Tightly-marked front players who do not know what they will do in advance, are tackled so quickly that they are not allowed to play. To be effective, the front players must 'look, move and play the ball whilst on the move'.

Because the time factor favours the defenders, the 'control, look,

## The theory of modern coaching

pass' sequence is no less out-dated for midfield and defence players. Running with the ball and giving square passes across the pitch wastes time. The ball must go forward quickly, and in the instant that possession of the ball is won, the entire team must switch from defence to attack.

If the players are going to be able to play at this speed they must be prepared for it in training and because there is no time to look and think in possession, the players must be drilled to do their looking and thinking 'off the ball'.

In the highest class, it can already be seen that the most effective moves are those carried out at top speed, i.e. based on first-time passing. It must be clear that if three or four players can participate in an attack based on four first-time passes then it follows that the players must have:

1. An awareness of the players around them (friend and foe).
2. The skill to play the ball first-time with accuracy.
3. The ability not only to read a situation but anticipate it.
4. A highly developed sense of team-play.

Under the supervision of a good coach, combinations will force the players to do all the things described above. If the player receiving the ball must decide for himself whether to *turn* or not, then he must be aware of the players around him. Similarly, the player giving the pass must become aware of other players if he has to advise his colleague man-on or turn.

Giving passes early, is one of the fundamentals in all the combinations and as this habit is acquired the players also improve their skill in this respect. Finally, with explanation and advice from the coach, the players are forced to anticipate the next move in each different combination and in time this leads to an understanding of the responsibilities of the individual player to his colleagues. In this respect the vital point in training is reached when the coach introduces maximum freedom into the various practices. Having learned each combination 'by heart' the individual players must now decide which variation is most suitable in each situation and these decisions must be made in conditions which closely resemble match play. It should be anticipated that at first, the combinations produced during matches will be in a stereotyped form. This will be particularly noticeable if the players are introduced to only one combination at a time. Later, when more combinations have been added to the players' repertoire, it will be seen that variations are introduced around the basic themes.

## *The theory of modern coaching*

At this point it will be clear that the players, as individuals, are looking, thinking and moving off the ball.

Coaching has always aimed to prepare the players for competitive play and following new conditions in match play, it will be clear that the basic approach of coaching must be adapted. Ten years ago, the aim of the coach was very largely to improve the players in terms of technique, but it is now clear that technique alone is not enough. More than ever before, the game demands a high level of intelligence and understanding and it is in this field that coaching must make its greatest contribution. While improving the technique of his players, the coach must also seek to develop an understanding of how technique can be used.

Through combinations the players will develop new habits. They will begin to give the ball early and turn when they have time. They will begin to look for colleagues running into space, and they will move off themselves (into space) after playing the ball. The players will now be looking, thinking and running before they receive the ball.

The first time the coach sees one of his combinations produced in a game it will provide conclusive proof that his work is bearing fruit. When the players begin to produce variations it will mean that they are beginning to *think for themselves.*

It must be understood that the aim in coaching via combinations is to offer the players a football education. When a place-changing element is introduced the education begins to reach a very high standard and success cannot be guaranteed. In football, there is no substitute for skill at any level and in the higher echelons there is no substitute for intelligence either. It follows, therefore, that only players with a high degree of ability and intelligence will be able to participate in a highly developed team game.

The experienced coach may be able to offer his players 100 different combinations, but in match play it must still be the individual player who decides where to run (and when), who to pass to (and where). From start to finish in every game, each individual player must constantly make decisions and it is the duty of the coach to prepare his players to make these decisions.

As the coach progresses from one combination to another he will also be given an opportunity to coach the defensive players as they face each new situation. This should not be done until the attacking players are all familiar with their respective roles, but when the

## The theory of modern coaching

practices reach the point where they become relatively 'free', the coach can then turn his attention to the defenders and suggest various ways of countering each particular move.

In the long term, the aim must be to produce a group of players who can take part in a team game. Collectivity must be the key-note now, with each individual able to play a full and positive role in every phase of the game.

Every individual must fully understand what is expected from him in every situation and he must not only be mentally prepared to take part in a collective effort but also be able to meet the physical demands made on him.

At any given moment, each player has a part to play. With his defence under pressure, the front player must show himself for a quick pass and constantly be acquainted with the positions of both colleagues and opponents around him. When possession is won following a successful tackle or by interception, the entire team must break out as one unit and only the goalkeeper and the two centre-backs should be excused from responsibilities in attack. For the other eight players there should be no hesitation, and the following rules should be observed:

1. The ball should go forward quickly to a front player.
2. Midfield players must come out at speed (a) to support the player in possession, and (b) to exploit space created within the enemy defence.
3. The player receiving the ball in possession must be given advice.
4. The attack must be pressed to a shot at goal with the minimum of delay.

When possession of the ball is lost and the attack breaks down, the entire team must switch back easily and naturally into a defensive posture. Other team rules are applicable here and they can be described as follows:

1. The front players must challenge the player in possession in a bid to prevent a quick counter-attack.
2. The midfield players must re-position themselves *goal-side* of their opposite numbers.
3. The defenders stranded upfield must sprint back to pick up their individual opponents.

Until the defences have been rebuilt the primary aim of players challenging for possession should be to delay the counter-attack. Front players, tackling back when they have lost possession, should be discouraged from using sliding tackles for though they may win the ball using this method, they will not be in a position to exploit their success. Seconds later, when the defences are intact once more, the major aim will be to regain possession but here again it must be emphasized that sliding tackles should be reserved for real emergencies. The purpose of a successful tackle is to gain possession of the ball in order that a quick counter-attack can be developed. Even the most perfectly executed sliding tackle can now be seen to be purely negative; for the player winning the ball is unable to make use of it while lying on his back.

## DEAD BALL RE-STARTS

A great deal of attention has already been devoted to this aspect of the game, particularly in Britain. Free-kicks, corner-kicks and throw-ins have all been given special treatment but in reality the approach of the players, in these situations, differs in no way from the principles outlined in combinations. If these principles are assimilated by the players they will be used freely in dead-ball situations. It seems clear that free-kicks and throw-ins have won special appeal because the dead ball gives a fixed point of reference for the players. In a fluid game, there are many fixed points of reference, i.e. when the right-back, the goalkeeper or the left-winger have possession, and it is these points of reference which form the foundations for combined play.

It is no more difficult to coach players in a fluid situation than it is at a dead ball re-start, as long as the coach predetermines the response of the opposition. Precisely the same conditions apply in both the fluid and the fixed situation for players who may receive the ball are just as tightly marked at a throw-in as they are in open play.

If the players can be taught to analyse the situation at a throw-in they can just as easily be coached to develop this ability in fluid play. Indeed, the results of rehearsed throw-ins and corner-kicks are no different from those achieved by combinations except that the players apply the principles involved only at re-starts if this is how they are introduced to them.

Diagram 99 illustrates a throw-in practice which is frequently used in professional football. With the right-back taking the throw-in his colleague on the right wing positions himself well down the touchline. As 2 shapes up to take the throw, 7 sprints towards the thrower and

## The theory of modern coaching

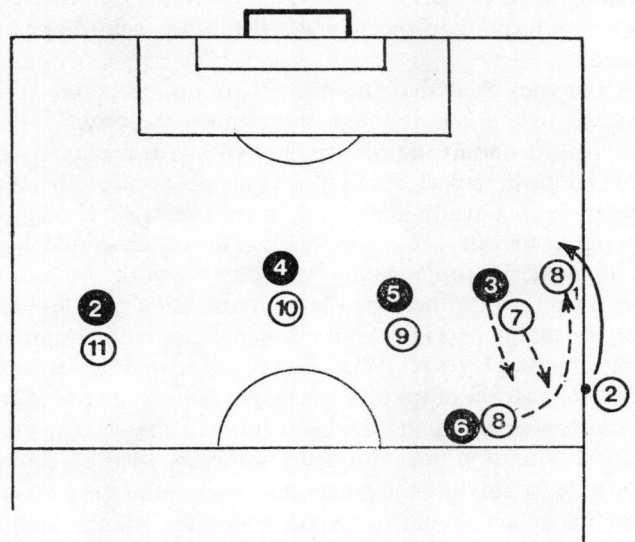

*Diagram 99*

with his opponent following right on his heels, the winger has made space. As the winger makes his run towards the thrower, the right-midfield sprints from a relatively deep position to exploit the created space as the ball is thrown beyond the advancing back.

To devote special attention to dead ball re-starts is to waste time. Through place-changing combinations the coach can establish general principles for play, which will apply equally in dead-ball situations and in fluid play. Once the players begin to look, to think and to move, they will apply these principles throughout the game.

## THE PSYCHOLOGY OF COACHING

When comparatively experienced players are first introduced to place-changing combinations, the coach is almost certain to meet with resistance and he should be prepared for it. Every effort should be made to persuade the players, individually and collectively, that combinations will considerably improve the performance of the team and that training must be approached with real enthusiasm.

Like anything else done half-heartedly, the results will be dis-

## *The theory of modern coaching*

appointing if the players do not devote themselves completely to the new form of training. If this happens then the coach will be forced to take action.

If it becomes clear that the players are not prepared to dedicate themselves to the new training programme, the coach should take action against one of the players. Preferably, this player should be one of the most respected and skilful members of the team and for whom there is a ready-made and proven reserve. Having decided which player he will take action against, the coach should choose the right moment. The opportunity will come when the bulk of the first XI are training with the coach in a combination play and the other players are taking part in a small side game supervised by an assistant.

If the chosen player remarks to a colleague that he disapproves of this particular form of training, or makes any other critical comment on the coach or his methods, this will be a suitable moment. If this favourable situation does not arise naturally, then an astute coach will be able to provoke the player at a moment of his own choice.

Now the coach should temporarily stop the training and without displaying any sign of anger he should suggest that the chosen player joins the other group. When the player has passed out of earshot, the coach can then address himself to the remaining players and ask if anyone else does not want to play in the next game.

With professional players and amateurs who are paid unofficially, this situation should never arise but if it does then the coach must be firm. The chosen player and any others who may have indicated that they did not want to play, must not be allowed to do so in any circumstances.

This approach may appear to be over-dogmatic, but it is quite clear that unless the coach, or manager, is firmly in control, it will be impossible to achieve the maximum in terms of results. To this end, the coach must assert himself as early as possible in his relationship with the players. In the words of one highly respected and extremely successful Continental coach—the trainer must be god.

If the coach is well advised to maintain a high standard of discipline, he must also be at great pains to discipline himself and his emotions. This is never more vital than when the team is doing badly.

A very small percentage of players may be impervious to criticism and unaware of their own failings, but the vast majority, amateurs and professionals alike, are very much aware of their mistakes. When a player fails to control the ball or makes a bad pass, he is

## The theory of modern coaching

immediately aware of his error and when he is playing badly, he does not need to be told. The team as a whole is no different to the individual in this respect and when a game goes badly it is the coach (or manager) above all who holds the key to revival. To criticize players at half-time is to invite disaster; to castigate the team after defeat is to demoralize the players and lay the foundations for defeat in the next match.

When players perform badly after being up half the night, drinking, dancing, or worse, then the coach has every right to be angry. Even in these circumstances, however, the coach must be careful to choose the right moment to show his displeasure.

Immediately before a match, during the interval or at the end of a game that has been lost, can never be the right time. Not in any circumstances. When players perform badly, all but the most insensitive will suffer a loss of confidence and worry about losing their place in the team.

The coach must understand that a worried player will be doubly prone to make mistakes and when a player or the team has lost its confidence, it is the first duty of the coach to restore it. In the short term it may help if the coach reassures an off-form player by telling him that he will not be dropped, but before doing this the coach must recognize that he must keep his word. Should the coach fail to keep his promise, then future attempts to reassure an off-form player will be of no value at all.

When the players return to the dressing-room after a poor first half, the coach must have it clear in his mind whether or not the players are doing their best. If they are, then the coach has no grounds for complaint and will be foolish to offer criticism. A few quiet words of encouragement, given individually to each of the players, can often work miracles and once the tension has been released it may be possible to re-motivate the team and effect a complete reversal of form in the second half.

When the game is over and the players return to the dressing-room, the coach begins immediately to prepare for the next match. If he is unfriendly or angry then the players will feel it and they will be apprehensive at the next training session. Amateurs may not attend the next training session in these circumstances and though professional players will be forced to attend, they cannot be *forced* to take part wholeheartedly.

Recognizing these factors, the coach must attempt to establish a

## The theory of modern coaching

personal relationship with each of his players, based on mutual trust and respect. Accepting that every player is an individual the coach must vary his method of approach from one player to another and having taken great pains to establish contact it would be foolish to destroy a good relationship in a moment of anger or disappointment.

The personality of the coach and his method of approach are at least as important as his understanding of the game and its problems. At every level, the coach must seek to capture the interest and enthusiasm of his players and constantly urge them to even greater achievements.